THE FATHERS OF THE CHURCH

A NEW TRANSLATION

VOLUME 94

THE FATHERS OF THE CHURCH

A NEW TRANSLATION

ORIGEN

HOMILIES ON LUKE
FRAGMENTS ON LUKE

Translated by

JOSEPH T. LIENHARD, S.J.
Fordham University
Bronx, New York

THE CATHOLIC UNIVERSITY OF AMERICA PRESS
Washington, D.C.

Printed in the United States of America
First paperback edition 2009

The paper used in this publication meets the minimum requirements of the American National Standards for Information Science—Permanence of Paper for Printed Library materials, ANSI Z39.48-1984.

LIBRARY OF CONGRESS CATALOGING-IN-PUBLICATION DATA

Origen.
[Homilies on Luke. English]
Homilies on Luke ; and, Fragments on Luke / Origen ; translated by Joseph T. Lienhard.
p. cm.—(The Fathers of the church ; v. 94)
Includes bibliographical references and indexes.
1. Bible. N.T. Luke—Sermons—Early works to 1800. 2. Sermons, Greek—Translations into English. I. Lienhard, Joseph T. II. Title. III. Title: Fragments on Luke. IV. Series.
BR60.F30686 1996
[BS2595]
226.4'07—dc20 95-39207

ISBN: 978-0-8132-1744-4 (pbk)

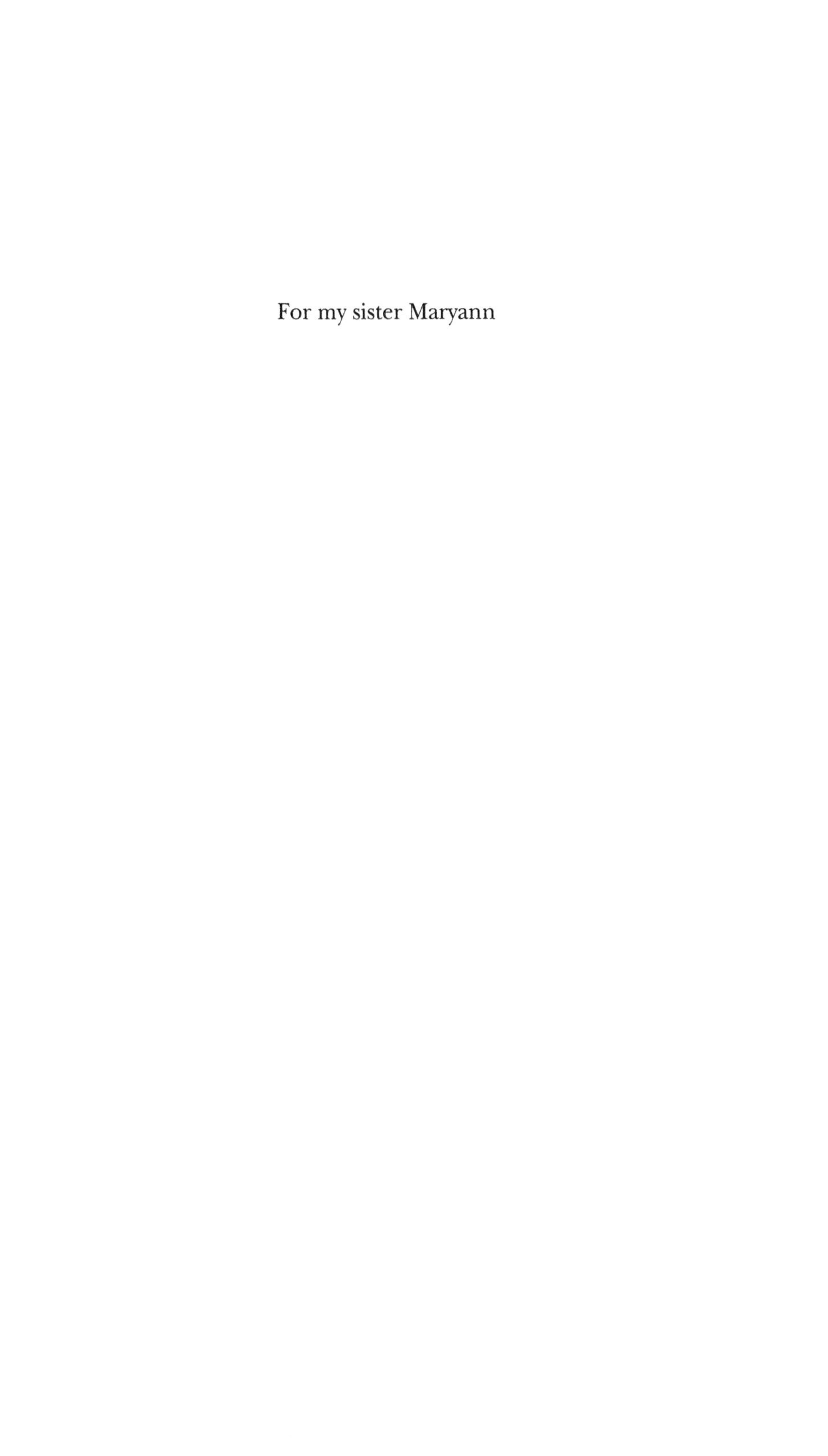

For my sister Maryann

CONTENTS

ABBREVIATIONS

ACW	Ancient Christian Writers. New York, New York/Mahwah, New Jersey: Newman Press, 1946–.
GCS	Die griechischen christlichen Schriftsteller der ersten drei Jahrhunderte. Leipzig: J.C. Hinrichs, 1897–1949. Berlin: Akademie-Verlag, 1953–.
JThS	*Journal of Theological Studies.* London, 1899–.
LCC	Library of Christian Classics. Philadelphia: Westminster Press, 1953–66.
LCL	Loeb Classical Library. Cambridge, Mass.: Harvard University Press. London: W. Heinemann, 1899–.
LXX	Septuagint
NPNF	A Select Library of Nicene and Post-Nicene Fathers of the Christian Church. Ed. P. Schaff and H. Wace. New York: Christian Literature Publishing Company, 1890. Reprints, 1956 and 1994.
PG	Patrologiae Cursus Completus: Series Graeca. Ed. J.-P. Migne. Paris, 1857–66.
PL	Patrologiae Cursus Completus: Series Latina. Ed. J.-P. Migne. Paris, 1878–90.
RSV	Bible: Revised Standard Version
SC	Sources chrétiennes. Paris: Éditions du Cerf, 1942–.
TU	Texte und Untersuchungen zur Geschichte der altchristlichen Literatur. Leipzig: J.C. Hinrichs, 1882-1949. Berlin: Akademie-Verlag, 1953–.

Abbreviations for Books of the Bible follow those used by *The New American Bible. Hom(s).* stands for *Homily(-lies)* and *Frag(s).* for *Fragment(s).*

SELECT BIBLIOGRAPHY

Texts and Translations

Origenes. *Die Homilien zu Lukas in der Übersetzung des Hieronymus und die griechischen Reste der Homilien und des Lukas-Kommentars.* Ed. Max Rauer. GCS. Origenes Werke 9. Berlin: Akademie-Verlag, 1959. (1st ed. 1931).

Origène. *Homélies sur s. Luc.* Intro., trans., and notes by Henri Crouzel, François Fournier, and Pierre Périchon. SC 87. Paris: Éditions du Cerf, 1962. (Rauer's text, with French translation of the 39 homilies and of 91 fragments.)

Origene. *Commento al Vangelo di Luca.* Trans. Salvatore Aliquò; intro. and notes by Carmelo Failla. Rome: Città Nuova, 1969. (Italian translation of the 39 homilies and of the same 91 fragments as in the SC volume.)

Origenes. *In Lucam Homiliae. Homilien zum Lukasevangelium.* Trans. and intro. by Hermann-Josef Sieben. 2 vols. Fontes Christiani, Band 4/1 and 4/2. Freiburg: Herder, 1991–1992. (Rauer's text, with German translation of the 39 homilies and of the same 91 fragments as in the SC volume.)

Reuss, Joseph, ed. *Lukas-Kommentare aus der griechischen Kirche: aus Katenenhandschriften.* TU 130. Berlin: Akademie-Verlag, 1984.

Smith, Harold. *Ante-Nicene Exegesis of the Gospels.* 6 vols. London: SPCK, and New York: Macmillan, 1925–1929.

Secondary Sources

Bertrand, Frédéric. *Mystique de Jésus chez Origène.* Théologie 23. Paris: Aubier, 1951.

Blanc, Cécile. "L'angélologie d'Origène." *Studia Patristica* 14 = TU 117 (Berlin: Akademie-Verlag, 1976) 79–109.

———. "Le baptême d'après Origène." *Studia Patristica* 11 = TU 108 (Berlin: Akademie-Verlag, 1972) 113–24.

Buchheit, Vinzenz. "Hippolyt, Origenes und Ambrosius über den Census Augusti." In *Vivarium. Festschrift Theodor Klauser zum 90. Geburtstag,* ed. Ernst Dassmann and Klaus Thraede. Jahrbuch für Antike und Christentum, Ergänzungsband 11, pp. 50–56. Münster: Aschendorff, 1984.

Cantalamessa, Raniero. "La primitiva esegesi cristologica di Romani I, 3–4 e Luca I, 35." *Rivista di storia e letteratura religiosa* 2(1966) 69–80.

Clark, Elizabeth A. *The Origenist Controversy: The Cultural Construction of an Early Christian Debate.* Princeton: Princeton University Press, 1992.

Courcelle, Pierre. *Late Latin Writers and Their Greek Sources.* Trans. Harry E. Wedeck. Cambridge: Harvard University Press, 1969.

Crouzel, Henri. "Les doxologies finales des homélies d'Origène selon le texte grec et les versions latines." *Augustinianum* 20(1980) 95–107.

———. *Les fins dernières selon Origène.* Collected Studies 320. Hampshire: Variorum, and Brookfield, Vt.: Gower, 1990. (Reprints of 14 articles.)

———. *Origen.* Trans. A. S. Worrall. San Francisco: Harper & Row, 1989.

———. *Origène et la "connaissance mystique".* Museum Lessianum, section théologique 56. Bruges and Paris: Desclée de Brouwer, 1961.

———. *Théologie de l'image de Dieu chez Origène.* Théologie 34. Paris: Aubier, 1956.

———. "La théologie mariale d'Origène." In Origène, *Homélies sur s. Luc* (SC 87), pp. 11–64.

———. *Virginité et mariage selon Origène.* Museum Lessianum, section théologique 58. Bruges and Paris: Desclée de Brouwer, 1963.

Daniélou, Jean. *Origen.* Trans. Walter Mitchell. New York: Sheed and Ward, 1955.

Gögler, Rolf. *Zur Theologie des biblischen Wortes bei Origenes.* Düsseldorf: Patmos, 1963.

Gorday, Peter. *Principles of Patristic Exegesis: Romans 9–11 in Origen, John Chrysostom, and Augustine.* Studies in the Bible and Early Christianity 4. New York: E. Mellen Press, 1983.

Holdcroft, I. T. "The Parable of the Pounds and Origen's Doctrine of Grace." JThS 24(1973) 503–4.

Kelly, J. N. D. *Jerome: His Life, Writings, and Controversies.* London: Duckworth, 1975.

Kilpatrick, George D. "Origenes, Homilie 1 in Lucam nach Codex 565." *Theologische Zeitschrift* 26(1970) 284–85.

Lienhard, Joseph T. "Christology in Origen's Homilies on the Infancy Narrative in Luke." *Studia Patristica* 26 (Louvain: Peeters, 1993) 287–91.

———. "Homily." In *Encyclopedia of Early Christianity* (New York and London: Garland, 1990), pp. 431–33.

———. "Origen and Augustine: Preaching on John the Baptist." *Augustinian Studies* 26(1995), pp. 37–46.

———. "Origen as Homilist." In *Preaching in the Patristic Age: Studies in Honor of Walter J. Burghardt, S.J.*, ed. David G. Hunter, pp. 36–52. New York: Paulist, 1989.

———. "Origen's Speculation on John the Baptist, or, Was John the Baptist the Holy Spirit?" In *Origeniana Quinta. Papers of the 5th International Origen Congress, Boston College, 14–18 August 1989*, ed. Robert J. Daly. Bibliotheca Ephemeridum Theologicarum Lovaniensium, 105, pp. 449–53. Louvain: University Press, 1992.

Lomiento, Gennaro. *L'esegesi origeniana del Vangelo di Luca (studio filologico).* Quaderni di Vetera Christianorum 1. Bari: Istituto di Letteratura Cristiana Antica, 1966.

Lubac, Henri de. *Histoire et Esprit. L'intelligence de l'Écriture d'après Origène.* Théologie, 16. Paris: Aubier, 1950. German trans. by Hans Urs von Balthasar, *Geist aus der Geschichte. Das Schriftverständnis des Origenes.* Einsiedeln: Johannes Verlag, 1968.

Monselewski, Werner. *Der barmherzige Samaritaner. Eine auslegungsgeschichtliche Untersuchung zu Lukas 10, 25–37.* Beiträge zur Geschichte der biblischen Exegese, 5. Tübingen: Mohr (Siebeck), 1967.

Nautin, Pierre. *Origène. Sa vie et son oeuvre.* Christianisme antique, 1. Paris: Beauchesne, 1977.

Nazzaro, A. V. "Il prologo del Vangelo di Luca nell'interpretazione di Origene." In *Origeniana Secunda*, ed. Henri Crouzel and Antonio Quacquarelli. Quaderni di Vetera Christianorum, 15, pp. 231–44. Rome: Ed. dell'Ateneo e Bizzarri, 1980.

Palma, José M. "Tapeinosis—virtud, Tapeinosis—estado: Origenes y la exegesis moderna de Luc 1:48." In *Diakonia pisteos al Reverendo Padre José Antonio de Aldama,* ed. Antonio Montero et al. Biblioteca teológica Granadina, 13, pp. 51–67. Granada: Facultad Teológica de Granada, 1969.

Rauer, Max. *Form und Überlieferung der Lukas-Homilien des Origenes.* TU 47, 3. Leipzig: J. C. Hinrichs, 1932.

Schlatter, Frederic W. "The Opus imperfectum in Matthaeum and the Fragments in Lucam." *Vigiliae Christianae* 39(1985) 384–92.

Simonetti, Manlio. "Eresia ed eretici in Origene." *Augustinianum* 25(1985) 735–48.

Torjesen, Karen Jo. *Hermeneutical Procedure and Theological Method in Origen's Exegesis.* Patristische Texte und Studien, 28. Berlin and New York: de Gruyter, 1986.

Trigg, Joseph Wilson. *Origen: The Bible and Philosophy in the Third-Century Church.* Atlanta: J. Knox, 1983.

Vogt, Hermann J. "Die Witwe als Bild der Seele in der Exegese des Origenes." *Theologische Quartalschrift* 165(1985) 105–18.

Wutz, Franz. *Onomastica Sacra. Untersuchungen zum Liber interpretationis nominum hebraicorum des hl. Hieronymus.* 2 vols. TU 41, 1 and 2. Leipzig: J. C. Hinrichs, 1914–1915.

Zahn, Theodor. "Die Predigten des Origenes über das Evangelium des Lukas." *Neue kirchliche Zeitschrift* 22(1911) 253–68.

Ziegler, J. "Ochs und Esel an der Krippe. Biblisch-patristische Erwägungen zu Is 1,3 und Hab 3,2(LXX)." *Münchener theologische Zeitschrift* 3(1952) 385–402.

INTRODUCTION[1]

Origen is the most important theologian of the Church before Nicaea, and one of the most influential Christian writers of all time. Unlike Justin Martyr, Origen did not come to Christianity after a long search through the philosophical schools; he was born into a Christian family. Unlike Irenaeus of Lyons, Origen did not devote his main energies to refuting error, but to explaining God's Word. Unlike Clement of Alexandria—who may have been his teacher—Origen saw no point in trying to make Christianity more palatable to the sophisticated and the curious; a determined ascetic, he expected his hearers to measure up to the highest Christian ideals.

Origen was, heart and soul, a man of the Bible. His mind was acute, his memory tenacious, his curiosity inexhaustible, and his patience unbreakable. He was a man who was most content when he could study, analyze, and comment upon a written text. All but one or two of his works are, in one form or another, commentaries on texts. Origen even helped shape the Bible. Five or six of the shorter books of the New Testament are in the canon largely because fourth-century writers appealed to Origen's authority. In and from his study of the Bible, Origen developed a theological system, perhaps the first in the history of Christianity. His system was intellectually

1. Some paragraphs of this Introduction are reprinted from Joseph T. Lienhard, "Origen as Homilist," in *Preaching in the Patristic Age: Studies in Honor of Walter J. Burghardt, S.J.*, ed. David G. Hunter (New York: Paulist, 1989), pp. 36–52, and used by permission of Paulist Press; © 1989 by David Hunter. The following introductions were also helpful: Max Rauer's in Origenes, *Die Homilien zu Lukas in der Übersetzung des Hieronymus und die griechischen Reste der Homilien und des Lukas-Kommentars*, GCS, Origenes Werke, 9, 2nd ed., (Berlin: Akademie Verlag, 1959), pp. vii-lxii; François Fournier's in Origène, *Homélies sur S. Luc*, SC 87 (Paris: Cerf, 1962), pp. 65–92; and Hermann-Josef Sieben's in Origenes, *In Lucam Homiliae, Homilien zum Lukasevangelium*, 2 vols., (Freiburg: Herder, 1991–92), I, 7–53.

rigorous, but it did not stop there. It had a practical goal, for it was a way of mysticism, a way that would lead the believer to union with God.

Theologians after Origen might criticize him, but they could not ignore him. Almost three centuries after Origen's death, the fifth ecumenical council, the Second Council of Constantinople (held in 553), condemned Origen as a heretic. G. L. Prestige has written, "Origen is the greatest of that happily small company of saints who, having lived and died in grace, suffered sentence of expulsion from the Church on earth after they had already entered into the joy of their Lord."[2]

But wariness of Origen, and outright rejection of him as one who merely adorned Platonic philosophy with a few Christian terms, continued well into the twentieth century, until scholars like Walther Völker, Jean Daniélou, Henri de Lubac, Antoine Guillaumont, Henri Crouzel, and others, took a fresh look at Origen, convincing much of the scholarly world to revise its picture of this great scholar and theologian.

Origen's Life

Origen was born ca. 185 in Alexandria, Egypt. Alexandria was a cosmopolitan city and, at the time, the center of Greek learning. Its library, founded by Alexander the Great, attracted scholars from the whole Mediterranean world. Origen's education was twofold, both Hellenistic and Biblical.

The way we read the Bible depends, to a large extent, on the way we learned to read. The student of rhetoric in the ancient world learned by analyzing a text word by word, pondering each word until every possible allusion and every conceivable relationship had been wrung out of it. That sort of education goes far in explaining Origen's approach to the Bible, which differs so markedly from modern exegesis. For modern readers, the unit of understanding is the sentence or

2. G. L. Prestige, *Fathers and Heretics: Six Studies in Dogmatic Faith with Prologue and Epilogue* (London: SPCK, 1968), p. 43.

the pericope; for Origen, the unit of understanding was the word. Again and again, in his homilies and commentaries, Origen puzzles over the meaning of a single word, a practice he learned as a young boy when he was taught Homer.

When Origen was about seventeen, his father Leonides died a martyr for the faith, and Origen became a teacher to support his mother and his six younger brothers and sisters. At the same time, he began to teach catechism—that is, to instruct pagans interested in Christianity. A few years later, probably when his brothers were able to support the family, Origen gave up teaching secular subjects and devoted himself—for the rest of his life, as it turned out—to studying and teaching the Scriptures. He also began to live an intensely ascetical life; Eusebius gives a moving account of Origen's ascetical regimen.[3]

Origen's career as a writer would have been severely limited if he had had to depend on a small income. But, when he was still young, he converted a wealthy man named Ambrose from Valentinian Gnosticism to orthodox Christianity. Ambrose became Origen's literary patron and virtually supplied Origen with his own publishing house. Eusebius writes,

> Ambrose . . . not only exerted verbal pressure and every kind of persuasion, but supplied him in abundance with everything needful. Shorthand-writers, more than seven in number, were available when he dictated, relieving each other regularly; and at least as many copyists; as well as girls trained in penmanship—all of them provided most generously with everything needful at Ambrose's expense. And not only that: in the devoted study of the divine teaching, he brought to Origen his own immeasurable enthusiasm.[4]

Origen lived at Alexandria until about 233, when he moved to Caesarea in Palestine. The precise reason for his move is not certain. That he was no longer welcome to live in Alexandria, but was quite welcome in Caesarea, is clear. As his

3. Eusebius, *Ecclesiastical History* 6.3; translated in *Eusebius. The History of the Church from Christ to Constantine,* trans. G. A. Williamson (Minneapolis: Augsburg, 1975), pp. 262–63.

4. *ibid.* 6.23.

reason for leaving Alexandria, some suggest a persecution of Christian teachers in Alexandria; others, that his theology was sharply criticized there. Opposition from Demetrius, the bishop of Alexandria, was almost certainly a factor. In the course of a journey Origen made in 232, Theoctistus, the bishop of Caesarea, ordained him a priest. This ordination, done without the consent of Demetrius of Alexandria, may have turned Demetrius against Origen. In any case, Origen took his library and his assistants with him, and spent the last twenty years of his life in Caesarea, greatly respected and free from rancorous controversy. He died in 254 or 255; his death was probably hastened by the torture he suffered in the persecution under the emperor Decius, the first of the three general persecutions of the Church.

Origen as Commentator and Preacher

Origen wrote on Scripture in three different literary genres: commentaries, scholia, and homilies. The commentaries and scholia are products of the library or the study, works in which a learned author writes for readers eager to learn. Scholia were the equivalent of scholarly footnotes. Commentaries treated a book of the Bible verse by verse, even word by word; the form of a commentary set no extraneous limit on the number of pages an author might spend on a point that intrigued him. Homilies, in contrast, a product of the pulpit, were naturally limited in length by the structure of the liturgy and the congregation's span of attention, and in scope by the hearers' ability to comprehend and use what the preacher said.

In Christian usage, the homily was a discourse on a Biblical text given before a congregation as part of a service of worship. In secular usage, the term had described the instruction that a philosopher gave his pupils in familiar conversation, distinct from the more formal oration or speech. A few Christian homilies survive from the time before Origen, but it would not be wrong to call Origen the "father of the Christian homily." He preached homilies on most of the Bible, and his homilies influenced preachers for centuries after his death.

In Origen's time, Pierre Nautin has written, Christian communities had three types of liturgical assemblies.[5] The first, and oldest, was the *synaxis* or assembly on Sunday, at which the Eucharist was celebrated. This assembly undoubtedly took place in the morning. On Wednesdays and Fridays there was also an assembly in the afternoon, perhaps at about three o'clock, which ended the fast customary on those two days.[6] This assembly included the celebration of the Eucharist. And finally, on every day but Sunday there was an assembly early in the morning, which was not Eucharistic.

The Eucharistic assembly on Sunday had three readings: one from the Old Testament, one from the apostolic writings, and one from the Gospels.[7] Because Origen's homilies on Luke are so much shorter than his homilies on the Old Testament, Nautin concludes that on Sunday a short homily was given after each of the three readings, perhaps by different preachers.

The Eucharistic assemblies on Wednesday and Friday also had a reading from the Gospels. If the Gospels were read three times a week at the rate of about eight verses to each reading (Origen's homilies on Luke treat six to ten verses each), then the four Gospels could be read in full during the course of three years.

The *synaxis* on weekday mornings had only one reading. According to Nautin, it was always from the Old Testament, since not only the baptized but also the catechumens attended, and the catechumens had not yet been introduced to the New Testament.[8] A homily followed to explain the reading, and prayers concluded the service. This assembly proba-

5. For what follows on the third-century liturgy, see Pierre Nautin, *Origène. Sa vie et son oeuvre*, Christianisme antique, 1 (Paris: Beauchesne, 1977), pp. 389–409.

6. The historian Socrates (*Ecclesiastical History* 5.22) mentions that Origen preached on Wednesdays and Fridays.

7. *Homilies* 12.2 and 31.5 imply that a reading from 1 Corinthians had preceded the one from Luke.

8. But the *Homilies on Luke* make it clear that catechumens heard Origen preaching on the Gospel; and the epistles were read at the same service (see above). Perhaps catechumens attended part of the Eucharistic service toward the end of their period of preparation.

bly lasted about an hour. The reading would be long, equivalent to two or even three chapters in our Bibles. And the reading was continuous—that is, a book was read from beginning to end, even if the preacher did not comment on the whole of the reading. At the rate of two or three chapters a day, the reading of the Old Testament would last about three years; and this, according to Hippolytus's *Apostolic Tradition*, was the duration of the catechumenate in the third century.[9] In Origen's time, apparently, candidates for Baptism were expected to attend a morning service six times a week for three years, and in the course of that service to hear an explanation of the entire Old Testament—certainly a rigorous initiation.

Origen's homilies give us a good picture of a third-century preacher.[10] Origen has no specific word for "preacher." He calls him simply διδάσκαλος, or "teacher"; that is, the preacher was one sort of educator. When Origen preached, he stood before the congregation and had the book of the Scriptures open before him; for the Old Testament, it was a corrected version of the Septuagint. By the third century, the office of preaching was generally restricted to bishops and presbyters.

Origen readily admitted that learning alone did not make a good preacher. Again and again, he asks his congregation to pray for him, and especially for his enlightenment, that he might understand the Scriptures and explain them correctly. Origen's congregations included catechumens, simple believers, and others who were more educated or spiritually advanced. But Origen did not preach catechetical homilies like those that Cyril of Jerusalem delivered during Lent in the fourth century to candidates for Baptism.

Origen acknowledges that some members of the congregation made him an object of adulation, while others accused him of teaching error (*Hom.* 25.6). Some objected to his method of interpreting the Scriptures, in particular to his dis-

9. Hippolytus, *Apostolic Tradition* 39.

10. The best treatment of this topic is by Pierre Nautin, "Origène prédicateur," in *Origène. Homélies sur Jérémie* 1, SC 232 (Paris: Cerf, 1976), pp. 100–91. See also Lienhard, "Origen as Homilist."

covery of a spiritual sense there; Biblical literalism is not only a modern temptation.

Most of Origen's extant homilies survive only in Latin translation. The full list is this: 16 on Genesis, 13 on Exodus, 16 on Leviticus, 28 on Numbers, 26 on Joshua, and 9 on Judges, all in Rufinus's Latin; 1 in Latin on 1 Samuel 1-2 and 1 in Greek on 1 Samuel 28, the passage on the witch of Endor; 9 on Psalms 36, 37, and 38 in Rufinus's Latin; 2 on the Song of Songs and 9 on Isaiah in Jerome's Latin; 20 in Greek and 14 in Jerome's Latin on Jeremiah (12 of the Latin homilies are translations of extant Greek texts); 14 on Ezekiel in Jerome's Latin; and, finally, the only homilies on the New Testament, 39 on Luke in Jerome's Latin.

St. Jerome, in his *Letter* 33 addressed to Paula, listed the works of Origen that he knew and included homilies on Deuteronomy, Job, Proverbs, Ecclesiastes, Matthew, Acts, 2 Corinthians, Thessalonians, Galatians, Titus, and Hebrews, besides homilies on Easter, peace, fasting, and monogamy; all are lost.

There is no evidence that Origen ever preached on the historical books after 1 Samuel; and he preached on 1 Samuel in Jerusalem, not in Caesarea. Nautin suggests that Origen may have broken off his course of homilies at Caesarea before he finished the three-year cycle because of objections to his allegorical exegesis, his doctrines, or his use of translations other than the Septuagint; all these complaints can be documented from his writings.[11]

Origen and Hermeneutics

If someone knows only one passage from Origen's writings, it is probably *On First Principles* 4.2.4, where Origen writes, "Just as man consists of body, soul, and spirit, so in the same way does the Scripture." The flesh of the Scripture, he writes, is "the obvious interpretation." The soul of the Scripture may edify "the man who has made some progress"—not, one notices, a definition. The spirit is for "the man who is perfect."

11. Nautin, *Origène*, p. 405.

Thus Scripture may have three senses, but their perception is conditioned by the reader's spiritual progress. In practice, Origen prefers other terms for the senses of Scripture, for example: historical, mystical, and allegorical; literal, mystical, and moral; the letter, the spirit, and the moral point. More often, though, Origen writes of only two senses of Scripture, and calls them the letter and the spirit, the literal meaning and the spiritual meaning, the flesh and the spirit, or the carnal meaning and the spiritual meaning.

Origen's consistent principle of interpretation was: explain the Bible by the Bible—that is, obscure or difficult passages should be explained by other passages, from anywhere else in the Bible, in which the same word or phrase or idea or situation occurs.[12]

In his *Commentary on the Psalms*, Origen related an intriguing comparison that he had heard from his Hebrew master: the Scripture is like one great house that has many, many rooms. All the rooms are locked. At each locked door there is a key, but not the key to that door. The scholar's task is to match the keys to their doors; and this is a great labor.[13]

The accusation most often made against Origen's exegesis—and for these purposes it is usually called "allegorical exegesis"—is that of utter arbitrariness. Origen, his critics contend, made a text mean whatever he wanted it to mean; allegorical exegesis meant the absence of any control over the interpretation of the text. But such assertions are most often made by those who have read only *On First Principles,* if that. For many years, this work (or even the anathemas of 553) were judged to contain the "real" Origen; the Origen of the homilies, especially, was considered a pious deceiver.

Henri de Lubac, in his brilliant book on Origen's exegesis, showed how wrong this is. De Lubac enunciated the principle, "Observe Origen at work"[14]—that is, to understand Origen's

12. On this important point see Rolf Gögler, *Zur Theologie des biblischen Wortes bei Origenes* (Düsseldorf: Patmos, 1963), esp. pp. 45–47.

13. On Ps 1, in *Philocalia,* ed. Marguérite Harl, SC 302 (Paris: Cerf, 1983), p. 245.

14. Henri du Lubac, *Histoire et Esprit. L'intelligence de l'Écriture d'après Origène,* Théologie, 16 (Paris: Aubier, 1950), p. 34.

method of exegesis, one has to observe what he does. It will not do to write about his methods only from the fourth book of *On First Principles.* Instead, we need many detailed studies of the commentaries and the homilies. De Lubac successfully, and fruitfully, shifted attention away from Origen's dogmatic work to his exegetical work. The task is formidable, but the results are rewarding.

In particular, de Lubac was able to show that Origen's exegesis is anything but arbitrary. He discovered two schemas in Origen's exgesis.[15] The first is echoed in the terms Origen uses in *On First Principles* 4.2.4. According to this scheme, the historical sense is found in an account of the events narrated in the Scriptures, or the text of the law. The moral sense refers to the soul, without any necessarily Christian dimension. The mystical sense refers to Christ, the Church, and all the other objects of faith. The other scheme, which Origen did not explain anywhere theoretically but often used in practice, is this: the historical sense is found in the events of Israel's history. The mystical sense refers to the mystery to be fulfilled in future ages, that is, Christ and the Church. The spiritual sense is found in applying the text to each single soul or person. This last, or "spiritual," sense differs from the "moral" of the first schema because it refers to the soul of the believer, "the soul in the Church," de Lubac says. In the believing soul, the mysteries of Christ are present and effective for the individual. Seen as a unity, the second schema means that, "Once signified by the narratives of the Old Testament (historical), the mystery of Christ (mystical) attains its full effect in the Christian believer (spiritual)."[16] This, too, is more typical of the mature Origen. In his surviving works, which span three decades, one can easily see a shift from cosmological interests, in his earlier works, to mystical and even pastoral interests (if he would have distinguished the two), in his later works. The homilies, in particular, show a clear and ever-present concern for the spiritual progress of his hearers.

15. *ibid.*, pp. 139–50.
16. *ibid.*, p. 144.

Homilies on Luke

Few patristic commentaries on the Gospel According to Luke survive. When the Fathers commented or preached on the Gospels, they concentrated on Matthew and John, said little about Luke, and practically ignored Mark. The only extant patristic works devoted to the Gospel According to Luke are Origen's 39 homilies; 156 homilies by Cyril of Alexandria, preserved in Syriac; and Ambrose's *Exposition of the Gospel According to Luke*, in ten books (the first two books of which depend heavily on Origen). Of lost works, fragments from the homiles of Titus of Bostra (died 378) are the most extensive. Origen's homilies are the only extant work on either Infancy Narrative before Hilary's commentary on Matthew, written ca. 355.

The date of Origen's *Homilies on Luke* must fall between Origen's move to Caesarea (probably in 233) and the *Commentary on Matthew* (244), which mentions the *Homilies on Luke*.[17] Max Rauer, who edited the homilies for the GCS series, dates them early in the period from 231 to 244.[18] François Fournier, who wrote the preface to the translation of the homilies in the series "Sources chrétiennes," suggests 233-234.[19] Nautin, in his well-known but controverted book on Origen, proposes that much of Origen's preaching took place at Caesarea in a three-year cycle between 238 and 243, perhaps from 239 to 242.[20] Sieben prefers Fournier's dates, 233-234.[21]

All of Origen's homilies on Luke, obviously enough, treat in succession several words or phrases from the Gospel passage that had been read. Origen sometimes ends a section rather mechanically, with a phrase like, "Let that suffice for an explanation." The homilies always end with a doxology (from 1 Pt 4.11), "To whom is glory and power for ages of ages. Amen." Origen often introduces the doxology with an

17. *Commentary on Matthew* 16.9 mentions *Hom.* 34 on Luke.
18. Rauer in Origenes, *Die Homilien zu Lukas*, p. viii.
19. Fournier in Origène, *Homélies sur S. Luc*, SC 87, p. 81.
20. Nautin, *Origène*, pp. 406–8.
21. Sieben in Origenes, *In Lucam Homiliae* I, 30–31.

exhortation to prayer. More interesting, perhaps, is Origen's practice of beginning some homilies by indirection, not with the exposition of the text but with some point other than the text at hand, a technique he may have learned from the rhetoricians. *Homily* 2, for example, begins with a consideration of whether it is possible to "be without sin"; *Homily* 3 with a distinction between seeing corporeal beings and seeing spiritual beings; *Homily* 19 with a refutation of the Ebionites; *Homily* 21 with a consideration of how prophecies are dated; *Homily* 25 with speculation on the limits of love; *Homily* 26 on the thought that God is spirit and fire; and *Homily* 30 with words on Christ and the Antichrist.

The 39 homilies on Luke are concentrated on the first four chapters of the Gospel. *Homilies* 1 to 33 treat Luke 1.1 to 4.27, with the exception of three passages: 1.33–38, 2.3–7, and 2.18–20. It seems unlikely that Origen would have skipped the three passages from Chapters 1 and 2; three homilies were probably lost (before the collection reached Jerome and Ambrose; see below). *Homilies* 34 to 39 treat isolated passages from Luke, from chapter 10 to chapter 20. These last six differ in tone from the first 33; they are generally longer, more complex, and more polished.

In his dedicatory letter to Paula and Eustochium, Jerome writes of translating "the thirty-nine homilies of our Adamantius on Luke, which are in Greek." It is unlikely that Jerome did not translate all the homilies he had available to him in Greek; by the late fourth century, the collection of 39 homilies on Luke was most probably the standard corpus, and the only one available. But at least some of the homilies on Luke had been lost already.[22]

Scripture and Its Interpretation in the Homilies on Luke

"I believe that every word of the Scriptures has its meaning," Origen writes (*Hom.* 35.7). But, even before he approached

22. In the *Commentary on Matthew* 13.29, Origen mentions a homily on Lk 15.4–7, and, in the *Commentary on John* 32.2, a homily on Lk 14.16–24.

the Scriptures, Origen knew what to expect of them. Even the simplest narrative had to speak to the Christian; what was written was written for our imitation (*Hom.* 11.3). The Scriptures contained nothing unworthy of their divine Author, and whatever might appear unworthy of that Author simply needed the right explanation. "The explanation both of what is said in Scripture and of the deeds recorded there should be worthy of the Holy Spirit and of faith in Christ, that faith to which we believers are called" (*Hom.* 9.1). Nothing is exempted from this rule. When Luke writes, "It happened in those days that an edict went out from Caesar Augustus, that the whole world should be registered" (Lk 2.4), Origen challenges Luke and says, "Evangelist, how does this narrative help me?" (*Hom.* 11.6)

But the task of the seeker is not always easy. Mary and Joseph sought Jesus, sorrowing (Lk 2.48). So too, Origen writes beautifully of his own labors, "sometimes you read the Scriptures and in them seek their meaning with a certain sorrow, and even pain. This is not because you think the Scriptures erred, or contain something wrong. Rather, they contain within themselves an expression and account of the truth. You cannot discover what is true. In just this way his parents sought Jesus" (*Hom.* 19.5). Origen also writes that the answer to his problems comes from contemplating the Logos, "We, too, often, when we carefully study the Scriptures and do not understand them, look up, as it were, with fixed attention as, for a moment, the Word shines 'in our hearts to illuminate the knowledge of his glory' (2 Cor 4.6); and 'he' is Christ" (*Frag.* 151).

Origen began his study with textual criticism. He knew, for example, that some manuscripts attribute the Magnificat to Mary, others to Elizabeth (*Hom.* 7.3). He knew that Marcion's disciples read "your bread," and not "our bread," in the Lord's Prayer (*Frag.* 180). Some Christians, he reports, believe that hedonists interpolated Jesus' words to the good thief, "Today you shall be with me in paradise" (Lk 23.43), into the Gospel (*Frag.* 248).

Origen, as the champion of spiritual exegesis, opposes an

exclusively literal interpretation of Scripture, because it leads to error. Marcion, Basilides, Valentinus, and the devil, all interpret the Scriptures literally (*Hom.* 31.2-3). But the plain narrative, or *historia,* is the foundation upon which all interpretation must be based; God's great deeds, in themselves, can edify the simple believer (*Frag.* 125). But, beyond the simple narrative, the Scripture has a deeper sense (*Hom.* 37.1), an elevated sense, ἀναγωγή, which only those who are advancing can profit by (*Hom.* 23.5). Allegorical interpretation was already a long-standing tradition in the Church; in a remarkable passage, Origen cites an allegorical interpretation of the parable of the Good Samaritan by an unnamed elder (*Hom.* 34.3), and then goes on to improve a little on the allegory.

Particularly in the fragments, Origen often explains a word with a simple equivalency, as if the correspondence were quite familiar. Egypt, for example, is the world (*Frag.* 182). The disciples' cloaks are deeds and words (*Frag.* 235). The word "house," interestingly, stands for the Church (*Frag.* 121b), this world (*Frag.* 122), the soul (*Frag.* 171), and man (*Frag.* 202). Numbers have a similar pattern of correspondence. Two stands for matter (*Frag.* 212), three for the Trinity (*Frag.* 182), five for the senses (*Frags.* 192, 202), six for creation (*Frag.* 139c), and seven for a multitude (*Frag.* 185).

Seeing a topic on two levels is a device that Origen makes great use of. Following Plato and a long tradition in philosophy, he distinguishes sensible reality from intelligible reality (*Frag.* 120). Baptism, too, can be either visible or invisible (*Hom.* 24.1). Each church has a visible bishop, and an invisible one (*Hom.* 13.5). Joseph gave earthly wheat to his brothers; Christ gives heavenly wheat (*Hom.* 28.5). Following Paul (2 Cor 4.16 and Rom 7.22), Origen distinguishes the outer man from the inner man (*Frag.* 196). He also distinguishes body from spirit, on many levels. Growth can be either corporeal or spiritual (*Hom.* 11.1); the age of the body is to be distinguished from the age of the soul (*Hom.* 206); Martha is somatic, Mary is spiritual (*Frag.* 171). Origen also finds the distinction of Jews and Gentiles signified in many places. Nazareth represents the Jews, Capernaum the Gentiles (*Hom.* 33.1); the woman with the flux of blood represents the Gentiles, while Jairus's daughter represents the Jews and the synagogue (*Frag.* 125); Martha stands for the synagogue, Mary for the Church (*Frag.* 171).

No word in the Scriptures is idle. Thus, for example, Origen asks how "to be just" differs from "to be just in God's sight" (Lk 1.6, *Hom.* 2.3). He also asks why Luke adds "without blame" to his praise of Zechariah and Elizabeth, "they walked in all the Lord's commandments and precepts" (Lk 1.6, *Hom.* 2.6). He wonders why Scripture speaks of seeing the Lord's voice, and seeing the Word (*Hom.* 1.4). And, in the homilies and fragments translated here, he is much concerned to discover, in Jesus' parables about servants who are given money to invest, the precise meaning of the different coins and the different rewards (*Hom.* 35.10-11; and *Frags.* 200 and 228).[23] The identity and character of the reader can also make a difference: the devil is not credible even when he quotes Scripture, whereas Paul can quote even secular writers and be convincing (*Hom.* 31.3).

Finally, Origen sometimes seems to be making notes to remind himself to investigate a question further, with phrases like, "You will seek to learn," or, "You will inquire" (*Frags.* 151 and 200). At one place, he even asks whether Jesus misquoted the Scriptures (*Hom.* 39.2).

Theology in the Homilies on Luke

Origen did not engage in much theological speculation when he preached on the Gospel According to Luke, since the homilies were addressed to catechumens, among others. He tried to inculcate some basic doctrines about God and about the person of Christ. Some statements about Mary and Joseph are also christological in intent. Origen is one of the earliest Christians to evince devotion to the infant Christ. He

23. For this reason I have retained the Greek and Latin names for measures of quantity (*sextarius*, *urna*, and *amphora* in *Hom.* 29.1) and for coins (*denarius*, *mina*, and *talent* in *Hom.* 35.11; *denarius*, *drachma*, *obol*, and *stater* in *Hom.* 35.15); to try to express the terms in English approximations would not foster clarity.

speculates a little on John the Baptist, but also with Christ in view.

Origen uses the names Father, Son, and Holy Spirit a few times (*Homs.* 3.2 and 37.5). He writes that "the Father is in the Son and the Son is in the Father" (*Hom.* 34.8), and elsewhere that some heretics, probably Marcionites, believe that the advocate promised in Jn 14.17 is Paul, so that a sort of Trinity of Father, Son, and Paul results (*Hom.* 25.5). But the truth is that the Holy Spirit is a distinct, divine person (*Hom.* 25.5).

On the person of Christ, Origen is fuller. The Ebionites deny Christ's divinity (*Hom.* 19.1), and the devil himself is an Adoptionist (*Frag.* 96) and a Psilanthropist (*Frag.* 98). Against Gnostic Docetism, Origen teaches that Christ had a true human body; it was not made of heavenly or sidereal matter (*Hom.* 14.4). Christ was the Son of God in the proper sense, and uniquely so (*Hom.* 29.2). He was a divine being who had a human body and a human soul (*Hom.* 19.1). The expression that the Son "assumed a man" is found (*Homs.* 29.5 and 34.7). But Origen can also write that after the resurrection Christ was no longer man, but God (*Hom.* 29.7); he seems to associate humanity with mortality, and mean that, when Christ was no longer mortal, he was not human in the way he had been.[24]

As is clear from other writings of his, Origen tried to work out his teaching about Christ by collecting the titles (ἐπίνοιαι[25]) of Christ. In the *Commentary on John,* Origen treated more than fifty titles. He is much more modest in his writings on Luke, but occasionally records single titles or short lists: Master Physician (*Hom.* 13.2); Word, Wisdom, Son of God (*Hom.* 19.5); Word, Wisdom, Justice, Truth (*Hom.* 30.1); Wisdom, Truth, God's Only-Begotten (*Hom.* 32.6); Way, Truth, Life (*Hom.* 35.9); Wisdom, Peace, Justice, Truth (*Hom.* 36.3); Word and High Priest (*Frag.* 140); Word, Wisdom, Justice

24. See also Joseph T. Lienhard, "Christology in Origen's Homilies on the Infancy Narrative in Luke," *Studia Patristica* 26 (Louvain: Peeters, 1993), pp. 287–91.

25. The word means "thought" or "conception," and designated the many ways the Bible provided for conceiving of Christ and his work.

(*Frag.* 162). Occasionally Origen compares John the Baptist with Christ by using Biblical terms: John is the lamp, Christ the light (*Hom.* 21.3); John is the voice, Christ the Word (*Hom.* 21.5). John is always Christ's precursor, even in the underworld (*Hom.* 4.5-6).[26]

Mary was perpetually a virgin, although some heretics say that Jesus repudiated Mary because, after his own birth, she bore Joseph's children (*Hom.* 7.4). But Joseph's children were not Mary's (*Hom.* 7.4). Although a virgin, Mary was betrothed to Joseph so that the birth of Jesus would not disgrace virginity (*Hom.* 6.4). Mary knew the Scriptures (and apparently the Septuagint) so well that, when the angel greeted her as "full of grace," she realized that this word is not found in the Scriptures, and hence she was afraid (*Hom.* 34.3). Joseph is Jesus' foster-father (*Homs.* 16.1, 17.1, and 18.2). Yet Joseph and Mary did not have perfect faith (*Hom.* 20.4).[27]

Origen's list of heretics is short. His intention is to warn his hearers or readers against basic doctrinal errors, and not to expound on and refute the heretics' erroneous teachings. His common list of heretics is: Marcion, Valentinus, and Basilides (*Hom.* 29.4 and *Frag.* 166. Cf. *Hom.* 20.2 and *Frag.* 242). He also named Dositheus, the heresiarch of Samaria (*Hom.* 25.4); Ebionites (*Frag.* 212); and Mani and the Manichees (*Frags.* 181 and 226).

Origen's most common objection to the Marcionites, of course, is that they reject the Old Testament and separate the Creator of the world from the Father of Jesus Christ. They say that the Creator, the God of the Law and the prophets, is not the Father of Christ (*Hom.* 20.2; cf. *Frag.* 226); that the Law and the prophets do not come from the Father of Jesus Christ (*Hom.* 18.5); and that Christ was not foretold by the prophets

26. See also Joseph T. Lienhard, "Origen's Speculation on John the Baptist, or, Was John the Baptist the Holy Spirit?" in *Origeniana Quinta. Papers of the 5th International Origen Congress, Boston College, 14–18 August 1989*, ed. Robert J. Daly, Bibliotheca Ephemeridum Theologicarum Lovaniensium, 105, (Louvain: University Press, 1992), pp. 449–53.

27. See also the excellent essay by Henri Crouzel, "La théologie mariale d'Origène," in Origène, *Homélies sur s. Luc*, SC 87, pp. 11–64.

(*Hom.* 17.5; cf. *Frag.* 162). The presentation of Christ in the temple refutes them (*Hom.* 14.7). Similarly, the Marcionites deny that Christ was born of a woman (*Hom.* 17.4), just as they deny the resurrection of the body (*Frag.* 242). One homily has some intriguing details about the claims of some Marcionites: that those who are to sit at the Savior's right and left (Mt 20.21) are Paul and Marcion; and that the advocate, the Spirit of Truth (Jn 14.17) is Paul (*Hom.* 25.5). In another, longer passage, Origen accuses heretics, clearly the Marcionites, of refusing to allegorize the Old Testament, but allegorizing a passage in the Gospel that embarrasses them (*Hom.* 16.4–6). At Lk 11.3 they read "your bread," but then have to allegorize the word, lest it mean material bread (*Frag.* 180).

Ebionites, in contrast, deny the virginal conception of Christ (*Hom.* 17.4), and philosophize about sensible, rather than intellectual, things (*Frag.* 212).

Although Origen mentions the Gnostics Basilides and Valentinus a few times, he does not distinguish their teachings from Marcion's dualism and docetism (cf. *Hom.* 20.2). Such heretics eat stones instead of bread (*Hom.* 29.4). Basilides wrote a gospel, as did other heretics (*Hom.* 1.2).

As already noted, Origen addresses catechumens several times in the homilies. He assures them that God has called them and exhorts them to courage (*Hom.* 7.7–8). He invites them to penance, as a preparation for Baptism (*Hom.* 21.4), and sternly warns them to turn away from sin (*Hom.* 22.6). He hopes that the eyes of all, including catechumens, will be fixed on Jesus (*Hom.* 32.6).

Given his concern for catechumens, it is not surprising that Origen mentions Christian Baptism several times. The homilies, of course, treat John the Baptist's baptism, and John's baptism of Jesus. When he speaks of specifically Christian Baptism, Origen tells the catechumens that they need to despise their sins before they come to Baptism, lest they not be forgiven (*Homs.* 21.4 and 22.5–6). The cleansing of Naaman was a type of Baptism (*Hom.* 33.5). Origen defends the Baptism of infants as the normal practice of the Church; and it is Baptism administered for the remission of sins (*Hom.* 14.5).

Even after the resurrection of the dead, another sacrament, akin to Baptism, will be needed for a final cleansing (*Hom.* 14.6). John's baptism was visible; Christ's Baptism, in the Holy Spirit and fire, is invisible. The Baptism with the Holy Spirit took place after the Ascension. The baptism with fire will be given to those who depart this life and still need cleansing; but only those who had been baptized with water, and with the Holy Spirit, will be eligible for this baptism in fire (*Hom.* 24.1–2). But in another homily, he apparently corrects himself and interprets baptism in the Holy Spirit as salvation, and baptism in fire as damnation (*Hom.* 26.3).

In contrast to the frequent mention of Baptism, Origen alludes to the Eucharist only once (*Hom.* 38.6).[28]

Jerome's Translation of the Homilies

In his preface to the homilies on Luke, Jerome writes that he translated the homilies at the request of Paula and her daughter Eustochium.[29]

Jerome himself is the best source of information on Paula; his *Letter* 108, written on the occasion of her death, provides a biographical sketch.[30] Paula was born in 347 into an old and distinguished Roman family. At the age of 15 she married the pagan senator Toxotius and bore him five children, among them their daughter Eustochium. When Paula was in her early thirties, her husband died. She thereupon joined the growing number of Christian widows and virgins in Rome who were dedicating themselves to Christian asceticism in the style of the Egyptian monks.

Soon after he returned to Rome in 382, Jerome became a sort of spiritual director to these women. He guided them in

28. For a further analysis of the *Homilies on Luke*, particularly from the aspect of spirituality, see Sieben in Origenes, *In Lucam Homiliae* I, 25–28.

29. Jerome also lists his translation of Origen's *Homilies on Luke* among his works in *On Illustrious Men* 135.

30. English translation by W. H. Fremantle in *The Principal Works of St. Jerome*, NPNF 2nd series, vol. 6, (Grand Rapids: Eerdmans, 1954), pp. 195–212. On Jerome and Paula, see also J. N. D. Kelly, *Jerome: His Life, Writings, and Controversies*, (London: Duckworth, 1975), pp. 91–152.

the study of the Scriptures, and taught some of them Hebrew. Jerome's involvement with these women was surely innocent, but it became the occasion for malicious gossip, all the more so because Jerome had not hesitated to criticize other clerics for fawning upon rich widows.

Once his patron, Pope Damasus, died in 384, opposition in Christian Rome to Jerome grew bitter. Jerome himself may have been disappointed at not being elected Damasus's successor. In any case, he left Rome in August of 385, never to return.

Meanwhile, Paula's dedication to asceticism deepened. Jerome's famous *Letter* 22 on asceticism, addressed to Paula's daughter Eustochium,[31] was also a treatise Paula could appreciate. In the wake of Jerome's spectacular departure, Paula also decided to leave Rome. She gave her property (and her children's) to the poor, and left Rome in 385. After a journey through parts of the East, she and Eustochium settled in Bethlehem, in the fall of 386, where Jerome was establishing a monastery. Paula had retained enough money to build a convent for women, and another for men, in Bethlehem. She also kept up her study of the Scriptures, and her contact with Jerome. In his book *On Illustrious Men*, Jerome mentions an indeterminate number of letters that he wrote to Paula and Eustochium, saying that he wrote to them daily.[32] Paula died in 404, and was buried near the grotto of the Nativity in Bethlehem. After Paula's death, Eustochium took over the leadership of the monastery of women in Bethlehem; she died in 418.

But Jerome's main reason for translating the homilies on Luke may not have been Paula's and Eustochium's urgent request. Jerome's intense dislike for St. Ambrose of Milan is attested by his entry on Ambrose in his book *On Illustrious Men*: "Ambrose, bishop of Milan, at the present time is still writing. I withhold my judgment on him, because he is still

31. English translations by F. A. Wright, *Select Letters of St. Jerome*, LCL (Cambridge: Harvard University Press, 1933), pp. 52–159, and Charles Christopher Mierow, *The Letters of St. Jerome*, ACW 33, (New York: Newman, 1963), pp. 134–79.

32. Jerome, *On Illustrious Men* 135.

alive, fearing either to praise or blame lest, in the one event, I should be blamed for adulation, and in the other for speaking the truth."[33] The reason for Jerome's dislike of Ambrose—and this is only speculation—may have been that Ambrose did not support Jerome in the papal election of 384. Thereafter, Jerome made a point of trying to embarrass Ambrose.

Ambrose read Greek well. In 381 he published a book entitled *On the Holy Spirit.* In 387 Jerome published a translation of Didymus the Blind's book of the same name, with one clear intention—to show that Ambrose had cribbed much of his book from Didymus. In 390 or 391, Ambrose published his *Exposition of the Gospel According to Luke* in ten books. In this work, Ambrose followed Origen closely, at least in the first two of his ten books on Luke; some parts of Ambrose's work are so close to Origen's that they can be used to clarify doubtful readings in the text of Origen. Jerome's reference in the preface to the black crow that adorns itself in other birds' brightly-colored feathers is clearly aimed at Ambrose.[34] The commentary that Jerome calls "childish in expression and dull in content" is, again, Ambrose's. Modern standards of plagiarism did not prevail in antiquity, but Jerome clearly thought that he could embarrass Ambrose by showing how unoriginal his work was.

The date of Jerome's translation depends on the date of the publication of Ambrose's *Exposition of the Gospel According to Luke.* Rauer dated it to 390; Sieben prefers 391. The date of Jerome's translation would be a year or so later, but certainly before the Origenist controversy broke out in 393.

Jerome's translation retains evidence of the Greek original. In some places, he glosses a Greek term (cf. *Homs.* 1.3,6; 8.29; 16.10; 34.3; and 35.7,14). In others he retains Greek words and explains their meanings. Most are from the Gospel itself. In *Homily* 1.3 he transcribes the word πεπληροφορημένων (Lk 1.1; RSV: "the things that have been accomplished"), and explains that no one Latin word can express its meanings. Luke

33. *ibid.* 124.

34. Rufinus of Aquileia (*Apology* 2.23–24) identifies Ambrose as the object of Jerome's scorn.

calls Theophilus κράτιστος (Lk 1.3), which means both "excellent" and "very strong" (*Hom.* 1.6). The angel's greeting to Mary, κεχαριτωμένη (Lk 1.28; usually "full of grace"), is unique in Scripture (*Hom.* 6.7). In *Homily* 8.7, Jerome follows Origen's explanation of κράτος (Lk 1.51), "strength," and considers two Latin translations. In the parable of the Good Samaritan, the injured man is brought to the *pandochium* (Lk 10.34, Latinized from πανδοχεῖον); Jerome keeps the word and glosses it as "stable," because Origen noted that πανδοχεῖον means "a place that accepts everyone," which he interprets as the Church (*Hom.* 34.3 and 7). Once Jerome keeps in Greek a word that Origen noted from the Septuagint, ἀπολιθοόντωσαν (Ex 15.16, *Hom.* 22.10), which implies that the Egyptians were turned to stone until the Hebrews could cross the Red Sea.

Apart from the text of the Bible, Jerome often has a problem with the Greek word λόγος (which he never retains in Greek). The word means both "word" and "reason," and Jerome often translates it with both terms (cf. *Homs.* 1.3; 5.1,3; and 19.5-6). In *Homily* 5.3, he retains the Greek word ἄλογος, which the Septuagint uses of Moses (Ex 4.10). In the original, Moses simply says that he is not eloquent; but Origen takes ἄλογος to mean that Moses was without speech and reason until God gave the Law.

In an interesting passage (*Hom.* 8.4-5), Origen tries to persuade his audience that humility is a virtue; they are obviously not used to thinking of it that way. Jerome keeps the Greek names of two other virtues Origen mentions, ἀτυφία ("modesty") and μετριότης ("moderation"), in his effort to explain what humility is.

Finally, Jerome retains the name of a figure of speech, ἀπὸ κοινοῦ (*Hom.* 32.4), in Greek; he liked the phrase and used it often.[35] He also retains the name ἀναγωγή for the elevated sense of Scripture, another word he favored.[36]

35. Pierre Courcelle, *Late Latin Writers and Their Greek Sources*, trans. Harry E. Wedeck, (Cambridge: Harvard University Press, 1969), p. 51, n. 10, lists fifteen other places where Jerome uses the Greek expression.

36. Courcelle, *ibid.*, lists more than twenty-five examples.

In the late-nineteenth and early-twentieth centuries, it was fashionable to disdain the Latin translations of Origen's works, and almost any Greek fragment was considered more trustworthy than the Latin versions. But such suspicion was unjustified. When Rufinus sought to criticize Jerome's translations, he accused Jerome of changing the text of the *Homilies on Luke* in two places. One is in *Homily* 4.4; Rufinus writes that Jerome added the words "and nature" to Origen's term "substance."[37] If that was the worst inaccuracy that Rufinus could find—and he had every reason to want to find more—then Jerome's translation is remarkably faithful. Jerome even leaves in passages that would be theologically problematic to him, such as Origen's reference to Mary's and Joseph's imperfect faith (*Hom.* 20.4).

Moreover, the Greek fragments are not always trustworthy. Most of them come from *catenae*, the running commentaries on books of the Bible pieced together from the writings of the Fathers, compiled from the sixth century on. The editors of the *catenae* often shortened, condensed, or rearranged the passages from the Fathers that they used. Hence, contemporary scholarship has a high estimate of the accuracy of Jerome's translation; it can be read with confidence that one is reading Origen himself, and not some other Origen whom it pleased Jerome to construct.

The Fragments

Besides the 39 extant homilies on the Gospel of Luke, Origen preached at least two more, which are lost.[38] He also wrote a *Commentary on Luke* in five books, also lost.[39] The extant books of the *Commentary on Matthew* show that, in that work, Origen generally commented on all the synoptic parallels together. Hence, in his *Commentary on Luke* he needed to treat only the passages that are unique to Luke. Origen finished the *Commen-*

37. See note to *Hom.* 4.4.

38. See above, note 22.

39. See Jerome's letter to Paula and Eustochium, below, the preface to the *Homilies on Luke*; he mentions the commentary there. Jerome's *Letter* 33 to Paula speaks of 15 books of commentary, but the number is probably a scribal error.

tary on Matthew in 244; the work on Luke would have been later.

Fragments of Origen's lost commentaries and homilies are preserved in the *catenae*. The oldest of these is the *Ps-Titus Commentary* (so called because it quotes often from Titus of Bostra), which dates from the sixth century.[40]

Once Rauer had catalogued all the *catenae*, and the manuscripts and printed editions in which they exist, he wrote a sentence that is at once pithy and accurate: "Hier beginnen die Schwierigkeiten," "This is where the problems start."[41] To sort out and order the vast amount of material in the *catenae* is a great labor.

Editors before Rauer tried to collect fragments of Origen's writings on Luke. De la Rue began the process in 1740; Gallardi's edition (1781) added more; and Angelo Mai, in 1838, added still more, as did Lommatsch.[42] Rauer himself carried out the difficult task of gathering the fragments, trying to establish a trustworthy text, and judging their authenticity, a task made somewhat easier by the fact that, from the late-fourth (and more so from the mid-sixth) century, Origen was considered a heretic, especially in the East. Hence the tendency of the *catenae* would be conservative: compilers would probably not attribute to Origen passages that were not his work.

Rauer divides the fragments into two groups. Those that are clearly parallel to passages in the Latin version of the homilies he prints next to the corresponding Latin passage. This process is no guarantee that the Greek is more accurate than the Latin; but having the Greek text on the same page as the Latin makes evaluation easier.

The second group of fragments comprises those that have no parallel in the Latin homilies. Some of those that treat a passage from Luke's Gospel are in fact from Origen's writings

40. To name and describe all the *catenae* here would be pointless; Rauer, in his detailed introduction to his critical edition, did so accurately and fully, and what he wrote cannot be condensed.

41. Rauer in Origenes, *Die Homilien zu Lukas*, p. lviii.

42. Once again, Rauer's introduction provides all the necessary details.

on Matthew. In these cases, Rauer prints only the opening and closing words of the fragment and refers the reader to the GCS volume where the fragments on Matthew are printed. The fragments that Rauer prints in full are those he believes to be from the lost homilies on Luke and from the *Commentary on Luke.* To judge from their tone and content, most of them come from the commentary rather than from lost homilies.

To establish beyond any doubt that all the fragments are authentic is, short of the discovery of a complete Greek manuscript of Origen's work, impossible. But Rauer's final judgment commands respect. He writes, "Der grösste Teil ist aber wohl sicher echt"—"But the greatest part is surely genuine."[43]

Editions and Translations—This Translation

The 39 homilies on Luke in Jerome's Latin version were first printed by Jacques Merlin at Paris in 1512. Merlin used a single manuscript. The homilies were edited again by the Maurist Charles de la Rue in 1740, and Jacques Paul Migne reprinted de la Rue's text in Patrologia Graeca, volume 13. Carl Heinrich Eduard Lommatsch published an edition of the homilies in 1835. But de la Rue and Lommatsch both simply used Merlin's text, while trying to improve it with some conjectured readings. Both also included some Greek fragments, which Merlin had not done.

Max Rauer published the first true critical edition in 1931. He used a dozen new manuscripts and added many Greek fragments. Rauer published a second edition of his work in 1959, for which he collated some additional manuscripts and, in response to critical reviews, removed some Greek fragments as unauthentic.

Three modern translations have been published. In 1962, François Fournier and Pierre Périchon, along with Henri Crouzel, published a volume in the series "Sources chrétiennes" that contained a translation of the 39 Latin homilies and of 91 Greek fragments; they also reprinted Rauer's text of the

43. Rauer, in Origenes, *Die Homilien zu Lukas,* p. 225.

homilies and the fragments. In 1969, Salvatore Aliquò and Carmelo Failla published an Italian translation of the same homilies and fragments. In 1991–1992 Hermann-Josef Sieben published a German translation of the homilies and of the 91 fragments, along with Rauer's text.

For this volume, I have translated the 39 homilies from Jerome's Latin in Rauer's edition, drawing on the parallel Greek fragments only at points where they could clarify the Latin, the course also followed by the French, Italian, and German translators. For the Greek fragments, however, I departed from their model and translated all the fragments in Rauer's edition from the fragment on Luke 4.1 on, with two exceptions: those that Rauer assigned to Origen's work on Matthew, and a few other fragments that were either so short as to be useless or duplicated what Origen wrote in the Latin homilies. Origen's thought on Luke 1 to 3 is covered well enough in the homilies. The authenticity of every fragment, of course, cannot be guaranteed. My goal was to supply Origen's thought, or what is most probably Origen's thought, on as much of the Gospel According to Luke as possible. I drafted the translation from the original, but compared my work with the French translations of François Fournier and Pierre Périchon, and the German translation of Hermann-Josef Sieben, and received much help from them.

In preparing the translation, I have had the sage advice of Fr. Roland J. Teske, S.J., of the Department of Philosophy at Marquette University in Milwaukee, who read much of the translation and suggested improvements, and Ms. Colleen Hoffman, at Fordham University, who patiently checked many of the references. I am grateful to the editors of The Catholic University of America Press for accepting this translation into the series "Fathers of the Church."

Fordham University
Solemnity of the Sacred Heart, 1994

HOMILIES ON LUKE

PREFACE OF JEROME THE PRESBYTER

Jerome to Paula and Eustochium[1]

A few days ago you said you had read the commentaries of some writers on Matthew and Luke. One of them was weak in content and expression, the other childish in expression and dull in content.[2] So you despised those trivial books and asked me to translate at least the thirty-nine homilies of our Adamantius[3] on Luke, which are in Greek. Translation is a distressing task, like a torture—as Tullius says, it is writing with someone else's taste and not one's own.[4] But I shall do it, because you do not ask for something more difficult. Once, at Rome, the holy Blesilla begged me to translate Origen's twenty-six books on Matthew, five more on Luke, and thirty-two on John into our language.[5] You realize that such an undertaking is beyond my strength, my time, and my ability to work. Notice how much weight your authority and your desires have with me! I have laid aside the books of Hebrew Questions[6] for a little while and have dictated the translation of a work that, in your opinion, is valuable; whatever it is worth is not mine,

1. The manuscripts begin with this note: "Here begins the preface of blessed Jerome, the presbyter, to Origen's homilies on Luke the Evangelist." On Paula and Eustochium, see the Introduction.

2. The first is probably the commentary on the Gospels by Fortunatianus of Aquileia (died 361), which is lost. The second is surely Ambrose's *Exposition of the Gospel According to Luke.* See the Introduction about Jerome's dislike for Ambrose.

3. A honorific name for Origen; it means "man of steel."

4. Cicero, *Letter* 127.2.

5. Eight books (10 to 17) of the *Commentary on Matthew* are extant in Greek, and a Latin translation (called the *Commentariorum series*) preserves Origen's commentary on Mt 16.13 to 27.25. The *Commentary on Luke* is lost except for fragments, some of which are translated in this volume. Of the thirty-two books of the *Commentary on John*, some were already lost in antiquity; eight are still extant, in Greek.

6. *Hebrew Questions on the Book of Genesis,* translated ca. 389.

but another's. On my left I hear an ominous crow cawing; in remarkable fashion it gleams with the colored feathers of all the birds, although the bird itself is black as night.[7] So I admit, before he objects, that in these sermons Origen is like a boy playing at dice. The works of his full manhood, and the writings of his old age, are of another sort.[8]

If I get myself to do it, and if I am able, and if the Lord gives me the time to make a translation into Latin, and if I finish the work I interrupted earlier, then you will be able to see—or rather, through you the Roman tongue will recognize—how much good it previously was ignorant of and now begins to know. Besides this task, I have arranged to have the *Commentary on Matthew* of Hilary,[9] a very eloquent man, and that of the blessed martyr Victorinus,[10] sent to you within a few days. They wrote their books in differing styles but by the one grace of the Spirit. I do not want you to be unaware of how much our people also once studied the Sacred Scriptures.[11]

7. Jerome means Ambrose.

8. Jerome seems to disdain the simplicity of the homilies on Luke because they lack the flights of imaginative interpretation that Origen displays in other commentaries. But modern studies suggest that Origen grew more cautious in his interpretation as he grew older.

9. Hilary of Poitiers, *Commentary on Matthew,* written ca. 353–355.

10. Victorinus of Petau, died 304. His commentary is lost.

11. The manuscripts have this note: "Here ends the preface. Now begin the homilies of Origen on Luke, thirty-nine in number, translated into Latin by Eusebius Jerome, and preached on Sundays. Now begins the first homily."

HOMILY 1

Luke 1.1–4

On the prologue of Luke, up to the point where it says, "to write to you, most excellent Theophilus."

N THE PAST, many claimed to prophesy among the Jewish people. Some were false prophets; among these was Hananiah, son of Azzur.[1] Others were true prophets. The people, like "well-trained money-changers,"[2] had the gift of the discernment of spirits. Through this gift they accepted some as prophets and rejected others. Now, in the New Testament also, "many have tried" to write gospels, but not all have found acceptance.[3] You should know that not only four Gospels, but very many, were composed. The Gospels we have were chosen from among these gospels and passed on to the churches. We can know this from Luke's own prologue, which begins this way: "Because many have tried to compose an account."[4] The words "have tried" imply an accusation against those who rushed into writing gospels without the grace of the Holy Spirit. Matthew, Mark, John, and Luke did not "try" to write; they wrote their Gospels when they were filled with the Holy Spirit. Hence, "Many have tried to compose an account of the events that are clearly known among us."[5]

2. The Church has four Gospels. Heretics have very many.

1. See Jer 28.1–17.

2. Origen is alluding to an ἄγραφον, or unwritten saying of Jesus. The saying is, "Be ye competent money-changers." On the ἄγραφα, see J. Jeremias, "Isolated Sayings of the Lord," in E. Hennecke, *New Testament Apocrypha* (London: SCM, 1963) I, 85–90.

3. Cf. 2 Pt 2.1.

4. Lk 1.1.

5. Lk 1.1.

One of them is entitled *According to the Egyptians*,[6] another *According to the Twelve Apostles.*[7] Basilides, too, dared to write a gospel and give it his own name.[8] "Many have tried" to write, but only four Gospels have been approved. Our doctrines about the Person of our Lord and Savior should be drawn from these approved Gospels. I know one gospel called *According to Thomas*,[9] and another *According to Matthias.*[10] We have read many others, too, lest we appear ignorant of anything, because of those people who think they know something if they have examined these gospels. But in all these questions we approve of nothing but what the Church approves of, namely only four canonical Gospels.[11]

We have said all this because the beginning of the Gospel reads, "Many have tried to compose an account of the events that have been accomplished among us."[12] Those other authors have attempted and "have tried" to write about these events, but for us they are clearly established.

3. Luke makes his intention known by the word he uses, πεπληροφορημένων, that is, "that have been clearly shown to us,"[13] a concept that the Latin language cannot express in one word.[14] It means that Luke knew by firm faith and by careful consideration, and did not waver on any point, wondering whether it should be this way or that. This certitude comes to

6. Little is known of this gospel except for a saying about Salome quoted by Clement of Alexandria. It existed in Egypt during the second century and may have had Gnostic traits. See W. Schneemelcher, "The Gospel of the Egyptians," in Hennecke, *Apocrypha* I, 166–78.

7. Virtually unknown; perhaps it was Jewish-Christian. See Hennecke, *Apocrypha* I, 263–64.

8. Basilides was a Gnostic who taught in Egypt during the first half of the second century. His gospel may have used parts of the four canonical Gospels. See Hennecke, *Apocrypha* I, 346–48.

9. The gospel Origen means is apparently the one discovered ca. 1945 in the Coptic Gnostic library near Nag Hammadi. See Hennecke, *Apocrypha* I, 278–307.

10. Clement of Alexandria quotes a few passages from this work. It may have been Gnostic. See Hennecke, *Apocrypha* I, 308–313.

11. Origen's phrase is "Gospels to be received."

12. Lk 1.1.

13. Lk 1.1.

14. Obviously Jerome's gloss. He puts the principle into practice and varies his translation of the word, using "known," "established," "accompanied," and "shown."

those who have faithfully believed and have attained what the prophet prays for. They say, "Confirm me in your words."[15] The Apostle, too, says of those who were steadfast and strong, "That you may be rooted and grounded in faith."[16] If anyone is rooted and grounded in faith, he will not be torn up or fall down, even if a storm should arise and winds blow and rain pour down, for his house has been built upon rock with a firm foundation.[17] We should not think that steadfastness in faith comes to us through our carnal eyes; mind and reason have imparted it. Let unbelievers trust the signs and portents that human sight beholds. The faithful, prudent, and strong man should follow reason and the Word,[18] and so distinguish truth from error.

4. "Just as those who from the beginning saw and were ministers of the Word[19] handed it down to us."[20] Scripture says, in Exodus, "The people saw the voice of the Lord."[21] Obviously a voice is heard rather than seen. But the Scripture says this to show us that those who deserve to "see God's voice" see it with different eyes.[22] In the Gospel, however, it is not a voice that is seen but a word, which is more excellent than a voice. So the Gospel now says, "Just as those who from the beginning saw and were ministers of the Word handed it down to us."[23] The apostles themselves saw the Word, not because they had beheld the body of our Lord and Savior, but because they had seen the Word. If seeing Jesus' body meant seeing God's

15. Ps 119.28.

16. Eph 3.17; Col 1.23 and 2.7.

17. Origen tries to combine the allusion to Eph and Col (see preceding note) with an allusion to Mt 7.25 and Lk 6.48, thereby mixing the metaphors of a tree and a building.

18. Jerome translates the one Greek word λόγος by its two meanings, "reason" and "word." He discusses the difficulty of translating this word in *Hom.* 5.3.

19. Throughout this homily Origen played on two terms: "voice" (φωνή) and "word" (λόγος). Jerome expands the list to three: "voice" (*vox*), "word" (*sermo*), and "Word" (*verbum*), translating λόγος as *sermo* or *verbum* as the context required. Words are superior to mere sound, and the Word is superior to words.

20. Lk 1.2.

21. Ex 20.18.

22. Origen regularly distinguishes physical from intellectual vision, and to the two kinds of vision there correspond two sorts of eyes. Here faith is the condition for understanding who Jesus was. Cf. *Hom.* 3.3–4, where Origen speaks of seeing who Jesus truly was as a grace.

23. Lk 1.2.

Word, then Pilate, who condemned Jesus, saw God's Word; so did Judas the traitor and all those who cried out, "Crucify him, crucify him, remove such a one from the earth."[24] But far be it that any unbeliever should see God's Word. Seeing God's Word means what the Savior says: "He who has seen me has also seen the Father who sent me."[25]

5. "Just as those who from the beginning saw and were ministers of the Word handed it down to us."[26] Luke's words implicitly teach us that the goal of one discipline is the discipline itself, while the goal of another discipline is its application. For example, the science of geometry has as its goal only the science and discipline itself. But the goal of another science, like medicine, includes its application. I ought to know the theory and principles of medicine not merely to know what I should do, but to do it. In other words, I should incise wounds; prescribe a regulated and controlled diet; detect the heat of fevers in the pulse of the veins; and dry up, regulate, and restrain an excess of humors with periodic treatments.[27] If someone merely knows these principles and does not follow them up with an application, his knowledge is pointless. There is a relation like that of the science of medicine to its application in the knowledge and service of the Word. Hence Scripture says, "Just as those who from the beginning saw and were ministers of the Word."[28] We should realize that the words "they saw" indicate a discipline and a science, while the words "they were ministers" refer to applications.

6. "It seemed right for me, too, following the same course from the beginning . . . ."[29] He makes his point and repeats it. He did not learn from rumors what he is going to write; he himself has grasped it from the beginning. Hence the Apostle praises him deservedly when he says, "He is praised for his

24. Jn 19.15; Acts 22.22.
25. Jn 14.9.
26. Lk 1.2.
27. Origen is thinking of the ancient medical theory that the human body contains four humors or fluids: blood, phlegm, choler (yellow bile), and melancholy (black bile). When he writes that good health depends on a balance among the four humors. Origen is probably following Galen, a physician who lived during the second century A.D.
28. Lk 1.2.
29. Lk 1.3.

Gospel throughout all the churches."[30] Scripture says this about no one else; it uses the expression only for Luke. "It seemed right for me, too, following the same course from the beginning, carefully to write down all those events for you in order, most excellent Theophilus."[31] Someone might think that Luke addressed the Gospel to a specific man named Theophilus. But, if you are the sort of people God can love, then all of you who hear us speaking are Theophiluses,[32] and the Gospel is addressed to you. Anyone who is "Theophilus" is both "excellent" and "very strong"; this is what the Greek word κράτιστος actually means.[33] No "Theophilus" is weak. Scripture says of the people of Israel, when they were going out from Egypt, "There was no weakling in their tribes."[34] I could say boldly that everyone who is a "Theophilus" is robust. He has vigor and strength from both God and His Word. He can recognize the "truth" of those "words, by which he has been instructed" and understand the Word of the Gospel in Christ, to whom is glory and power for ages of ages. Amen.[35]

30. 2 Cor 8.18. Although Paul does not identify the "brother" he mentions there as Luke, Origen thinks that Paul knew the Gospel According to Luke and was praising Luke for that.

31. Lk 1.3.

32. The name Theophilus means "beloved of God."

33. Again, Jerome's gloss. In the Greek text, Luke calls Theophilus κράτιστος; Jerome translates it correctly.

34. Ps 105.37.

35. All 39 homilies end with this doxology, which is taken from 1 Pt 4.11.

HOMILY 2

Luke 1.6

On the passage, "But both were just in God's sight and walked without blame in all the Lord's commandments and precepts."

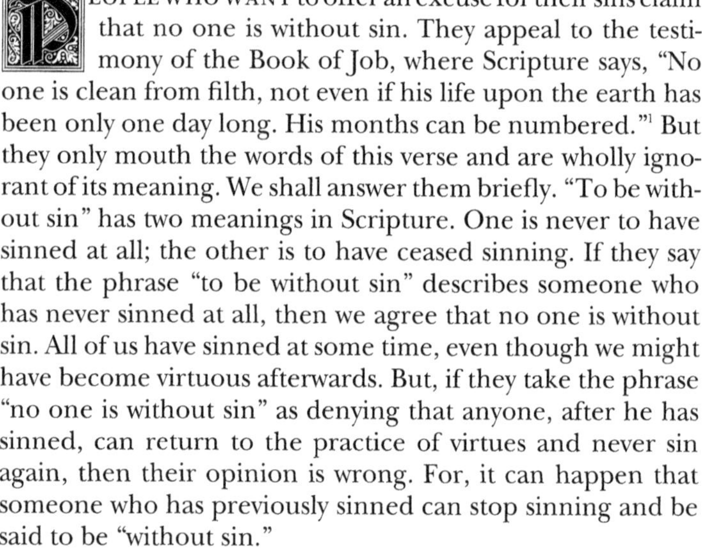

PEOPLE WHO WANT to offer an excuse for their sins claim that no one is without sin. They appeal to the testimony of the Book of Job, where Scripture says, "No one is clean from filth, not even if his life upon the earth has been only one day long. His months can be numbered."[1] But they only mouth the words of this verse and are wholly ignorant of its meaning. We shall answer them briefly. "To be without sin" has two meanings in Scripture. One is never to have sinned at all; the other is to have ceased sinning. If they say that the phrase "to be without sin" describes someone who has never sinned at all, then we agree that no one is without sin. All of us have sinned at some time, even though we might have become virtuous afterwards. But, if they take the phrase "no one is without sin" as denying that anyone, after he has sinned, can return to the practice of virtues and never sin again, then their opinion is wrong. For, it can happen that someone who has previously sinned can stop sinning and be said to be "without sin."

2. Our Lord Jesus Christ "presented to himself a glorious Church, which had no stain"[2]—not because the members of the Church never had a stain, but because they were later free from stain. Scripture adds, "and no wrinkle," not because the members of the Church did not have the wrinkles "of the old

1. Jb 14.4–5.
2. Eph 5.27.

man"[3] at one time, but because they have ceased to have them. The words that follow should be understood in the same way: "So that the Church may be holy and spotless"[4]—not because their souls were spotless from the beginning (one cannot even suspect that they were not stained), but because they are counted as pure and unblemished after they have ceased being stained. We say this to teach that someone who has stopped sinning can be called "without sin and spotless." Hence, Scripture says clearly of Zechariah and Elizabeth, "Both were just in God's sight and walked without blame in all the Lord's commandments and precepts."[5]

3. Let us consider more attentively the praises of Zechariah and Elizabeth that St. Luke writes in his narrative. We want not only to understand that they deserved praise, but also to make their holy zeal our own and become worthy of praise ourselves. Luke could have written simply, "Both were just and walked in all the commandments."[6] But he had to add, "Both were just in God's sight."[7] For, it can happen that someone is just in the sight of men without being just "in God's sight." For example, someone has nothing evil to say about me. He considers everything about me and finds nothing to reproach me with. Then I am just in the sight of men. Imagine that everyone has the same opinion of me. They seek something to reproach me with but cannot find anything. They praise me unanimously. Then I am just in the sight of many. But the judgment of men is uncertain. They do not know whether I once sinned in the hidden depths of my heart—whether I looked at a woman and desired her, and adultery was born in my heart.[8]

4. When men see me giving alms according to my means, they do not know whether I am doing it because of God's commandment or because I am seeking human praise and applause.[9] To be just "in God's sight" is a difficult undertaking. It means that you do something good only for the sake of the

3. Eph 4.22 and Col 3.9.
4. Eph 5.27.
5. Lk 1.6.
6. Lk 1.6.
7. Lk 1.6.
8. Cf. Mt 5.28.
9. Cf. Mt 6.2–4.

good and you seek only God, who rewards a good work. The Apostle says something like that: "Their praise is not from men but from God."[10] Blessed is he who is just and praiseworthy "in God's sight." For, although men seem to have clear judgment, they cannot judge inerrantly. It happens from time to time that they praise someone who is not praiseworthy and reproach someone who deserves no reproach at all. Both in praise and in censure God alone is a just judge.

5. Thus Luke rightly adds to the praise of those two just people, "Both were just in God's sight."[11] Solomon, too, in the Book of Proverbs, urges us on to a goal like this when he says, "Look for good in the sight of God and men."[12]

There follows more praise of Zechariah and Elizabeth: "They walked in all the Lord's commandments and precepts."[13] We walk "in the Lord's precepts" when we judge well and rightly. We walk "in his commandments" when we do some deed well and rightly. I think St. Luke wanted to commend them with perfect praise when he said, "Both were just and walked in all the Lord's commandments and precepts."[14]

6. Someone might say to me, "If this praise is perfect, what does Scripture mean when it adds, 'without blame'? It was enough to say, 'they walked in all the Lord's ways and precepts,'[15] unless it can happen that someone might walk in all God's commandments and still not walk 'without blame.' How is it possible that someone who walks 'in all God's commandments and precepts' is subject to blame?" I shall answer briefly. Unless it were possible, we would not understand what another passage means, namely, "Follow justly what is just."[16] For, unless there were a just act that we might not do justly, the commandment to "follow justly what is just" would be enjoined upon us in vain.

7. We can fulfill God's commands but have our consciences spattered with the filth of vainglory because we are pleasing men. We might be motivated to do good deeds by a reason

10. Rom 2.29.
11. Lk 1.6.
12. Prv 3.4.
13. Lk 1.6.
14. Lk 1.6.
15. Lk 1.6.
16. Dt 16.20

that displeases God. In these cases we are carrying out God's commandment, but we are not doing it "without blame," and are following unjustly what is just. Thus it is difficult to "walk without blame in all the Lord's commandments and precepts," following the testimony and praise of God in Christ Jesus. This praise has to be given on the day of judgment by him "before whose tribunal all of us must stand, so that each one might receive recompense for what he has done in his body, whether good or evil."[17] "For, we shall all stand before God's tribunal"[18] to receive what we merit in Christ Jesus, to whom is glory and power for ages of ages. Amen.

17. 2 Cor 5.10.
18. Rom 14.10.

HOMILY 3

Luke 1.11

On the passage, "The angel of the Lord appeared to him, standing at the right side of the altar of incense."

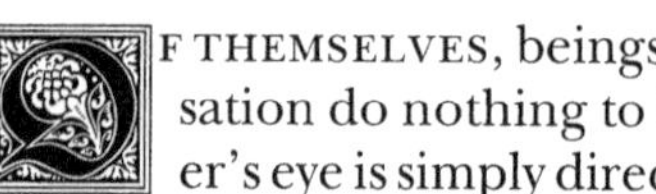

F THEMSELVES, beings that are corporeal and lack sensation do nothing to be seen by another. The observer's eye is simply directed toward them. Whenever the observer directs his gaze and his regard at them, he sees them, whether the objects will it or not. What can a man or any other object that is enclosed in a solid body do to avoid being seen, when they are in fact there? In contrast, things that are from above and divine are not seen, even when they are there, unless they themselves will it. It lies within their will to be seen or not. It was by an act of his grace that God appeared to Abraham and the other prophets. The eye of Abraham's heart was not the only cause that allowed him to see God; God offered his grace to the sight of a just man to let him see.

2. You should understand this not only of God the Father, but also of our Lord and Savior and of the Holy Spirit and—to come to lesser beings—of cherubim and seraphim. Perhaps an angel is helping us as we are speaking now, but we cannot see him because we do not deserve to. Even though the eye of our body or our soul makes an effort to see, the man who wants to see will not, unless the angel willingly appears and offers himself to sight. Thus, wherever Scripture says, "God appeared" to someone—just as here, for example, "The angel of the Lord appeared to him, standing at the right side of the altar of incense"[1]—understand it as I explained. Whether it is

1. Lk 1.11.

God or an angel, and whether he appears to Abraham or to Zechariah, he will be seen or not, depending on whether he wishes it or not.

3. And we say this not only "of the present age"[2] but also of the age to come. When we depart from the world, God or the angels do not appear to everyone, as if anyone who departs from the body immediately deserves to see the angels, the Holy Spirit, the Lord and Savior, and God the Father himself. Only one who has a pure heart and shows himself worthy of the vision of God will see them. One will be pure of heart; another will still be stained with some filth. Although they will be in the same place, the place itself will not be able to help or hinder them. Whoever has a pure heart will see God.[3] Whoever does not will not see what the other beholds.[4] I think we should understand something similar of Christ, too, when he was seen in the body. Not everyone who laid eyes on him was able to see him.

4. They saw his body, but, insofar as he was Christ, they could not see him. But his disciples saw him and beheld the greatness of his divinity. I think this is why, when Philip entreated the Savior and said, "Show us the Father and it is enough for us," the Savior answered him, "Have I been with you for so long a time, and you do not know me? Philip, he who sees me sees the Father also."[5] Pilate, who saw Jesus, did not gaze upon the Father. Neither did Judas the traitor. Neither Pilate nor Judas saw Christ as Christ. Nor did the crowd, which pressed around him.[6] Only those whom Jesus judged worthy of beholding him really saw him.[7] Let us, too, therefore, work so that God might appear to us at this moment. The holy word of Scripture has promised, "He is found by those who do not test him, and he appears to those who do

2. Gal 1.4.
3. Cf. Mt 5.8.
4. Origen believed that the soul, after death, underwent a sort of education, and was led into higher and higher truths until it gazed on the very causes of things and finally saw God. He imagined that this education took place as the soul journeyed upwards through the spheres of the heavens. See *On First Principles* 2.11.6–7.
5. Jn 14.8–9.
6. Cf. Lk 8.45.
7. See the parallel discussion of the two kinds of vision in *Hom.* 1.4.

not doubt him."[8] In the age to come may he not be hidden from us; may we see him "face to face."[9] May we have the assurance of a good life and enjoy the vision of Almighty God in Christ Jesus and in the Holy Spirit, to whom is glory and power for ages of ages. Amen.

8. Wis 1.2.
9. 1 Cor 13.12.

HOMILY 4

Luke 1.13–17

On the passage from, "Do not be afraid, Zechariah," up to the point where it is said of John, "He will go before him in the spirit and power of Elijah."

WHEN ZECHARIAH SAW the angel, he was terrified. If the human gaze beholds a strange form, the mind is agitated and the soul is unsettled. The angel understands that human nature reacts in this way, so he first settles Zechariah's agitation and says, "Do not be afraid, Zechariah."[1] He revives the trembling man and gladdens him by announcing his news.[2] He says, "Your prayer has been heard. Your wife Elizabeth will bear a son. You shall name him John. He will bring you joy and elation."[3] When a just man is born into the world and enters the course of this life, those responsible for his birth rejoice, and their hearts soar upward. But, when someone who is destined for an evil life is born, one who is virtually banished to a prison as a punishment, the one responsible for his birth is thrown into confusion and loses heart.

2. Do you want an example of a holy man, all of whose deeds are praiseworthy? Consider Jacob. He fathered twelve male offspring. All of them became patriarchs, princes of God's people and of Jacob's heritage.[4] Jacob, their father, rejoiced in all of them. The Gospel proclaims joy for all people because of John's birth. Once a man engages in the task of begetting

1. Lk 1.13.

2. Origen refers to his understanding of the "Gospel," which he defines as, "A discourse containing a promise of things that, on account of the advantages they bring, naturally bring joy to the hearer as soon as he hears the news" (*Commentary on John* 1.5.27).

3. Lk 1.13–14.

4. Cf. Dt 32.9.

children to benefit others and willingly devotes himself to this service, he should pray to God and ask that any son of his who comes into the world might be like John, one whose birth would bring him joy. Scripture says of John, "He will be great in the Lord's sight."[5] This phrase, "He will be great in the Lord's sight," shows the greatness of John's soul. God's eyes beheld this greatness. There is also a "smallness" of soul, which properly looks to the soul's virtue.

3. This is how I understand the passage in the Gospel that says, "Do not despise one of these least ones in the Church."[6] "Least one" is to be understood in contrast with someone greater. The Gospel does not command me not to despise a great one; a great one cannot be despised. But it tells me, "Do not despise one of these least ones." You should realize that the words "least" and "little" are not used haphazardly. Scripture says, for the reason we just mentioned, "whoever scandalizes one of these least ones."[7] A "least one" can be scandalized; a great one cannot.

4. Then the Gospel says of John, "He will be filled with the Holy Spirit even from his mother's womb."[8] John's birth is filled with miracles. An archangel announced the coming of our Lord and Savior; an archangel also announces John's birth: "He will be filled with the Holy Spirit even from his mother's womb."[9] The Jewish people did not recognize our Lord when he performed "signs and wonders"[10] and cured their illnesses.[11] But, when John is still in his mother's womb, he rejoices and cannot be restrained. When Jesus' mother arrives, he tries to burst out of the womb. Elizabeth says, "For behold, when your greeting sounded in my ears, the infant leapt for joy in my womb."[12] John was still in his mother's womb when he received the Holy Spirit, but the Spirit was not the principle of his being or nature.[13]

5. Lk 1.15.
6. Mt 18.10.
7. Mt 18.6.
8. Lk 1.15.
9. Lk 1.15.
10. Cf. Jn 4.48.
11. Lk 5.15.
12. Lk 1.44.
13. An anti-Gnostic phrase. John the Baptizer was not the Holy Spirit incarnate, as some Gnostics asserted. See Rufinus of Aquileia, *Apology against Jerome* 2.27 (PL 21.606), who writes that Jerome inserted the words "or nature" into Origen's text.

5. Then Scripture says, "He will convert many of the sons of Israel to the Lord their God."[14] John converts many; the Lord converts not many but all. This is the Lord's work, to convert all to God the Father. "He will go before Christ in the spirit and power of Elijah."[15] Luke does not say, "in the soul of Elijah," but, "in the spirit and power of Elijah."[16] Power and spirit dwelt in Elijah as in all the prophets and, with regard to his humanity, in the Lord and Savior as well. A little later in the Gospel the angel says to Mary, "The Holy Spirit will come upon you, and the power of the Most High will overshadow you."[17] So the spirit that had been in Elijah came upon John as well, and the power that Elijah had also appeared in John. Elijah was carried off to heaven. John was the Lord's precursor and died before him so that he could go down to the underworld and proclaim his coming.

6. I believe that the mystery of John is still being achieved in the world today. If anyone is going to believe in Christ Jesus, John's spirit and power first come to his soul and "prepare a perfect people for the Lord."[18] It makes the roads in the heart's rough places level and straightens out its paths.[19] Not only at that time were the roads made ready and the paths straight; even today John's spirit and power precede the coming of our Lord and Savior. How great are the Lord's mysteries and his plan! Angels go before Jesus, and today angels go up or down[20] for the salvation of men in Christ Jesus, to whom is glory and power for ages of ages. Amen.

14. Lk 1.16.
15. Lk 1.17.
16. Origen is denying a doctrine of metempsychosis, or the transmigration of souls. John does not have Elijah's soul, but his spirit.
17. Lk 1.35.
18. Lk 1.17.
19. Cf. Is 40.3–4 and Lk 3.4–5.
20. Cf. Jn 1.51.

HOMILY 5

Luke 1.22

On the fact that Zechariah fell mute.

HEN THE PRIEST Zechariah offers incense in the temple, he is condemned to silence and cannot speak. Or better, he speaks only with gestures. He remains mute until the birth of his son John. What does this mean? Zechariah's silence is the silence of prophets in the people of Israel.[1] God no longer speaks to them. His "Word, which was with the Father from the beginning, and was God,"[2] has passed over to us. For us Christ is not silent; for the Jews he is silent even to this day. Therefore, Zechariah the prophet was also silent. His words make it quite clear that he was both a prophet and a priest. But what does the phrase that follows mean, namely, "He kept nodding to them"[3]—that is, he compensated for the loss of his voice with signs? I think that there are deeds that are no different from empty signs because they lack words and reason.[4] But, when words and reason come first and the deed follows, the deeds are not mere signs; they are endowed with rationality.

2. Consider the Jewish practices. They lack words and rea-

1. Cf. Ambrose, *Exposition of the Gospel According to Luke* 1.40.

2. Jn 1.1–2.

3. Lk 1.22.

4. Jerome here translates λόγος awkwardly as "word and reason." What follows makes it clear that, in Origen's view, Jewish practices (and more generally, the entire Old Testament) remain mere gestures if they lack the fulfillment that λόγος—that is, the Word himself, the principle of intelligibility—brings to them. Origen's disparagement of the Jews, sometimes expressed rather sharply, rests on his conviction that, in rejecting Jesus as Messiah, they rejected God's Word and hence the very principle that rendered their Scripture and their practices intelligible.

son.[5] The Jews cannot give a reason for their practices. Realize that what happened in the past in Zechariah is a type of what is fulfilled in the Jews even to this day. Their circumcision is like an empty sign. Unless the meaning of circumcision is provided, it remains an empty sign, a mute deed. Passover and other feasts are empty signs rather than the truth. To this very day the people of Israel are mute and dumb. The people who rejected the Word from their midst could not be anything but mute and dumb.

3. Moses himself once said, "I am ἄλογος (wordless)."[6] The Latin version uses a different expression, but we can translate the word ἄλογος exactly as "without words and reason." After he said this, he received reason and speech, which he admitted that he did not have before. When the people of Israel were in Egypt, before they had received the Law, they too were without words and reason and thus, in a sense, mute. Then they received the Word; Moses was the image of it. So these people do not admit now what Moses had once admitted—that they are mute and wordless—but show by signs and silence that they have neither words nor reason. Do you not realize that the Jews are confessing their folly when none of them can give a reasonable explanation of the precepts of their Law and of the predictions of their prophets?[7]

4. Christ ceased to be in them. The Word deserted them. What Isaiah wrote was fulfilled, "The daughter of Zion will be deserted like a tent in the vineyard or like a hut in the cucumber patch; she is as desolate as a plundered city."[8] The Jews were left behind and salvation passed to the Gentiles. God meant to spur on the Jews with envy. We contemplate God's mysterious plan, how for our salvation he rejected Israel. We ought to be careful. The Jews were rejected for our sake; on

5. That is, the Jews lack the Λόγος.

6. Ex 4.10. Jerome keeps the Greek word here.

7. See Rom 11.11. Origen here states the Christians' principal objection to the Jews. Jews failed to understand the Old Testament—that is, they failed to interpret it christologically.

8. Is 1.8.

our account they were abandoned. We would deserve even greater punishment if we did nothing worthy of our adoption by God and of his mercy. In his mercy God adopted us and made us his sons in Christ Jesus, to whom is glory and power for ages of ages. Amen.

HOMILY 6

Luke 1.24–32

On the passage from, "But, when Elizabeth conceived, she kept herself hidden," up to the point where it says, "He will be great."

HEN ELIZABETH CONCEIVED, "she kept herself hidden for five months. She said, 'The Lord did this for me when he showed concern for me and took away the reason people reproach me.'"[1] I ask why she avoided public notice after she realized that she was pregnant.[2] Unless I am mistaken, the reason is this. Even those who are joined in marriage do not consider every season free for intercourse. At times they abstain from the use of marriage. If the husband and wife are both aged, it is a disgraceful thing for them to yield to lust and turn to mating. The decline of the body, old age itself, and God's will all inhibit this act. But Elizabeth had relations with her husband once again, because of the angel's word and God's dispensation.[3] She was embarrassed because she was an old and feeble woman, and had gone back to what young people do.

2. Hence "she kept herself hidden for five months"—not until the ninth month, when childbirth was impending, but until Mary also conceived. When Mary conceived and came to Elizabeth, and "her greeting resounded in [her] ears, the child in [Elizabeth's] womb leapt for joy."[4] Elizabeth prophesied. She was filled with the Holy Spirit. She spoke the words

1. Lk 1.24–25.
2. Cf. Ambrose, *Exposition of the Gospel According to Luke* 1.43.
3. The Greek word οἰκονομία, literally "the management of a household," was used by the Fathers to designate God's plan of salvation, and particularly the Incarnation. Jerome translated it with *dispensatio*.
4. Lk 1.44.

recorded in the Gospel account, and "these words spread through the entire hill country."[5] A rumor spread among the people that Elizabeth bore a prophet in her womb, and that what she was carrying was greater than a man. Then she does not hide her condition. In full freedom she appears in public and rejoices, because she is bearing the precursor of the Savior in her womb.

3. Scripture then relates that, six months after Elizabeth conceived, "the angel Gabriel was sent by God to a town of Galilee named Nazareth, to a Virgin betrothed to a man named Joseph of the house of David, and the Virgin's name was Mary."[6] Again I turn the matter over in my mind and ask why, when God had decided that the Savior should be born of a virgin, he chose not a girl who was not betrothed, but precisely one who was already betrothed.[7] Unless I am mistaken, this is the reason. The Savior ought to have been born of a virgin who was not only betrothed but, as Matthew writes, had already been given to her husband, although he had not yet had relations with her.[8] Otherwise, if the Virgin were seen growing big with a child, the state of virginity itself would be a cause of disgrace.

4. I found an elegant statement in the letter of a martyr—I mean Ignatius, the second bishop of Antioch after Peter. During a persecution, he fought against wild animals at Rome. He stated, "Mary's virginity escaped the notice of the ruler of this age."[9] It escaped his notice because of Joseph, and because

5. Lk 1.65.

6. Lk 1.26–27.

7. Cf. Ambrose, *Exposition of the Gospel According to Luke* 2.1.

8. Cf. Mt 1.24.

9. Ignatius of Antioch, *Ephesians* 19.1. Origen quotes accurately but shortens the sentence. Ignatius wrote, "Now, Mary's virginity and her giving birth escaped the notice of the prince of this world, as did the Lord's death—those three secrets crying to be told, but wrought in God's silence," in the translation of Cyril C. Richardson (in Early Christian Fathers, LCC 1 [Philadelphia: Westminster, 1953], p. 93). Ignatius's meaning has long been disputed; see William R. Schoedel, *Ignatius of Antioch: A Commentary on the Letters* (Philadelphia: Fortress, 1985) on the passage. Tradition makes Ignatius the third bishop of Antioch, after Peter the Apostle and Evodius. Ignatius was condemned to death under Trajan (100–118) and transported to Rome for execution, probably about A.D. 110. Seven of his letters, written during his journey to Rome, are extant. Cf. also Ambrose, *Exposition of the Gospel According to Luke* 2.3.

of their wedding, and because Mary was thought to have a husband. If she had not been betrothed or not had (as people thought) a husband, her virginity could never have been concealed from the "ruler of this age."[10] Immediately, a silent thought would have occurred to the devil: "How can this woman, who has not slept with a man, be pregnant? This conception must be divine. It must be something more sublime than human nature." But the Savior had so arranged his plan that the devil did not know that he had taken on a body. When he was conceived, he escaped the devil's notice. Later he commanded his disciples "not to make him known."[11]

5. When the Savior was tempted by the devil himself, he never admitted that he was the Son of God. He merely said, "It is not right for me to adore you or to turn these stones into loaves of bread or to throw myself down from a high place."[12] He said that, but never said he was the Son of God. Look in other books of Scripture, too. You will find that it was Christ's will that the devil should be ignorant of the coming of God's Son. For, the Apostle maintains that the opposing powers[13] were ignorant of his Passion. He writes, "We speak wisdom among the perfect, but not the wisdom of this age or the wisdom of the rulers of this age. They are being destroyed. We speak God's wisdom, hidden in a mystery. None of the rulers of this age knows it. If they had known it, they would never have crucified the Lord of glory."[14] Thus the mystery of the Savior was hidden from the rulers of this age.

6. An objection to this explanation can be raised, and I think I should resolve it before someone else raises it. The problem is why something that was hidden from the rulers of this age was not hidden from the demon who said in the Gospel, "Have you come here to torture us before the assigned time? We know who you are—the Son of God."[15] Bear this in mind. The demon, who is less evil, knew the Savior. But the

10. 1 Cor 2.6 and Jn 12.31.
11. Mt 12.16.
12. Cf. Mt 4.3–10 and Lk 4.3–13. Origen changes the order. Matthew's order is bread, temple, worship; Luke's is bread, worship, temple.
13. Origen's standard term for the forces of evil. Cf. *Homs.* 22.2, 23.4, and 31.6; *Frag.* 112; and *On First Principles* 3.2.
14. 1 Cor 2.6–8.
15. Mt 8.29.

devil's wickedness is greater; he is fickle and depraved. The fact that his wickedness is greater prevents him from knowing the Son of God. We ourselves can advance to virtue more easily if we are less sinful. But, if we are more sinful, then we need sweat and hard labor to be freed from our greater evil. This is my explanation of why Mary was betrothed.

7. The angel greeted Mary with a new address, which I could not find anywhere else in Scripture. I ought to explain this expression briefly. The angel says, "Hail, full of grace."[16] The Greek word is κεχαριτωμένη. I do not remember having read this word elsewhere in Scripture.[17] An expression of this kind, "Hail, full of grace," is not addressed to a male. This greeting was reserved for Mary alone.[18] Mary knew the Law; she was holy, and had learned the writings of the prophets by meditating on them daily. If Mary had known that someone else had been greeted by words like these, she would never have been frightened by this strange greeting. Hence the angel says to her, "Do not be afraid, Mary! You have found grace in God's eyes. Behold, you will conceive in your womb. You will bear a son, and you will name him 'Jesus.' He will be great, and will be called 'Son of the Most High.'"[19]

8. Scripture also says of John, "He will be great,"[20] and the angel Gabriel attests to this. But, when Jesus (who is truly great and truly exalted) comes, then John (who earlier had been "great") becomes less.[21] Jesus said, "He was a lamp, burning and shining, and at that hour you wished to rejoice in his light."[22] The greatness of our Savior was not manifested when he was born. It has shone forth only afterward, when his enemies seemed to have extinguished it.

16. Lk 1.28.

17. Origen is right. The word is never found in the Septuagint, although it does occur at Eph 1.6. Origen imagines that Mary had studied the Scriptures carefully and would have recognized the word if it had occurred in the Old Testament.

18. Cf. Ambrose, *Exposition of the Gospel According to Luke* 2.9.

19. Lk 1.30–32.

20. Lk 1.15. Cf. *Homilies on Leviticus* 12.2 and Ambrose, *Exposition of the Gospel According to Luke* 2.10.

21. Cf. Jn 3.30.

22. Jn 5.35.

9. Behold the Lord's greatness. "The sound of his teaching has gone out into every land, and his words to the ends of the earth."[23] Our Lord Jesus has been spread out to the whole world, because he is God's power.[24] And now he is with us, according to the Apostle's words: "You are gathered together in my spirit also, with the power of the Lord Jesus."[25] The power of the Lord and Savior is with those who are in Britain, separated from our world, and with those who are in Mauretania, and with everyone under the sun who has believed in his name. Behold the Savior's greatness. It extends to all the world. And still I have not expounded his true greatness.

10. Go up to the heavens.[26] See how he fills the celestial regions: "He appeared to the angels."[27] Go down in your mind to the nether world. See that he went down there, too. "He went down, the one who also went up, to fulfill everything,"[28] "so that at Jesus' name every knee might bend—those of heavenly beings, and earthly beings, and beings in the nether world."[29] Ponder the Lord's power, how it has filled the world—that is, the heavens, the earth, and the nether regions. He passed through heaven itself and rose to the regions above. We have read that the Son of God "passed through the heavens."[30]

If you understand this, you will also realize that Scripture does not say, "He will be great," carelessly, but the word has been fulfilled in deed. Jesus our Lord is great, both present and absent. He has endowed this assembly and gathering of ours with a share of his fortitude. That each of us may deserve to receive it, we pray the Lord Jesus, to whom is glory and power for ages of ages. Amen.

23. Ps 19.4. Also cited in Rom 10.18. Origen adds "of his teaching" and substitutes "his" for "their" twice.

24. Cf. 1 Cor 1.24.

25. 1 Cor 5.4.

26. Cf. Ps 139.8 and Rom 10.6.

27. 1 Tm 3.16.

28. Eph 4.10.

29. Phil 2.10.

30. Heb 4.14.

HOMILY 7

Luke 1.39–45

On the passage from, "But Mary rose up in haste and went into the mountain country," up to the point where it says, "He will be the fulfillment of what has been said."

ETTER MEN GO to weaker men to give them some advantage by their visits.[1] Thus the Savior came to John to sanctify John's baptism.[2] And as soon as Mary heard the angel announce that she would conceive the Savior and that her relative Elizabeth had a child in her womb, "she rose up in haste and went into the mountain country, and entered Elizabeth's house."[3] Jesus was in her womb, and he hastened to sanctify John, who was still in his own mother's womb. That is, before Mary came and greeted Elizabeth, the infant did not rejoice in her womb. But, as soon as Mary spoke the word that the Son of God, in his mother's womb, had supplied, "the infant leapt in joy."[4] At that moment Jesus made his forerunner a prophet for the first time.

2. Mary was the one most suitable to bear God's Son. After the angel spoke to her, it was also appropriate for her to go up to the mountain country and to stay in the higher regions. Hence Scripture says, "Mary rose up in those days and went into the mountain country."[5] She was eager, and not slothful.[6] Thus it was right for her to hasten on eagerly. She was filled with the Holy Spirit; it was appropriate for her to be led to the

1. Cf. Ambrose, *Exposition of the Gospel According to Luke* 2.22.
2. Cf. Lk 3.21.
3. Lk 1.39.
4. Lk 1.40–41.
5. Lk 1.39.
6. Cf. Rom 12.11.

higher regions and have God's power protecting her, for that power had already overshadowed her. Hence she went "into the city of Judah, and Zechariah's house, and she greeted Elizabeth. And it happened that, when Elizabeth heard Mary's greeting, the infant leapt in her womb, and she was filled with the Holy Spirit."[7]

3. So there is no doubt on this point. Elizabeth, who was filled with the Holy Spirit at that moment, received the Spirit on account of her son.[8] For the mother did not merit the Holy Spirit first. First John, still enclosed in her womb, received the Holy Spirit. Then she too, after her son was sanctified, was filled with the Holy Spirit. You will be able to believe this if you also learn something similar about the Savior. (In a certain number of manuscripts, we have discovered that blessed Mary is said to prophesy. We are not unaware of the fact that, according to other copies of the Gospel, Elizabeth speaks these words in prophecy.)[9] So Mary also was filled with the Holy Spirit when she began to carry the Savior in her womb. For, as soon as she received the Holy Spirit, who was the creator of the Lord's body, and the Son of God began to exist in her womb, she too was filled with the Holy Spirit.

4. Therefore "the infant in [Elizabeth's] womb leapt, and she was filled with the Holy Spirit. She cried out in a loud voice and said, 'Blessed are you among women.'"[10] At this point we ought to refute the heretics' usual objections;[11] otherwise some simpler people might be deceived. Someone or other gave vent to his madness and claimed that the Savior had repudiated Mary because she had been joined to Joseph after his birth.[12] This is what he said. I hope he knows what the state of his mind was when he said it. If heretics ever raise an objection like this to you, answer them and say, "Elizabeth surely was

7. Lk 1.40–41.

8. Cf. Ambrose, *Exposition of the Gospel According to Luke* 2.23.

9. Origen is right. Some manuscripts assign the *Magnificat* to Mary, while others attribute it to Elizabeth. Modern critics believe that the original editor meant it to be Mary's words.

10. Lk 1.41–42.

11. The identity of these heretics is uncertain.

12. Cf. Mt 1.25 and 12.48.

filled with the Holy Spirit when she said, 'Blessed are you among women.'[13] If the Holy Spirit called Mary 'blessed,' how could the Savior repudiate her?" Furthermore, they assert that Mary had marital relations after the birth of Jesus. But they have no source of proof. For the children who were called Joseph's[14] were not born of Mary. There is no passage in Scripture that mentions this.

5. "Blessed are you among women, and blessed is the fruit of your womb. And whence does this happen to me, that the mother of my Lord should come to me?"[15] Elizabeth says, "Whence does this happen to me?"[16] She is utterly filled with the Holy Spirit. She does not speak in ignorance, as if she did not know that, according to God's will, the mother of the Lord was coming to her. She rather speaks with this meaning: "What good have I done? What deeds of mine are so great that the mother of my Lord should come to me? By what justice, by what good works, by what fidelity of mind have I merited this, that the mother of the Lord should come to me?" "For behold, as your greeting sounded in my ears, the infant leapt for joy in my womb."[17] The soul of the blessed John was holy. While he was still enclosed in his mother's womb and still to come into the world, he recognized the one whom Israel did not know. Hence "he leapt"—and he did not simply leap, but he leapt "for joy." For he had perceived that his Lord had come to sanctify his servant before he went forth from his mother's womb. I hope that unbelievers might call me stupid because I have believed such things. The deed itself, and the truth, show that I have put my trust not in stupidity but in wisdom, because this, which they consider stupid, is the occasion of my salvation.

6. For, unless the Savior's birth had been heavenly and blessed, unless it had had something of the divine that surpassed human nature, his teaching would never have spread

13. Lk 1.42.
14. Cf. Mt 13.55 and Origen, *Commentary on Matthew* 10.17.
15. Lk 1.42–43.
16. Cf. Ambrose, *Exposition of the Gospel According to Luke* 2.25.
17. Lk 1.44.

to the whole world. If only a man had been in Mary's womb and not the Son of God, how could it happen—both at that time and now—that many diseases are cured, not only of bodies but also of souls? Who of us was not once foolish? Now, because of God's mercy, we have understanding, and we know God. Who of us believed in justice? Now, because of Christ, we possess justice and follow it. Who of us was not wandering aimlessly, and vacillating? Now, because of the Savior's coming, we are not tossed about by the waves or agitated. We are on our way—that is, we are in him who says, "I am the Way."[18]

7. When we collect the rest of the testimony, too, we can see that everything written about him is reported as divine, and worthy of wonder. His birth, his growth, his power, his Passion, and his Resurrection were effective not only in their own time but now too, in us. You catechumens—who gathered you into the Church?[19] What goad compelled you to leave your houses and come together in this assembly? We did not go to you from house to house. The Almighty Father put this zeal into your hearts by his invisible power. He knows you are worthy. He wills you to come to faith, reluctant and doubtful as you are, especially at the beginning of your religious faith. Timid and frightened, you received faith in salvation with fear.

8. Catechumens, I entreat you. Do not shrink back. None of you should be afraid or terrified. Follow Jesus, who goes before you. He draws you to salvation. He gathers you into the Church, which in this age is on earth. But, if you bear worthy fruit,[20] he will draw you into "the Church of the first-born, whose names are written in heaven."[21] "Blessed is she who believed," and blessed is he who believed, "because what the Lord said to them will be fulfilled."[22] Hence Mary glorifies the Lord Jesus. Her "soul glorifies the Lord," her "spirit glorifies God."[23] We shall inquire into and consider and discuss the

18. Jn 14.6 and cf. Origen, *Commentary on John* 1.51.

19. Origen also addresses the catechumens in *Homs.* 21.4 and 22.6. In *Hom.* 32.6 he acknowledges the presence both of catechumens and of the baptized in the assembly.

20. Cf. Lk 3.8.

21. Heb 12.23.

22. Lk 1.45.

23. Lk 1.46.

interpretation of this passage, if the Lord grants it, when we gather in church again, when you come to God's house in celebration, when you open your ears to the divine reading, in Christ Jesus, to whom is glory and power for ages of ages. Amen.

HOMILY 8

Luke 1.46–51

On the passage from, "My soul magnifies the Lord," up to the point where it says, "He gave strength to those who fear him."

LIZABETH PROPHESIES before John; before the birth of the Lord and Savior, Mary prophesies. Sin began from the woman and then spread to the man. In the same way, salvation had its first beginnings from women.[1] Thus the rest of women can also lay aside the weakness of their sex and imitate as closely as possible the lives and conduct of these holy women whom the Gospel now describes. Let us consider the Virgin's prophecy. She says, "My soul magnifies the Lord, and my spirit has rejoiced in God my Savior."[2] Two subjects, "soul" and "spirit," carry out a double praise. The soul praises the Lord, the spirit praises God. This is not because the praise of the Lord differs from the praise of God, but because he who is God is also Lord, and he who is Lord is also God.

2. We ask how a soul can magnify the Lord.[3] The Lord can undergo neither increase nor loss. He is what he is. Thus, why does Mary now say, "My soul magnifies the Lord"? I need to consider that the Lord and Savior is "the image of the invisible God,"[4] and realize that my soul is made "in the Creator's image,"[5] so that it is an image of the Image. My soul is not directly

1. Cf. Sir 25.24, and Ambrose, *Exposition of the Gospel According to Luke* 2.28.

2. Lk 1.46–47.

3. Origen here plays on the literal sense of the Greek word μεγαλύνειν, which means "to magnify," "to make great." (The same is true of *magnificare*, the word Jerome uses.) He asks how the soul can magnify God—that is, make God great. He answers that God can be made greater only in the sense that the soul that praises him can "grow."

4. Col 1.15.

5. Cf. Gn 1.26–27. Origen thinks of the Word, "through whom all things were made" (Jn 1.3), and not of the Father, as the Creator.

an image of God; it was created as the image of an Image that already existed. Then I shall understand. Take an example. Those who paint pictures take the one exemplar—for instance, the face of a king—and then use all their diligence and skill to copy the original likeness. So too each one of us shapes his soul into the image of Christ and makes either a larger or a smaller image of him. The image is either dingy and dirty, or it is clean and bright and corresponds to the form of the original. Therefore, when I make the image of the Image—that is, my soul—large, and magnify it by work, thought, and speech, then the Lord himself is magnified in my soul, because it is an image of him. And, just as the Lord is thus magnified in our image of him, so too, if we are sinners, he diminishes and decreases.

3. But surely the Lord is not diminished, nor does he decrease. Rather, we create other images in ourselves instead of the Savior's image. Instead of being the image of the Word, or of wisdom, justice, and the rest of the virtues, we assume the form of the devil. Then we can be called "serpents" and "a generation of vipers."[6] When we are venomous, cruel, or wily, we have taken on the character of the lion, the snake, or the fox. When we are prone to pleasure, we are like the goat. I recall once explaining that place in Deuteronomy[7] where it is written, "Do not make any image of a male or a female, or an image of any beast."[8] I said that, "because the law is spiritual"[9] the passage means this. Some make themselves into the image of a male, others into the image of a female. One has the likeness of birds, another of reptiles and serpents. Still another makes himself the image of God. Anyone who reads what I wrote will know how the passage can be understood.

4. So first Mary's soul magnifies the Lord, and afterwards her spirit rejoices in God.[10] Unless we have already grown

6. Mt 23.33.
7. Origen's *Homilies on Deuteronomy* are lost.
8. Dt 4.16–17.
9. Rom 7.14. I.e., the Old Testament requires a spiritual interpretation.
10. Lk 1.47.

great[11] we cannot rejoice. "Because he has looked upon the humility of his handmaid,"[12] she says. What humility of Mary's did the Lord look upon? The mother of the Savior was carrying the Son of God in her womb. What was humble and despised in her? What she says, "He looked upon the humility of his handmaid,"[13] is equivalent to saying, "He looked upon the justice of his handmaid," "looked upon her temperance," "looked upon her fortitude and her wisdom."[14] For it is right for God to look upon virtues. Someone might object and say, "I understand how God could look upon his handmaid's justice and wisdom. But it is not quite clear how he could look upon her humility." The one who asks such questions should consider that, in the Scriptures, humility is declared to be one of the virtues.[15]

5. For the Savior says, "Learn from me, for I am gentle and humble in heart, and you will find rest for your souls."[16] If you wish to hear the name of this virtue, how even the philosophers designate it, listen: the humility that God looks upon is the same virtue that they call ἀτυφία ("modesty") or μετριότης ("moderation").[17] We can also describe it with a circumlocution: it is the state of someone who is not conceited, but who lowers himself. For, according to the Apostle, one who is conceited falls "under the devil's judgment,"[18] since the devil had his beginnings in conceit and pride. Paul says, "so that he should not be conceited and fall into the devil's judgment."[19]

11. Origen again plays on "magnify," which means "grow great."

12. Lk 1.48.

13. Lk 1.48.

14. Christian writers took over reflection on the four cardinal virtues (prudence, justice, fortitude, and temperance) from Plato and Aristotle. Origen here uses "wisdom" for "prudence," as he does in *Hom.* 35.9 also.

15. The Greeks never considered humility to be a virtue, and the word used for it at Lk 1.48 always had, in secular Greek, a negative connotation. Morally, it meant "baseness" or "vileness," socially, "lowness of position." In this paragraph, Origen struggles to present humility as a virtue to an audience of catechumens who are not used to thinking of it as such.

16. Mt 11.29.

17. ἀτυφία means "freedom from arrogance," and was a characteristic of the Stoic sage. μετριότης means "moderation." Origen is still struggling to convey a positive sense of ταπεινότης, Luke's word for "humility."

18. 1 Tm 3.6.

19. 1 Tm 3.6.

"He looked upon the humility of his handmaid."[20] She is saying, "God looked upon me because I am humble and pursue the virtues of gentleness and submission."

6. "For behold, from now on all generations will call me blessed."[21] If I take "all generations" literally, I apply it to believers. But, if I search for something more profound, I will notice how valuable it is to join to it, "because he who is powerful has done great things for me."[22] For, "everyone who humbles himself will be exalted."[23] But God looked upon the blessed Mary's humility, and on account of it "he who is powerful did great things for [her], and holy is his name."[24] "And his mercy extends to generations of generations."[25] God's mercy is not for one generation, nor for two, nor for three. It is not for five; but it stretches "from generation to generation." "To those who fear him he has shown strength in his arm."[26] You may approach the Lord as a weak man. If you fear him, you will be able to hear the promise the Lord makes to you on account of your fear of him.

7. What is this promise? He says, "He made himself the power of those who fear him." *Virtus* or *imperium* is royal power.[27] For κράτος,[28] which we can call in Latin *imperium*,[29] is derived from him who commands, or holds everything under himself. So, if you fear the Lord, he gives you courage or authority; he gives you the kingdom, so that you might be placed under the "king of kings,"[30] and possess the kingdom of heaven in Christ Jesus, to whom is glory and power for ages of ages. Amen.

20. Lk 1.48.
21. Lk 1.48.
22. Lk 1.49.
23. Lk 14.11.
24. Lk 1.49.
25. Lk 1.50.
26. Lk 1.50–51. Origen divides the verse differently than do modern editors.
27. Jerome explains the Latin word *virtus*. It originally meant "manly qualities," especially as displayed in war or contests. It then came to mean a specific trait of character, and thus "virtue." *Imperium* is a technical term from Roman government, and means the supreme administrative power, or the authority possessed by some higher magistrates.
28. Jerome keeps the Greek word that Luke uses here.
29. Jerome's gloss.
30. Rv 19.16.

HOMILY 9

Luke 1.56–64

On the passage from, "She remained with her for three months," up to the point where it says, "and he spoke, praising God."

OUR EXPLANATION BOTH of what is said in Scripture and of the deeds recorded there should be worthy of the Holy Spirit and of faith in Christ, that faith to which we believers are called. Hence, we should now ask why Mary went to Elizabeth after she conceived and "remained with her for three months."[1] We should also ask why Luke, who was writing a narrative of the Gospel,[2] also inserted the words, "She remained with her for three months and afterwards returned to her home."[3] Surely there ought to be some explanation; and, if the Lord opens our hearts, the discourse that follows will provide it. The mere fact that Mary came to Elizabeth and greeted her made Elizabeth's infant "leap with joy"[4] and made "Elizabeth, filled with the Holy Spirit,"[5] prophesy those things which have been written in the Gospel. In one hour, Elizabeth made that much progress. We are left to conjecture what progress John made in the three months during which Mary dwelt with Elizabeth.[6]

2. In a moment or an instant, the infant leapt up and, as it were, frolicked for joy, and Elizabeth was filled with the Holy Spirit. It would be most inappropriate if neither John nor Elizabeth profited from the immediate presence, for three

1. Lk 1.56.
2. "Gospel" here means the Good News itself, and not a written account.
3. Lk 1.56.
4. Lk 1.41.
5. Lk 1.41.
6. Cf. Ambrose, *Exposition of the Gospel According to Luke* 2.29.

months, of the Lord's mother and of the Savior himself. Hence, John was being trained; for three months, as it were, he was being rubbed down on the athletes' practice field and made ready in his mother's womb. His birth was marvelous, but his rearing was even more marvelous. John was not reared in the usual way. Scripture does not report how he was nursed at his mother's breasts or how he was placed in the bosom of the one who bore him. Instead, it immediately adds, "And he was in the wilderness up to the day of his revelation to Israel."[7]

3. Then we read, "But Elizabeth's time to bear was fulfilled, and she bore a son."[8] Many think it is superfluous to say, "But Elizabeth's time to bear was fulfilled, and she bore a son." For what woman can bear unless the time for bearing is already fulfilled? But one who ponders the Scriptures diligently and understands what Paul means when he says, "Attend to the reading,"[9] can search both the Old and the New Testaments to find a place where it is written of a sinner's birth, "the time to bear was fulfilled." He will never find a single instance. But, whenever a just man is born, then the days "are fulfilled." In that instance, his coming into the world is fulfilled. The birth of a just man is marked by a fullness, whereas emptiness and futility, so to speak, mark the birth of a sinner.[10] This is the explanation of the words, "the time for her to bear was fulfilled."[11]

4. Thereupon, after John was born, the Gospel reads, "Neighbors and relatives were congratulating"[12] his mother and wished to give the boy a name to honor his father; they wanted to call him Zechariah.[13] But Elizabeth, at the prompting of the Holy Spirit, kept saying, "His name is John."[14] Then they sought good reasons why in particular he should be called "John." No one in his family had this name. They asked his father. Zechariah was unable to answer, and spoke by writing

7. Lk 1.80.
8. Lk 1.57.
9. 1 Tm 4.13.
10. Cf. Origen, *Homilies on Genesis* 12.3.
11. Lk 1.57.
12. Lk 1.58–59.
13. Cf. Ambrose, *Exposition of the Gospel According to Luke* 2.31–32.
14. Lk 1.63. On the name "John," see Origen, *Commentary on John* 2.196–198.

letters and gesturing. "He wrote" on a tablet, "His name is John."[15] As soon as the stylus marked the wax,[16] "his tongue," which had been bound, "was loosed," and he received superhuman eloquence. As long as his tongue was bound, it was human, for unbelief had bound it. As soon as his tongue was loosed, it ceased to be human. "And he was speaking and glorifying God."[17] He prophesied what has been written in the Gospel. We shall speak about it when the time comes, if the Lord Jesus Christ helps us; to him is glory and power for ages of ages. Amen.

15. Lk 1.63.

16. Ordinary writing was done with a stylus on a thin board dipped in wax; the wax could later be smoothed over and the tablet reused.

17. Lk 1.67.

HOMILY 10

Luke 1.67–76

On the passage from, "Filled with the Holy Spirit, he prophesied," up to the point where it says, "for you will go before the Lord to prepare his ways."

ILLED WITH THE Holy Spirit, Zechariah utters two general prophecies: the first about Christ, the second about John. This is clearly shown by his words. He speaks of the Savior as if he were already present and active in the world; then he speaks of John. "Filled with the Holy Spirit, he prophesied and said, 'Blessed be the Lord, the God of Israel, because he visited his people and worked their redemption.'"[1] For, when God visited and willed to redeem his people, "Mary remained for three months"[2] with Elizabeth after the angel had spoken to her. By some ineffable power, the Savior, by his presence, instructed not only John, as we said already, but also Zechariah, as the Gospel now declares.

2. Gradually, in the course of three months, Zechariah kept receiving spiritual sustenance from the Holy Spirit. Although he did not realize it, he was being instructed. Then he prophesied about Christ and said, "He brought redemption to his people, and raised up a horn of salvation for us in the house of David,"[3] because Christ was born "of the seed of David according to the flesh."[4] He was truly "a horn of salvation in the house of David,"[5] since the following passage reinforces it: "For a vineyard was planted on the horn-shaped ridge."[6]

1. Lk 1.68.
2. Lk 1.56.
3. Lk 1.69.
4. Rom 1.3.
5. Lk 1.69.
6. Is 5.1. Both Greek and Latin permit a pun here, since the word "horn" in either language can mean either an animal's horn or a horn-shaped plot of land, like the ridge of a hill. Origen probably had in mind Jesus' identifying himself as

Which horn was it planted on? On Christ Jesus, him of whom Scripture now says, "He raised up a horn of salvation for us in the house of David, his servant, as he spoke by the mouths of his holy prophets."[7]

3. "Deliverance from our enemies."[8] We should not think this means corporeal enemies, but rather spiritual ones. For the Lord Jesus came, "strong in battle,"[9] to destroy all our enemies and free us from their snares, namely, from the hand of all our enemies "and from the hand of all who hate us."[10] "To bring about mercy for our fathers."[11] I believe that, when our Lord the Savior came, Abraham, Isaac, and Jacob were blessed with God's mercy. Previously, they had seen his day and rejoiced.[12] It is not believable that they did not profit from it later, when he came and was born of a virgin. And why do I speak of the patriarchs? I shall boldly follow the authority of the Scriptures to higher planes,[13] for the presence of the Lord Jesus and his work benefited not only what is earthly, but also what is heavenly. Hence, the Apostle too says, "Establishing peace through the blood of his cross, both on earth and in heaven."[14] But, if the Lord's presence was beneficial in heaven and on earth, why do you fear to say that his coming also benefited our ancestors? What Scripture said is fulfilled: "To bring about mercy for our fathers, and to be mindful of his holy covenant, the oath that he swore to Abraham our father,"[15] to grant us deliverance "without fear from the hand of the enemies."[16]

4. Men are frequently delivered from the hand of enemies, but not "without fear."[17] For, when fear and danger have preceded and someone is removed from the hand of enemies under these circumstances, he is in fact freed, but not "without fear." Yet the coming of the Lord Jesus removed us "without

---

the true vine (Jn 15.1). Christ the vine is planted in the land of David, whence salvation comes.

7. Lk 1.69–70.
8. Lk 1.71.
9. Ps 24.8.
10. Lk 1.71.
11. Lk 1.72.
12. Cf. Jn 8.56.
13. Cf. *Homilies on Leviticus* 1.3.
14. Col 1.20.
15. Lk 1.72–73.
16. Lk 1.74.
17. Lk 1.74.

fear from the hand of enemies."[18] We did not perceive our enemies or see them fighting back, but—without our knowing it—we were suddenly snatched from their jaws and their ambushes. "In a moment and an instant,"[19] he transported us "into the inheritance and the share of the just"[20] and we have been freed "without fear from the hand of enemies, to serve God in holiness and justice before his face all our days."[21]

5. "And you, child, shall be called a prophet of the Most High."[22] In my own mind, I sought the reason why Zechariah speaks not about John, but to John himself, when he prophesies and says, "And you, child, shall be called a prophet of the Most High," and so on. It was pointless to speak to one who could not hear, to address an infant at the breast, unless, as I think, I have discovered the explanation. John was born miraculously. He came into the world by an angel's prophecy. After Mary had stayed with Elizabeth for three months, John was born. So everything that is written about him reports some miraculous event. Perhaps you doubt that an infant who just issued from his mother's womb can hear and understand his father's words. Then what does this mean, which is addressed to John: "And you, child, shall be called a prophet of the Most High"?[23] Consider the fact that what preceded was more miraculous: "Behold, as the words of your greeting sounded in my ears, the infant leapt for joy in my womb."[24]

6. So John heard Jesus while he was still enclosed in his mother's womb, and leapt up and rejoiced when he heard him. Why might you not believe that, once he was born, he could understand his father's prophecy, as Zechariah said to him, "And you, child, shall be called a prophet of the Most High, for you will go before the Lord to prepare his ways."[25] So I suppose that Zechariah hastened to speak to the infant because he knew John would soon be living in the desert, and he would no longer enjoy John's presence. "For, the boy was in the wilderness up to the day of his revelation to Israel."[26]

18. Lk 1.74.
19. Cf. 1 Cor 15.52.
20. Col 1.12–13.
21. Lk 1.74–75.
22. Lk 1.76.
23. Lk 1.76.
24. Lk 1.44.
25. Lk 1.76.
26. Lk 1.80.

7. Moses, too, dwelt in the desert. After he completed the fortieth year of his age, he fled from Egypt and, for another forty years, pastured Jethro's herds.[27] But John went out to the wilderness as soon as he was born. "Greatest among the sons of women,"[28] he was evidently worthy of a greater upbringing. The prophet says of him, "Behold I send my angel before your face."[29] One who had been sent into the Lord's presence, and who, as soon as he was born, could hear and understand his father's prophecies, is rightly called an angel. We believe such great miracles. We should believe with equal confidence in the resurrection, and in the promises of the Kingdom of Heaven, which will be fulfilled. The Holy Spirit promises these to us each day. Scripture expresses all these truths in a marvelous way, more marvelous than we can realize. We shall receive them in Christ Jesus, to whom is glory and power for ages of ages. Amen.

27. Cf. Ex 2.15; Acts 7.23 and 30.
28. Mt 11.11.
29. Mal 3.1. Cf. Ex 23.20, Mt 11.10, Mk 1.2, and Lk 7.27.

HOMILY 11

Luke 1.80–2.2

On the passage from, "But the boy grew and was strengthened in spirit," up to the point where it says, "This is the first census that was made under Cyrinus, the governor of Syria."

IN THE HOLY SCRIPTURES, something is said to "grow" in two senses. One sense is corporeal, that is, when the human will contributes nothing. The other sense is spiritual, that is, when human effort is the cause of the growth. The evangelist now speaks of this latter sense, that is, the spiritual one—which we laid out second—when he says, "But the boy grew and was strengthened in spirit."[1] What it means follows: "He grew in spirit." His spirit did not remain in the same condition in which it had begun, but always kept growing in him. In each hour and each moment, as the spirit grew, his soul too kept developing. And not only his soul, but also his senses and his mind kept following the growth of his spirit. The Lord commanded, "Grow and multiply."[2] I do not know how those who take this passage simply and literally can explain it. Granted that "multiply" refers to numbers, when they become more in number than they were previously, they "multiply." But what precedes, to "grow," that is not in our power.

2. For, what man would not want to "add to his stature,"[3] to become taller? Something is commanded so that it will be done; it is stupid to command what the one you command cannot do. We are commanded to grow. Hence we are able

1. Lk 1.80.

2. Gn 1.22. The usual translation is "increase and multiply," but the word for "increase" is the same as the one for "grow" in Lk 1.80, both in Greek and in Latin.

3. Mt 6.27.

to do what is commanded. Do you want to know how "grow" should be understood? Listen to what Isaac did. Scripture says of him, "Isaac progressed and became greater, until he became great, and very much so."[4] His will always tended toward the better, and kept making progress. His mind kept contemplating something more divine, and he kept exercising his memory, to store up more in his treasure-house and retain it more securely. So this is the way it came about. Isaac cultivated all his virtues in the field of his soul, and thus fulfilled the command that ordered him to "grow."

3. Wherefore John too, while still a little boy, grew and multiplied. But it is exceedingly difficult, and very rare among mortals, for one who is still a little child to grow in spirit.[5] "But the boy grew and was strengthened in spirit." It is one thing to "grow," another to "be strengthened." Human nature is weak. It needs divine help to become stronger. We read, "The flesh is weak."[6] What forces can strengthen it? The Spirit, of course, "for the spirit is quick to respond, but the flesh is weak."[7] Someone who wants to become stronger should be strengthened only in spirit. Many are strengthened in the flesh, and their bodies become more powerful. But an athlete of God[8] should become more powerful in spirit. Thus strengthened, he will crush the wisdom of the flesh. Spiritual activity will subject the body to the soul's command.[9] We should not think that, when Scripture says, "He grew and was strengthened in spirit," what was written about John was just a narrative that does not pertain to us in any way. It is written for our imitation. We should take "growth" in the sense we have explained, and be multiplied spiritually.

4. "And he was in the wilderness until the day of his revelation to Israel."[10] I said recently that even John's conception had something astonishing about it. "The infant leapt in the womb,"[11] and, before he was born, he recognized his Lord.

4. Gn 26.13. Cf. *Homilies on Genesis* 12.5.
5. Lk 1.80.
6. Mt 26.41.
7. Mt 26.41.
8. Cf. 2 Tm 2.3–5.
9. Cf. Rom 8.7.
10. Lk 1.80.
11. Lk 1.41,44.

His birth was just as much a wonder. Zechariah spoke to him as to one who could hear and prophesied, "And you, child, shall be called a prophet of the Most High."[12] John had been conceived and born thus. So it was right for him not to expect to be reared by his father and mother "until the day of his revelation to Israel."[13] He withdrew, fleeing from the tumult of cities, the crowds of people, and the vices of the towns. He went into the wilderness, where the air is purer and the sky more open, and God is closer. Neither the mystery of his baptism nor the time for preaching had come yet. He gave himself to prayers and associated with angels. He called upon God and heard him answer and say, "Behold I am here."[14] Just as "Moses spoke and God answered him,"[15] so, I think, John spoke in the desert and the Lord answered him.

5. I believe this, because I am impressed by the clear account of the Scriptures. For, if "none among those born of women was greater than John the Baptist,"[16] and God answered Moses,[17] then it was fitting that he also answered John. For, John was greater than Moses. John was reared in the wilderness. The same archangel announced John's birth as announced the Lord's. John's father, who did not believe John was to be born, fell dumb. Hence, John "was in the desert."[18] He was nourished in a new way, not according to human customs. Matthew mentions this: "But his food was locusts, and honey from the woodland."[19] John was a servant of the Lord's first coming, and spoke only of the Lord's coming in flesh. A prophecy of his foretold him who had been born of a virgin. Hence, he did not have household honey, filtered by human attention. He had woodland honey, and a flying insect that was his food. This insect is not large; it does not fly high. It is a small insect; it scarcely rises from the ground; it leaps rather than flies. Why should I say more? Scripture says quite clearly that his food was locusts—a small and clean animal. Ponder

12. Lk 1.76.
13. Lk 1.80.
14. Ex 3.4.
15. Ex 19.19.
16. Lk 7.28.
17. Cf. Ex 3.13–14.
18. Lk 1.80.
19. Mt 3.4.

this, dearest brethren, that he was born in a new fashion, and reared in a new fashion.

6. After this Scripture adds, "It happened in those days that an edict went out from Caesar Augustus, that the whole world should be registered. This was the first census made under Cyrinus, the governor of Syria."[20] Someone might say, "Evangelist, how does this narrative help me? How does it help me to know that the first census of the entire world was made under Caesar Augustus; and that among all these people the name of 'Joseph, with Mary who was espoused to him and pregnant,'[21] was included; and that, before the census was finished, Jesus was born?" To one who looks more carefully, a mystery seems to be conveyed. It is significant that Christ should have been recorded in the census of the whole world. He was registered with everyone, and sanctified everyone. He was joined with the world for the census, and offers the world communion with himself. After this census, he could enroll those from the whole world "in the book of the living"[22] with himself. Whoever believed in him would be later "inscribed in heaven,"[23] along with his saints. To him is glory and power for ages of ages. Amen.

20. Lk 2.1–2.
21. Lk 2.4–5.
22. Rv 20.15 and Phil 4.3.
23. Lk 10.20.

HOMILY 12

Luke 2.8–11

On the passage that says an angel came down from heaven and announced the birth of the Lord to shepherds.

Y LORD JESUS[1] has been born, and an angel has come down from heaven to announce his birth. Let us see whom the angel sought out to announce his coming. He did not go to Jerusalem. He did not seek out Scribes and Pharisees. He did not enter a synagogue of the Jews. Instead, he found "shepherds in the fields keeping watch over their flock"[2] and said to them, "Today a Savior is born for you, who is Christ the Lord."[3]

2. Do you think that the words of the Scriptures signify nothing else, nothing more divine, but only say this, that an angel came to shepherds and spoke to them? Listen, shepherds of the churches! Listen, God's shepherds! His angel always comes down from heaven and proclaims to you, "Today a Savior is born for you, who is Christ the Lord."[4] For, unless that Shepherd comes, the shepherds of the churches will be unable to guard the flock well. Their custody is weak, unless Christ pastures and guards it along with them. We just read in the Apostle, "We are coworkers with God."[5] A good shepherd, who imitates the Good Shepherd, is a coworker with God and Christ. He is a good shepherd precisely because he

1. Origen's expression for his own love of Jesus; it recurs in *Homilies* 18.1 and 22.4. Origen is probably the first Christian to use it.

2. Lk 2.8.

3. Lk 2.11.

4. Lk 2.11.

5. 1 Cor 3.9. A passage from 1 Corinthians had been read at the same service as this passage from the Gospel According to Luke. Cf. *Hom.* 31.5.

has the best Shepherd with him, pasturing his sheep along with him. For, "God established in his Church apostles, prophets, evangelists, shepherds,[6] and teachers. He established everything for the perfection of the saints."[7] Let this suffice for a simpler explanation.

3. But we should ascend to a more hidden understanding.[8] Some shepherds were angels that governed human affairs.[9] Each of these kept his watch. They were vigilant day and night. But, at some point, they were unable to bear the labor of governing the peoples who had been entrusted to them and accomplish it diligently. When the Lord was born, an angel came and announced to the shepherds that the true Shepherd had appeared. Let me give an example. There was a certain shepherd-angel in Macedonia who needed the Lord's help. Consequently, he appeared to Paul in his dreams as a Macedonian man "and said, 'Cross over to Macedonia and help us.'"[10] Why do I speak of Paul, since the angel said this not to Paul but to Jesus, who was in Paul?[11] So shepherds need the presence of Christ. For this reason, an angel came down from heaven and said, "Do not fear. For behold, I announce great joy to you."[12]

4. It was indeed a great joy to these shepherds, to whom the care of men and provinces had been entrusted, that Christ had come into the world. The angel who administered the affairs of Egypt received a considerable advantage after the Lord came down from heaven, for the Egyptians could become Christians. It profited all who governed the various provinces, for example, the guardian of Macedonia, the guardian of Achaea, and the guardians of the other regions. It is not right to believe that wicked angels govern individual provinces, and good angels do not have the same provinces and regions entrusted to them. I think that what Scripture says about individual provinces should also be believed more generally about all people. Two angels attend each human being.

6. Or "pastors."
7. Eph 4.11–12. 1 Cor 12.28.
8. Cf. *Homilies on Numbers* 20.3.
9. Cf. Dn 10.13.
10. Acts 16.9.
11. Cf. Gal 2.20.
12. Lk 2.10.

One is an angel of justice, the other an angel of iniquity.[13] If good thoughts are present in our hearts and justice springs up in our souls, the angel of the Lord is undoubtedly speaking to us. But, if evil thoughts turn over in our hearts, the devil's angel is speaking to us. Just as there are two angels for individuals, so, I believe, there are different angels in individual provinces, some good and some evil.

5. For example, very wicked angels kept watch over Ephesus, on account of the sinners who lived in that city. But, because there were many believers in that city, there was also a good angel for the church of the Ephesians. What we have said about Ephesus should be applied to all the provinces. Before the coming of the Lord and Savior, those angels could bring little benefit to those entrusted to them, and their efforts were not powerful enough to bring about success. What indicates that they were hardly able to help those under their charge? Listen to what we say.[14] When the angel of the Egyptians was helping the Egyptians, hardly one proselyte came to believe in God. And this took place when an angel was administering the Egyptians.

6. But then many proselytes among the Egyptians and the Idumaeans[15] received faith in God. That is why Scripture says, "You shall not detest the Egyptian, because you were strangers in the land of Egypt. Nor shall you despise the Idumaean, because he is your brother. If sons are born to them, they will enter the Church of God in the third generation."[16] And thus it happened. From every nation some became proselytes. The angels, who had these nations subject to them, strove to attain this. Now nations of believers come to faith in Jesus. The angels to whom the churches have been entrusted have been strengthened by the presence of the Savior and bring in many

13. On the two angels, cf. *Hom.* 35.3. For Origen's teaching on angels, see *On First Principles* 1.8.1 and 3.4; *Homilies on Joshua* 23.3; *Homilies on Numbers* 11.4 and 20.3. Cf. also Hermas, *Shepherd* 36.2–10 and *Epistle of Barnabas* 18–20.

14. Origen, an Egyptian, betrays some local patriotism in the rest of the homily.

15. Inhabitants of a territory between Egypt and Palestine.

16. Dt 23.7–8. Clearly this is not the sense of the original, but it is the way Origen understands the text.

proselytes. Assemblies of Christians come together throughout the whole world. For this reason, let us rise up[17] and praise the Lord.[18] Let us become a spiritual Israel in place of the carnal Israel. Let us bless Almighty God by deed and thought and word in Christ Jesus, to whom is glory and power for ages of ages. Amen.

17. The same request to stand recurs in *Hom.* 36.3 and 39.7.
18. Cf. 1 Cor 10.18.

HOMILY 13

Luke 2.13–16

On the passage from, "And there was a great number of the heavenly army," up to the point where it says, "They found Mary and Joseph, and Jesus laid in a manger."

OUR LORD and Savior is born in Bethlehem. And a "great number of the heavenly army"[1] praises God and says, "Glory to God on high, and peace on earth among men of good will."[2] This "great number of the heavenly army" speaks thus because they had already failed to provide assistance to men. They realized they could not fulfill the task that had been entrusted to them without him who could truly save and who could also help the governing angels themselves, so that men could be saved. The Gospel records[3] that certain men were ploughing the sea with oars against contrary winds. They were already exhausted. They had toiled for twenty-five or thirty *stadia*[4] and could not reach port. Afterwards the Lord came to them. He made the swelling waves grow calm and freed the ship, whose hull was being buffeted on both sides, from imminent danger.

2. Understand the passage in the following way. The angels wanted to offer men help and to provide them with a cure for their diseases. "All spirits are servants, sent to minister on account of those who are to attain salvation."[5] As much as they could, they helped men. But they realized that their remedy fell far short of what men's cure required. Take it a step fur-

1. Lk 2.13.
2. Lk 2.14.
3. Jn 6.18–21.
4. The Roman *stadium* was about one-ninth of a mile.
5. Heb 1.14.

ther, so that you can understand from an example what we are saying. Picture a city in which very many people are sick and a large band of doctors is employed. There are various wounds. Every day spreading gangrene infects the moribund flesh. But still, the doctors who are employed to provide a cure are unable to discover any more remedies and thus overcome the great evil by the knowledge of their art. With the situation in such a state, a master physician arrives, one who possesses full knowledge of his art. Those doctors who previously could not heal see the gangrene in the wounds halted by the master's hand. They do not envy him, nor are they wracked with jealousy. Instead they break forth into praise of the master physician and thus exalt God, who sent a man of such great knowledge both for themselves and for the sick.

3. It is for a reason like this that a great number of the army of angels was heard saying, "Glory to God on high, and peace on earth among men of good will."[6] For, after the Lord came to the earth, "he established peace through the blood of his cross, both for those upon the earth and those who are in heaven."[7] And the angels wanted men to remember their Creator. They had done everything in their power to cure them, but they were unwilling to be cured. Then the angels behold him who could effect a cure. They give glory and say, "Glory to God on high, and peace on earth."[8]

4. The careful reader of Scripture might ask how the Savior can say, "I have not come to spread peace upon the earth, but a sword,"[9] while now at his birth the angels chant "peace on earth." In another passage, he says in person, "My peace I give to you, peace I leave for you. I do not give peace as this world gives peace."[10] Let the reader consider the argument we advance; perhaps it can answer his question. If Scripture said, "peace on earth," and the sentence ended there, then the objection would be valid. But something is added. After "peace," that is, Scripture says, "among men of good will." This

6. Lk 2.14.
7. Col 1.20.
8. Lk 2.14.
9. Mt 10.34.
10. Jn 14.27.

answers the objection. The peace on earth that the Lord does not give is not the peace "of good will." For he did not say simply, "I have not come to spread peace." He added "upon earth." Nor, on the other hand, did he say, "I have not come to spread peace upon the earth of good will."[11]

5. The angels spoke these words to the shepherds. They spoke not only at that time, but in the present day also. Unless the angels had spoken to the pastors and added their own works to theirs, those pastors would have heard the words, "Unless the Lord build the house, they who build it have labored in vain; unless the Lord guard the city, they who guard it watch in vain."[12] If it is appropriate for one who follows the sense of the Scriptures to speak boldly, I shall say that in each of the churches there are two bishops. One is visible, the other invisible. One is visible to the flesh, the other invisible to the senses. A man who carries out well a task committed to him is praised by the Lord. If he does it badly, he is subject to blame and guilty of a fault. The same is true of an angel. In the Apocalypse of John we read, "But you have there a few names that have not sinned."[13] Or again, you have this: "You have there those who teach the doctrine of the Nicolaitans."[14] And then, "You have those who commit these or those sins." And the angels to whom the churches are entrusted are blamed.

6. But, if angels are concerned about how churches are governed, what do we have to say about men?[15] How much they should fear! What if they would not be able to obtain salvation as they labor alongside laboring angels. I think that both an angel and a man can be discovered together as the good bishops of a church. In a sense, they both share in one work. Since this is so, let us ask Almighty God that both angels and men might help us as bishops of the churches. We should realize that the Lord judges both of them on our account. But, if they are judged, and a fault or a sin is uncovered, not in their indifference, but in our own negligence, then we shall be

11. Origen distinguishes earthly peace, which is not the Lord's, from heavenly peace, which the Lord gives to men of good will.

12. Ps 127.1.

13. Rv 3.4.

14. Rv 2.15.

15. That is, the visible bishops.

blamed and punished. Should they make every effort and struggle for our salvation, we shall nevertheless remain open to sin. But it often happens that we struggle, while they do not fulfill their task and are at fault.

7. The passage continues: "And it happened that, when the angels had left them and returned to heaven, the shepherds said to one another, 'Let us go over to Bethlehem and see this word which has been done, which the Lord revealed to us.' And they hastened and went, and they found Mary and Joseph and the child."[16] They hastened—not proceeding cautiously, nor at a slow pace—and they went. Thus they found Joseph, who arranged matters[17] for the Lord's birth, and Mary, who bore Jesus in childbirth, and the Savior himself, "lying in a manger."[18] That was the manger of which the inspired prophet said, "The ox knows his owner and the ass his master's manger."[19] The ox is a clean animal, the ass an unclean animal.[20] "The ass knows his master's manger." The people of Israel did not know their Lord's manger, but an unclean animal from among the Gentiles did. Scripture says, "Israel, indeed, did not know me, and my people did not understand me."[21] Let us understand this manger. Let us endeavor to recognize the Lord and to be worthy of knowing him, and of taking on not only his birth and the resurrection of his flesh, but also his celebrated second coming in majesty, to whom is glory and power for ages of ages. Amen.

16. Lk 2.15–16.
17. Origen's term suggests Joseph's role in the divine economy of salvation.
18. Lk 2.16.
19. Is 1.3. Origen, at this place, is the first Christian writer to mention the ox and the ass in the stable at Bethlehem.
20. See Philo, *On the Virtues* 146; and Jerome, *Commentary on Isaiah* 1.1.3.
21. Is 1.3.

HOMILY 14

Luke 2.21–24

On the passage from, "But, when the days of his circumcision were fulfilled," to the point where it says, "a pair of turtle doves or two young doves."

HEN CHRIST DIED, "he died to sin"[1]—not that he himself sinned; "for he did not commit sin, and treachery was not found in his mouth."[2] He died so that, once he had died to sins, we who were dead might no longer live to sin and vices. Hence Scripture says, "If we have died with him, we shall also live with him."[3] So, when he died, we died with him, and, when he rose, we rose with him. So too we were circumcised along with him. After the circumcision, we were cleansed in a solemn purification. Hence, we have no need at all for a circumcision of the flesh. You should know that he was circumcised on our account. Listen to Paul's clear proclamation. He says, "All the fullness of divinity dwells in him bodily. You are filled in him, who is the head of every rule and power. In him you have been circumcised by a circumcision done without hands, when the body of the flesh was despoiled in the circumcision of Christ. We were buried with him in Baptism, and we have risen up with him through faith in the work of God, who raised him from the dead."[4] Therefore, his death, his resurrection, and his circumcision took place for our sake.

2. Scripture says, "When the days for circumcising the child had been fulfilled, his name was called 'Jesus,' which he had

1. Rom 6.10.
2. 1 Pt 2.22.
3. Rom 6.8.
4. Col 2.9–12.

been called by the angel before he was conceived."[5] The word "Jesus" is glorious, and worthy of all adoration and worship. It is "the name above every name."[6] It was not fitting that this name should first be given by men or brought into the world by them, but by some more excellent and greater nature. The evangelist indicated this when he added, "His name was called 'Jesus,' which he had been called by the angel before he was conceived in the womb."[7]

3. Then the Gospel says, "When the days of their purification were fulfilled, according to the law of Moses, they brought him into Jerusalem."[8] The passage says, on account of "their" purification. Who are "they"? If Scripture had said, "on account of 'her' purification"—that is, Mary's, who had given birth—then no question would arise.[9] We would say confidently that Mary, who was a human being, needed purification after childbirth. But the passage reads, "the days of their purification." Apparently it does not signify one, but two or more. Did Jesus therefore need purification? Was he unclean, or polluted with some stain? Perhaps I seem to speak rashly; but the authority of Scripture prompts me to ask. See what is written in the book of Job: "No man is clean of stain, not even if his life had lasted but a single day."[10] The passage does not say, "No man is clean of sin," but, "No man is clean of stain." "Stain" and "sins" do not mean the same thing. "Stain" is one thing, "sin" another. Isaiah teaches this clearly when he says, "The Lord will wash away the stains of the sons and daughters of Zion, and he will cleanse the blood from their midst. By the spirit of judgment he will purge the stain, and by the spirit of burning the blood."[11]

4. Every soul that has been clothed with a human body has its own "stain."[12] But Jesus was stained through his own will, because he had taken on a human body for our salvation.

5. Lk 2.21.
6. Phil 2.9.
7. Lk 2.21.
8. Lk 2.22.
9. Cf. *Homilies on Leviticus* 8.2.
10. Jb 14.4–5.
11. Is 4.4.
12. Cf. *Homilies on Leviticus* 9.6.4. Cf. also Tertullian, *Against Marcion* 3.7.6 and *Against the Jews* 14.7.

Listen to the prophet Zechariah. He says, "Jesus was clothed with stained garments."[13] Zechariah says this to refute those who deny that our Lord had a human body, but say that his body was made of heavenly and spiritual substance.[14] They say this body was made of heavenly matter or, they falsely assert, of sidereal matter, or of some other more sublime and spiritual nature. Let them explain how a spiritual body could be stained, or how they interpret the passage we quoted: "Jesus was clothed with stained garments." If this difficulty drives them to assume that the "stained garment" means the spiritual body, then they should be consistent and say this, that what is said in the prophecies has been fulfilled, that is, "an animal body is sown, a spiritual body rises."[15] Do we thus rise soiled and stained? It is an impiety even to think this, especially when one knows what Scripture says: "The body is sown in corruption, but will rise in incorruption; it is sown in obscurity, but will rise in glory; it is sown in weakness, but will rise in strength; our animal body is sown, but a spiritual body will rise."[16]

5. Thus, it was fitting that those offerings that, according to the law, customarily cleanse stain, should be made. They were made for our Lord and Savior, who had been "clothed with stained garments"[17] and had taken on an earthly body. Christian brethren often ask a question. The passage from Scripture read today encourages me to treat it again. Little children are baptized "for the remission of sins."[18] Whose sins are they? When did they sin? Or how can this explanation of the baptismal washing be maintained in the case of small children, except according to the interpretation we spoke of a little earlier? "No man is clean of stain, not even if his life upon the earth had lasted but a single day."[19] Through the mystery of

13. Zec 3.3. But the Greek translation, which Origen was reading, transliterated the Hebrew name "Joshua" as "Jesus," so Origen applies what the Scripture says of Joshua to Jesus.

14. Origen probably means Gnostics like Marcion or Apelles.

15. 1 Cor 15.44.

16. 1 Cor 15.43–44.

17. Zec 3.3.

18. Acts 2.38. On the baptism of infants, cf. *Homilies on Leviticus* 8.3.5.

19. Jb 14.4–5.

Baptism, the stains of birth are put aside. For this reason, even small children are baptized. For, "unless a man be born again of water and spirit, he will not be able to enter into the kingdom of heaven."[20]

6. The Gospel continues: "When the days of their purification were fulfilled. . . ."[21] Days are also fulfilled mystically. For a soul is not purified as soon as it is born, nor does it gain perfect purity in birth itself. It is written in the law, "If a mother bears a male child, she will sit for seven days in unclean blood, and then for thirty-three days in clean blood. At the end she and the infant will sit in the purest blood."[22] But "the Law is spiritual"[23] and "has a shadow of good things to come";[24] so we can understand that true purification will come about after time. I think that we shall need a sacrament to wash and cleanse us even after resurrection from the dead.[25] No one will be able to rise without stains, nor will any soul be found that immediately lacks all vices. So the rebirth of Baptism contains a mystery: just as Jesus, in the economy of the flesh, was purified by an offering, so we too are purified by spiritual rebirth.

7. "According to the law of Moses, they brought him into Jerusalem, to make an offering in the sight of the Lord."[26] Where are those who deny the God of the Law, who say that not he, but another god, was proclaimed by Christ in the Gospel?[27] "God sent his Son, born from a woman, subject to the Law."[28] Should we therefore suppose that the good God made his Son under the law of the creator god, and under the law of an enemy, a law that he himself had not given? No; rather, he was made under the Law "to redeem those who were under

20. Jn 3.5.

21. Lk 2.22.

22. Lv 12.2–4. The sense of Origen's text differs from the Hebrew here, especially in the last phrase. See *Homilies on Leviticus* 8.2–3.

23. Rom 7.14.

24. Heb 10.1.

25. Cf. *Hom.* 24.1–2 on baptism in fire after death, and the corrections in *Hom.* 26.3. On purification after death, cf. also *Hom.* 3.3; *Homilies on Numbers* 25.4; *Homilies on Leviticus* 8.4.1; *On First Principles* 2.10; and *Commentary on Matthew* 15.23.

26. Lk 2.22.

27. Origen clearly means the Marcionites.

28. Gal 4.4.

the Law"[29] and to subject them to another Law. Scripture had already said of this Law, "Listen, my people, to my Law,"[30] and so on. So "they brought him to place him in the sight of the Lord."[31] What scriptural commands were they fulfilling? This one: "As it is written in the law of Moses, every male that opens the womb shall be called holy to the Lord,"[32] and, "Three times in the year every male shall appear in the sight of the Lord God."[33] Males were sacred because they opened their mothers' wombs. They were offered before the altar of the Lord. Scripture says, "Every male that opens the womb. . . ." This phrase has a spiritual meaning. For you might say that "every male is brought forth from the womb" but does not open the womb of his mother, in the way that the Lord Jesus did. In the case of every other woman, it is not the birth of an infant but intercourse with a man that opens the womb.[34]

8. But the womb of the Lord's mother was opened at the time when her offspring was brought forth, because before the birth of Christ a male did not even touch her womb, holy as it was and deserving of all respect. I dare to say something. At that moment of which Scripture says, "The Spirit of God will come upon you, and the power of the Most High will overshadow you,"[35] the seed was planted and the conception took place; without an opening of the womb, a new offspring began to grow. Hence the Savior himself says, "But I am a worm, and not a man, reproached by men and rejected by the people."[36] In his mother's womb he saw the uncleanness of bodies. He was walled in on both sides by her innards; he bore the straits of earthly dregs. So he compares himself with a worm and says, "'I am a worm and not a man.' A man is normally born from a male and female; but I was not born from a male and a female, according to nature and the ways of men. I was born like a worm. A worm does not get seed from outside itself.[37] It

29. Gal 4.5.
30. Ps 78.1.
31. Lk 2.22.
32. Lk 2.23, formulated from Ex 13.2 and Nm 8.16.
33. Ex 34.23.
34. Cf. Ambrose, *Exposition of the Gospel According to Luke* 2.56.
35. Lk 1.35
36. Ps 22.6.
37. The same theory is found in Augustine, *Letter* 140.8.21.

reproduces in itself and from itself, and it produces offspring from its own body alone."

9. Because "every male that opens the womb shall be called holy to the Lord," he was brought "into Jerusalem," to appear before the face of God; and also for the following reason, "that the gift might be offered for him that is prescribed in the law of the Lord: a pair of turtle-doves or two young pigeons."[38] We see a pair of turtle-doves and two young pigeons offered for the Savior. I myself believe that those birds that were offered for the Lord's birth are blessed. I marvel at Balaam's ass[39] and heap blessings on it, because it was worthy not only to see the angel of God, but even to have its mouth opened and break into human speech. Much more do I praise and extol those birds, because they were offered before the altar for our Lord and Savior. "To offer a pair of turtle-doves or two young pigeons for him."[40]

10. Perhaps I seem to introduce something new and hardly worthy of the dignity of this matter. The new birth of the Savior came not from a man and a woman, but solely from a virgin. So too, that "pair of turtle-doves or two young pigeons" were not the sort that we see with fleshly eyes. They were the sort that the Holy Spirit is, who "came down in the form of a dove and settled"[41] upon the Savior, when he was baptized in the Jordan. The pair of turtle-doves were also like this. Those birds were not like the ones that fly through the air. Something divine, and more majestic than the human mind can contemplate, appeared under the form of a pigeon and a dove. He who for the sake of the whole world was born and had to suffer was not purified in the Lord's sight by such victims as purify all other men. Rather, just as he had arranged everything in a new manner,[42] so too he had new offerings, according to the will of Almighty God in Christ Jesus, to whom is glory and power for ages of ages. Amen.

38. Lk 2.24.
39. Nm 22.25–35.
40. Lk 2.24.
41. Mt 3.16; Mk 1.10; and Lk 3.22.
42. Cf. Rv 21.5.

HOMILY 15

Luke 2.25–29

Concerning Simeon, that he came to the temple in the Spirit, up to the point where it says, "Now you dismiss your servant, Lord, in peace."

E MUST SEEK an explanation worthy of God's purpose as to why, as is written in the Gospel, "Simeon, a holy man and one pleasing to God, awaiting the consolation of Israel, received an answer from the Holy Spirit that he would not perish in death before he saw the Lord's Anointed."[1] What did he gain from seeing Christ? Did he have only this promised to him, that he would see him, and derive no profit from seeing him? Or is some gift worthy of God concealed here, a gift that the blessed Simeon both merited and received? "The woman touched the fringe of Jesus' garment and was healed."[2] If she derived such an advantage from the very edge of his garment, what should we think of Simeon, who "received" the infant "into his arms"?[3] He held him in his arms, and kept rejoicing and exulting. He saw that the little child he was carrying had come to release captives and to free Simeon himself from the bonds of the body. Simeon knew that no one could release a man from the prison of the body with hope of life to come, except the one whom he enfolded in his arms.

2. Hence, he also says to him, "Now you dismiss your servant, Lord, in peace."[4] For, as long as I did not hold Christ, as long as my arms did not enfold him, I was imprisoned, and unable to escape from my bonds." But this is true not only of Simeon, but of the whole human race. Anyone who departs from this

1. Lk 2.25.
2. Lk 8.44.
3. Lk 2.28.
4. Lk 2.29.

world, anyone who is released from prison and the house of those in chains, to go forth and reign, should take Jesus in his hands. He should enfold him with his arms, and fully grasp him in his bosom.[5] Then he will be able to go in joy where he longs to go. Consider how great a saving act had taken place earlier, so that Simeon should deserve to hold the Son of God. First he had received an answer from the Holy Spirit, that "he would not see death unless he had first seen the Lord's Anointed."[6]

3. Then he entered the temple—but not by chance, or naively. He "came to the temple in the Spirit of God."[7] "For, as many as are led by the Spirit of God, these are sons of God."[8] Therefore the Holy Spirit led him into the temple. If you wish to hold Jesus, and to embrace him with your hands, and to be made worthy of leaving prison, you too must struggle with every effort to possess the guiding Spirit and come to God's temple. See, you stand now in the temple of the Lord Jesus—that is, in his Church. This is the temple "built from living stones."[9] But you stand in the Lord's temple when your life and your conduct are worthy of the title "church."

4. If you come "to the temple in the Spirit," you will find the child Jesus. You will lift him up in your arms and say, "Now you dismiss your servant, Lord, in peace, according to your word."[10] At the same time, notice that "peace" has been added to the dismissal and the sending forth. For he does not say, "I wish to be dismissed," but to be dismissed with the addition of "in peace." This same thing was promised to the blessed Abraham: "But you will go to your fathers in peace, after you have been cared for in a good old age."[11] Who is the one who dies "in peace" if not he who has "the peace of God, which surpasses every perception and guards the heart"[12] of him who

5. This passage is among the earliest witnesses in Christian literature to devotion to the child Jesus. See also the end of this homily, where Origen encourages prayer to the child Jesus.

6. Lk 2.26.

7. Lk 2.27.

8. Rom 8.14.

9. 1 Pt 2.5.

10. Lk 2.29.

11. Gn 15.15.

12. Phil 4.7.

possesses it? Who is the one who departs "in peace" from this world if not he who understands that "God was in Christ, reconciling the world to himself"?[13] Who if not he in whom nothing is hostile to God or opposed to him, but who by good works has acquired all peace and harmony in himself? Thus he is dismissed "in peace" to go on to the holy fathers, to whom Abraham also went forth.

5. Why do I speak about the fathers? He is to go to the very prince and Lord of the patriarchs, to Jesus, of whom it is said, "It is better to be released and to be with Christ."[14] He who dares to say, "I live, now not I, but Christ lives in me,"[15] he possesses Jesus. Therefore, let us pray that we too might stand in the temple, hold the Son of God, and embrace him, and that we might be worthy of release and of going on to better things. Let us pray to Almighty God, and let us pray to Jesus himself, the little child. We long to speak to him and hold him in our arms, to whom is glory and power for ages of ages. Amen.

13. 2 Cor 5.19.
14. Phil 1.23.
15. Gal 2.20.

HOMILY 16

Luke 2.33–34

On the passage from, "His father and mother were astonished at these things that were being said about him," up to the point where it says, "Behold, he has been destined for the falling and the rising of many in Israel."

HE GOSPEL SAYS, "And his father and mother were astonished at these things that were being said about him."[1] Let us gather into one those things that were said and written about Jesus at his birth. Then we shall be able to know the single points, each of which merits our astonishment. Wherefore, both his father—for Joseph has also been called this because he was his foster-father—and his mother were astonished at all that was being said about him. What are these things that had been reported about the infant Jesus? "There were shepherds in that region, who stayed awake and kept the night watch over their flock."[2] At the very hour of Jesus' birth, an angel came and said to them, "I announce a great joy to you. Go and you will find an infant wrapped in swaddling clothes and laid in a manger."[3] The angel had hardly finished speaking and behold, "a great number of the heavenly army"[4] began to praise and bless God. When the shepherds pondered this message anxiously and "the angel had left them, they said to one another, 'Let us go to Bethlehem and see the event that the Lord has revealed to us.'"[5] They went, and they found the infant. Both they and the parents were astonished at what had taken place.

1. Lk 2.33.
2. Lk 2.8.
3. Lk 2.10 and 12.
4. Lk 2.13.
5. Lk 2.15.

2. Moreover, Scripture also says of Simeon that he added to Jesus' fame and even caused much of the amazement. For, he held the boy in his arms and said, "Now, Lord, you dismiss your servant in peace, according to your word, because my eyes have seen your salvation."[6] Simeon's discourse was the high point and, so to speak, the pinnacle of what was being said about Jesus, and what his mother and father were astonished at. For, it was not enough for him to hold the infant and to speak the words that are recorded as his. He blessed Jesus' father and mother, and also prophesied about the infant himself. He said, "Behold, this child has been destined for the falling and the rising of many in Israel, and for a sign that will be contradicted. And a sword will pierce your very soul to reveal the thoughts of many hearts."[7]

3. What does this passage mean? It says, "Behold, this child has been destined for the falling and the rising of many in Israel." I found something similar to this written in the Gospel According to John. It says, "I came into this world for judgment, so that those who are blind might see, and those who see might become blind."[8] He came "for judgment," so that the blind among the Gentiles might see, and those of Israel who had previously had their sight might become blind.[9] Thus too, he came "for the falling and the rising of many." For, at the coming of our Lord and Savior, those who previously had stood fell down, and those who had fallen rose up. This is one interpretation of what has been said: "Behold, this child has been destined for the falling and the rising of many in Israel."

4. But there is also something more profound to be understood here, most especially in opposition to those who yelp against the Creator.[10] From every place in the Old Testament, which they do not understand, they gather testimony "and deceive the hearts of the simple."[11] They say, "Behold the god

6. Lk 2.29–30.

7. Lk 2.34–35.

8. Jn 9.39.

9. Cf. *Homilies on Leviticus* 3.1.2.

10. For Origen's arguments against Marcion, cf., for example, *Homilies on Exodus* 6.9; *Homilies on Numbers* 19.2; and *On First Principles* 2.5. Crouzel notes that "yelp" is typical of Jerome; Origen did not insult his adversaries.

11. Rom 16.18.

of the law and the prophets! See what sort of god he is! He says, 'I shall kill and I shall make alive. I shall strike and I shall heal. There is no one who can escape my hands.'"[12] They hear, "I shall kill," and do not hear, "I shall make alive." They hear, "I shall strike," and refuse to hear, "And I shall heal." With instances like this they misrepresent the Creator.

5. Before I explain the sense of the passage, "I shall kill and I shall make alive; I shall strike and I shall heal," I shall set the testimony of the Gospel against them. There are countless heresies that accept the Gospel According to Luke. I shall say this against the heretics. You say that the Creator is savage, and only a judge, and cruel, because he says, "I shall kill and I shall make alive; I shall strike and I shall heal." Then it is absolutely clear that Jesus is his Son, since the same things have been written about him: "Behold, he is destined for the falling and the rising of many in Israel"—not only "for the rising," but also "for the falling." If it is evil to kill, then acknowledge that it is also evil to cause someone to fall. What will they answer? Will they cease worshipping him, or will they seek another interpretation and take refuge in figures of speech, so that what comes "for the falling" implies benevolence rather than severity?[13]

6. How can it be just, when something like this is found in the Gospel, to take refuge in allegories and new interpretations, but, in the case of the Old Testament, immediately to make accusations and not to accept any explanation, no matter how probable? This passage follows: "I came into this world for judgment, so that those who are blind might see, and those who see might become blind."[14] Although they seek to expound it, they will be unable to succeed. But I hope to be a man of the Church. I hope to be addressed not by the name of some heresiarch, but by the name of Christ. I hope to have his name, which is blessed upon the earth. I desire, both in

12. Dt 32.39.

13. Ironically, Origen, the defender of spiritual interpretation, accuses the Marcionites of hiding behind allegory.

14. Jn 9.39.

deed and in thought, both to be and to be called a Christian.[15] I ask for an equal accounting for both the Old Law and the New.

7. God says, "I shall kill." I willingly concede that God kills. For, when the old man is in me and I still live as a man, I desire to have God kill the old man in me and raise me up from among the dead. For Scripture says, "The first man was from the earth, and earthly; the second man is from heaven, and heavenly. As we have carried about the image of the earthly man, let us also bear the image of the heavenly man."[16] The passage, "I came into the world for judgment, so that those who are blind might see and those who see might become blind,"[17] is interpreted according to this sense. All of us human beings have both sight and blindness in us. Adam both saw and did not see. Eve, too, before her eyes were opened, is said to have seen. Scripture says, "The woman saw the tree, that it was good to eat and excellent to behold with the eyes. She took from the fruit of the tree and ate, and she gave some to her husband, and they ate."[18] So they were not blind; they could see.

8. Then Scripture says, "And their eyes were opened."[19] Therefore, they had been blind and could not see. Afterwards their eyes were opened. But beforehand they could see well. After they disobeyed the command of the Lord, they began to see poorly.[20] Afterwards, as their sin seeped into them, they lost the vision that is obedience. Thus I also understand that passage where God says, "Who made a man dumb and deaf, seeing and blind? Is it not I, the Lord God?"[21] There is a corporeal eye, by which we see those earthly things, an eye according to the sense of the flesh. Scripture says of it, "He walks in vain, puffed up by the sense of the flesh."[22] We have another eye,

15. Hans Urs von Balthasar chose this passage as the epigraph for his anthology of Origen's writings, *Origenes. Geist und Feuer: Ein Aufbau aus seinen Schriften* (Salzburg: Müller, 1938). See also Henri de Lubac, *Histoire et esprit. L'intelligence de l'Écriture d'après Origène,* Théologie 16, (Paris: Aubier, 1950) 47–91 (Ch. 2: "Origène homme d'Église")

16. 1 Cor 15.47–49.

17. Jn 9.39.

18. Gn 3.6.

19. Gn 3.7.

20. Cf. *Homilies on Numbers* 17.3.

21. Ex 4.11.

22. Col 2.18.

opposed to this one.[23] It is better, and perceives divine things. But it was a blind eye in us. Jesus came to enable it to see, so that those who were blind might see, and those who saw might become blind. Therefore, the passage that we now have at hand, namely, "Behold, he is destined for the falling and the rising of many in Israel,"[24] should be interpreted according to this meaning.

9. I have something within me that wrongly stands upright and rears itself up in the pride of sin. Let this thing fall; let it be destroyed. If it falls, then what had previously fallen will rise up and stand. My "interior man"[25] once lay broken, and the "exterior man"[26] stood straight. Before I believed in Jesus, the good in me lay low, while the evil was standing. After he came, what was evil in me collapsed. And Scripture has been fulfilled: "Always carrying about in the body the death of Jesus . . . ,"[27] and, "Put to death your members upon earth: fornication, impurity, licentiousness, idolatry, sorcery,"[28] and the rest.

10. The fall of all these vices is advantageous. Of this fall Scripture says, "Wherever the cadaver is, there will the eagles gather."[29] The word "cadaver" comes from the verb "to fall."[30] This fall is good. First of all, Jesus came because of it. Nor could he bring about a rising unless a falling had come first. Let him first come to destroy what is evil in me. Once that has been destroyed and put to death, let what is good arise in me and receive life, so that we may obtain the kingdom of heaven in him, to whom is glory and power for ages of ages. Amen.

23. Cf. *Homilies on Numbers* 17.3 and *Homilies on Ezekiel* 2.3.
24. Lk 2.34.
25. Rom 7.22.
26. 2 Cor 4.16.
27. 2 Cor 4.10.
28. Col 3.5.
29. Mt 24.28.
30. Jerome is right. The same is true in Greek, where πτῶμα, the word for "corpse," has the same derivation.

HOMILY 17

Luke 2.33–38

Again on the passage from, "His father and mother were astonished at these things that were being said about him," up to the point where Anna is written of.

IT IS LUKE who wrote, "The Holy Spirit will come upon you, and the power of the Most High will overshadow you. For this reason, what will be born is holy. He will be called the Son of God."[1] He clearly handed down to us that Jesus was the son of a virgin, and was not conceived by human seed. But Luke has also attested that Joseph was his father when he said, "And his father and mother were astonished by the things that were being said about him."[2] Therefore, what reason was there that Luke should call him a father when he was not a father?[3] Anyone who is content with a simple explanation will say, "The Holy Spirit honored Joseph with the name of 'father' because he had reared Jesus." But one who looks for a more profound explanation can say that the Lord's genealogy extends from David to Joseph. Lest the naming of Joseph, who was not the Savior's father, should appear to be pointless, he is called the Lord's "father," to give him his place in the genealogy.[4] Thus "his father and mother were astonished by the things that were being said about him"[5]—both by the angel and by the great number of the heavenly army, as well as by the shepherds. When they heard all of these things, they were greatly astonished.

1. Lk 1.35.
2. Lk 2.33.
3. Cf. *Homilies on Leviticus* 12.4.1.
4. Origen believed that Luke named Joseph in the genealogy of Jesus to establish Jesus' Davidic descent. Cf. *Commentary on Romans* 1.5.
5. Lk 2.33.

2. Then Scripture says, "Simeon blessed them and said to Mary, his mother, 'Behold, he is destined for the falling and the rising of many in Israel, and for a sign that will be contradicted. And a sword will pierce your very soul, to reveal the thoughts of many hearts.'"[6] We must ponder how the Savior came "for the falling and the rising of many." One who explains the passage in a simple way can say that he came "for the falling" of unbelievers and "for the rising" of believers. But one who is a diligent interpreter says that the only one who falls is he who had been standing. Answer me, therefore: Who is the one who stood, and for whose falling the Savior came? And who is he who rises up? For, surely, he who earlier had fallen rises up. Therefore, we have to see whether perhaps the Savior came not for the falling of some and the rising of others, but for the falling and the rising of the same ones. He says, "I came for judgment, so that those who were blind might see and those who could see might become blind."[7] Among us, it is one thing that someone could first see, and afterwards ceased to see, and another thing that he did not see and afterwards began to see. For example, I wish to see with those eyes with which I did not see earlier, and which afterwards are opened for me, because, after their disobedience, both Adam's and Eve's eyes were opened.[8] We treated these eyes in our earlier discourse.[9]

3. But now we have to interpret the meaning of the passage that says, "Behold, this child is destined for the falling and the rising of many in Israel."[10] It is right that I should first fall and then, after I have fallen, rise up aright. Otherwise, the Savior would be the cause of an evil fall for me. But he made me fall for this reason, that I might rise up. My fall was to be very beneficial to me—much more than the time when I seemed to stand. For, at that time when I lived by sin, I was standing by sin. Because I was standing by sin, the first benefit I received was to fall and die to sin. Then too, when the holy prophets contemplated something more august, they fell on their faces.

6. Lk 2.34–35.
7. Jn 9.39.
8. Gn 3.7.
9. Cf. *Hom.* 16.7.
10. Lk 2.34.

They fell to purge their sins more fully by this fall. The Savior, too, first granted you this very thing—that you should fall. You were a Gentile. Let the Gentile in you fall. You loved prostitutes. Let the lover of prostitutes in you perish first. You were a sinner. Let the sinner in you fall. Then you can rise again and say, "If we have died with him, we shall also live with him,"[11] and, "If we have been made like him in death, we shall also be like him in resurrection."[12]

4. For, he "has been destined for the falling and the rising of many in Israel"[13]—that is, among those who can see[14] with full acuteness and reason—and "for a sign that is contradicted."[15] Everything that the plain narrative recounts about the Savior is contradicted. The virgin is a mother. This is "a sign that is contradicted." The Marcionites contradict this sign and insist that he was not born of a woman.[16] The Ebionites[17] contradict this sign and say that he was born of a man and a woman in the same way as we are born. He had a human body. This too is "a sign that is contradicted." For, some say that he came down from heaven. Others say that he had a body like ours, so that he could also redeem our bodies from sin by the likeness of his body to ours and give us hope of resurrection. He rose from the dead. This is also "a sign that is contradicted." How did he rise? Was he just as he was when he died, or did he surely rise into a body of a better substance?

5. There is endless contention on this point. Some say, "He showed Thomas the mark of the nails in his hands." Others argue from another line of thought: "If he had the same body, how 'did he enter through closed doors and stand there'?"[18] So you see how even the question of his resurrection is beset with various arguments and is "a sign that is contradicted." I

11. 2 Tm 2.11

12. Rom 6.5.

13. Lk 2.34.

14. From Philo onwards, the name "Israel" was understood as meaning "vision of God" or "one who sees God." Cf. Philo, *On Drunkenness* 82; *Who Is the Heir?* 78; and *Questions and Answers on Genesis* 3.49. Cf. also Origen, *Homilies on Numbers* 11.4 and 17.4.

15. Lk 2.34.

16. Cf. *Homilies on Ezekiel* 1.4.

17. A Jewish-Christian sect; the name "Ebionites" (from a Hebrew word that means "the poor") had been in use since Irenaeus.

18. Cf. Jn 20.26.

myself think that even the fact that he was foretold by the mouths of the prophets is a sign that is contradicted. For, there are many heretics who assert that he was simply not foretold by the prophets.[19] Why must I furnish many examples? Everything that the plain narrative recounts about him is "a sign that is contradicted." It is not as if those who believe in him contradict them; we know indeed that everything that Scripture records is true. But, for unbelievers, all things that are written about him are "a sign that is contradicted."

6. Thereupon Simeon says, "a sword will pierce your very soul."[20] Which sword is this that pierced not only others' hearts, but even Mary's? Scripture clearly records that, at the time of the Passion, all the apostles were scandalized. The Lord himself said, "This night you will all be scandalized."[21] Thus, they were all so scandalized that Peter too, the leader of the apostles, denied him three times. Why do we think that the mother of the Lord was immune from scandal when the apostles were scandalized? If she did not suffer scandal at the Lord's Passion, then Jesus did not die for her sins. But, if "all have sinned and lack God's glory, but are justified by his grace and redeemed,"[22] then Mary too was scandalized at that time.

7. And this is what Simeon now prophesies when he says, "And your very soul." You know, Mary, that you bore as a virgin, without a man. You heard from Gabriel, "The Holy Spirit will come upon you, and the power of the Most High will overshadow you." The "sword" of infidelity "will pierce" you,[23] and you will be struck by the blade of uncertainty, and your thoughts will tear you in pieces when you see him. You had heard him called the Son of God. You knew he was begotten without a man's seed. You knew he was crucified, and died, and subjected to human punishment. You knew that at the end he lamented and said, "Father, if it is possible, let this chalice pass from me."[24] Thus the Scripture, "and a sword will pierce your very soul."[25]

19. For example, Marcion and the Gnostics.
20. Lk 2.35.
21. Mk 14.27.
22. Rom 3.23.
23. Lk 1.35.
24. Mt 26.39.
25. Lk 2.35.

8. ". . . to reveal the thoughts in the hearts of many."[26] Men had evil thoughts. They were revealed to bring them into the open and destroy them. Once they had been slain and are dead, they would cease to exist. He who died for us would kill them. For, as long as such thoughts were hidden and not brought out into the open, it was quite impossible to kill them. Thus, if we ourselves have sinned, we ought to say, "I made my sin known to you, and I have not hidden my iniquity. I said, 'Against myself shall I proclaim my injustice to the Lord.'"[27] For, if we have done this and revealed our sins not only to God but also to those who can heal our wounds and our sins,[28] our sins will be blotted out by him who says, "I shall blot out your transgressions like a cloud, and like a mist your sins."[29]

9. Because it was necessary that women too should be saved, after Simeon there came a woman who was a prophetess. Of her Scripture says, "And Anna was a prophetess, a daughter of Phanuel, from the tribe of Asher."[30] How beautiful the order is! The woman did not come before the man. First came Simeon, who took the child and held him in his arms. Then came the woman. Her exact words are not recorded. But the account says in general terms that "she gave praise to the Lord and spoke about him to everyone who was awaiting the redemption of Jerusalem."[31] The holy woman justly deserved to receive the spirit of prophecy, because by a long life of chastity and long fasts she had risen to this high state.

10. Women, look on Anna's testimony and imitate it! If it ever happens to you that you lose your husbands, ponder what Scripture has said of Anna. "For seven years from her virginity she lived with her husband,"[32] and so on. For that reason she was a prophetess. The Holy Spirit did not dwell in her accidentally or by chance. It is a good thing, and first in value, if a woman can possess the grace of virginity.[33] If she cannot do

26. Lk 2.35.
27. Ps 32.5.
28. An allusion to second penance, or reconciliation after Baptism. In Origen's time it included *exomologesis,* or confession of sins.
29. Is 44.22.
30. Lk 2.36.
31. Lk 2.38.
32. Lk 2.36.
33. Cf. *Frag.* 35 on 1 Cor 7.8, ed. Claude Jenkins, "Origen on I Corinthians III," JThS 9 (1908) 503–505.

this, but she happens to lose her husband, let her persevere as a widow. In fact, she should have this idea in mind not only after the death of her husband, but even while he is still living. Then, if what she wills and proposes does not occur, she will be crowned by the Lord and can say, "If something happens in the course of life,[34] although I do not hope for it, I shall do nothing else but persevere uncorrupted as a widow. "But now second, third, and fourth marriages—and I keep my silence about even more—are found in the Church. We know that such a union will eject us from the kingdom of God. Not only fornication, but also a second marriage, excludes someone from office in the Church. Anyone twice married may be neither a bishop nor a presbyter nor a deacon nor a widow.[35] Perhaps in this sense will a twice-married man be ejected from the assembly "of the first-born and the spotless,"[36] "the Church, which has neither spot nor wrinkle"[37]—not to be cast into eternal fire, but to be denied a place in the kingdom of God.

11. I recall that, when I was explaining what is written to the Corinthians, namely, "To the Church of God, which is at Corinth, together with all who invoke" him,[38] I said that there was a difference between "the Church" and "those who invoke the name of the Lord." For I think that the man who married only once, and the virgin, and he who perseveres in abstinence, belong to the Church of God. He who marries twice, even if he has good morals and is outstanding in the other virtues, is not "of the Church" or of that number who "have neither wrinkle nor spot, or anything else of that sort."[39] He is rather of the second rank, and among those "who invoke the name of the Lord." They are saved in the name of Jesus Christ, but they are not crowned by him, to whom is glory and power for ages of ages. Amen.

34. That is, if her husband dies.
35. Cf. 1 Tm 5.9–16.
36. Heb 12.23.
37. Eph 5.27.
38. 1 Cor 1.2. Origen's homilies on 1 Cor are lost, except for fragments; cf. *Frag.* 1 on 1 Cor 1.2, ed. Claude Jenkins, "Origen on I Corinthians," JThS 9 (1908) 232.
39. Eph 5.27.

HOMILY 18

Luke 2.40–49

On the passage from, "But the boy grew and was strengthened," up to the point where it says, "Do you not know that I should be in my Father's house?"

ESUS MY LORD has been born. His parents have gone up to Jerusalem to fulfill what was commanded in the law. They went to offer "a pair of turtle-doves or two young pigeons"[1] for him. Simeon held him in his arms, as was read earlier. He prophesied about him those things that the narrative relates. After everything was accomplished in the traditional way, his parents returned. How old was Jesus then? Certainly he was still but a small child. Yet "he grew and was strengthened, and he was filled with wisdom" and grace.[2] He had not yet completed the forty days of purification, nor had he come to Nazareth, but he was already receiving full wisdom. Scripture could say, "He grew and was strengthened, and he received the Spirit."[3] "He had emptied himself by taking the form of a slave."[4] But, as soon as a sacrifice was offered for his purification, he filled up what he had emptied out. It was not his body that was made greater at that moment. Something more sacred is manifested when Scripture reports, "The boy grew and was strengthened, and was filled with wisdom."[5]

2. Let us find out whether Scripture says of a small child, "he grew and was strengthened," anywhere else. By comparing many instances, we can understand what more is being said about our Lord. We read about John, "but the boy grew and

1. Lk 2.24.
2. Lk 2.40.
3. Origen adds to Lk 2.40 a phrase from Lk 1.80.
4. Phil 2.7.
5. Lk 2.40.

was strengthened."[6] But Scripture does not add, "and he was filled with wisdom,"[7] but "he was strengthened in spirit."[8] Scripture says of the Lord, "He grew and was strengthened, and was filled with wisdom, and the grace of God was upon him."[9] All of this is said of a boy who has not yet completed his twelfth year. But, when he is twelve years old, he remains in Jerusalem. His parents do not know this. They seek him anxiously and do not find him. They seek him "among their relatives." They seek him "in the accompanying crowd." They seek him "among their acquaintances."[10] And in none of these places do they find him. Thus Jesus is sought by his parents. He is sought by his father, who was his foster-father, and who accompanied him when he went down to Egypt. And still, he does not find him as soon as he seeks him. For, Jesus is not found among their relatives—those near to him according to the flesh—not among these, who are joined to him corporeally. My Jesus cannot be found in the crowd of the many.

3. Learn where they who seek him find him. Then you too, when you seek him along with Joseph and Mary, might be able to find him. They sought him and, Scripture says, "they found him in the temple":[11] not in any other place, but "in the temple"; and not simply "in the temple," but "in the midst of the teachers, listening to them and asking them questions."[12] You too, therefore, seek Jesus "in the temple" of God. Seek him in the Church. Seek him among the teachers who are "in the temple" and do not leave it. For, if you seek him in this way, you will find him. But, if anyone says he is a teacher and does not possess Jesus, he is a teacher only in name and Jesus, who is God's Word and Wisdom, cannot be found with him. He was found, Scripture says, "in the midst of the teachers." You should understand the words, "in the midst of the teachers," in the sense in which Scripture, in another passage, speaks about the prophets. It says, "If a revelation is given to another

6. Lk 1.80.
7. Lk 2.40.
8. Lk 1.80.
9. Lk 2.40.
10. Lk 2.44.
11. Lk 2.46.
12. Lk 2.46.

one who is sitting, let the first be silent."[13] They find him "sitting in the midst of the teachers"—and not only sitting, but "asking them questions and listening to them." Jesus is present now as well. He interrogates us and hears us speaking. Scripture says, "And all were astonished."[14] What were they astonished about? Not about his questions, even though they too were remarkable, but "about his answers."[15] For it is one thing to ask questions, another to answer them.

4. He was questioning the teachers and, since from time to time they could not answer, he himself would answer the question he had asked. Let the divine law itself teach you that in the Holy Scriptures the word "answer" does not mean the give and take of ordinary conversation, but the teaching found in the Scriptures. "Moses was speaking, and God was answering him with his voice."[16] That answer concerned matters that Moses was ignorant of, and in which the Lord instructed him. Sometimes Jesus asks questions, sometimes he answers. As we said earlier, as astonishing as his questions are, his answers are still more astonishing. Let us implore him and beg him with great earnestness and sorrow to allow us to hear him, and to ask us questions that he himself would solve. Then we shall be able to find him whom we seek. Scripture says, and not in vain, "Your father and I were seeking you and grieving."[17]

5. He who seeks Jesus should do so not carelessly, not laxly, not halfheartedly, as some seek him and cannot find him. We should say, "We seek you grieving." And, when we have said this, he will answer our souls in their distress, as they seek him in sorrow, and say, "Do you not know that I should be in my Father's house?"[18] Where are the heretics,[19] where are the impious ones and the madmen, who claim that the Law and the prophets do not come from the Father of Jesus Christ? Surely Jesus was in the temple that Solomon had built. He confesses

13. 1 Cor 14.30.
14. Lk 2.47.
15. Lk 2.47.
16. Ex 19.19(LXX). The Hebrew text has, "God answered him in thunder."
17. Lk 2.48.
18. Lk 2.49.
19. Gnostics and Marcion, who divided creation from redemption and the Old Testament from the New.

that it is the temple of his Father, whom he revealed to us, and whose Son he said he was. Let them answer and say how one God can be good and the other one just. Because the Savior is the Son of the Creator, let us praise the Father and the Son together. His is the Law, and his is the temple. To him is glory and power for ages of ages. Amen.

HOMILY 19

Luke 2.40–46

Again on the passage from, "But the boy grew and was strengthened," up to the point where the elders in the temple were questioning him.

OME WHO APPEAR to believe the Sacred Scriptures deny the Savior's divinity for the sake—as they think—of the glory of Almighty God.[1] Hence, it seems right to me that they should be instructed by the authority of those very Scriptures. They should learn that a divine being came into a human body—and not only into a human body, but also into a human soul. Yet, if we pay careful attention to the meaning of Scripture, we realize that his soul had something more than the souls of other men. Every human soul, before it turns to virtue, is stained with vices. But the soul of Jesus was never defiled with the stain of sin.[2] In the Gospel of Luke, the Holy Spirit writes this of him before he reached the age of twelve: "But the boy grew and was strengthened, and he was filled with wisdom."[3] Human nature itself does not permit this, that wisdom is perfected before the twelfth year of life. It is one thing to participate in wisdom, another thing to be filled with wisdom.

2. Hence, we may not doubt that a divine being appeared in the flesh of Jesus—and a being that is not only superior to human nature, but even superior to every rational creature. Scripture says, "he grew." For, "he humbled himself, taking the form of a slave."[4] By that same power by which he humbled himself, he grows. He had appeared as weak, because he had

1. Ebionites. Cf. *Hom.* 17.4.
2. On Jesus' soul, cf. *On First Principles* 2.6.3–7.
3. Lk 2.40.
4. Phil 2.7.

assumed a weak body, and, for that reason, once more he is strengthened. The Son of God "had emptied himself,"[5] and, for that reason, again he is filled with wisdom. "And the grace of God was upon him."[6] He possessed the grace of God not when he reached young manhood, not when he taught openly, but already when he was a small child. Just as everything else about him was extraordinary, so his boyhood was extraordinary as well, that it might be filled with the wisdom of God.

3. "Thus, according to their custom, his parents went to Jerusalem for the solemn day of the Pasch. And, when he was twelve years old . . . ."[7] Observe carefully. Before he was twelve years old, he was filled with the wisdom of God and with the other gifts that Scripture records. As we said, when he was twelve years old, and, according to custom, the days of the feast were completed and his parents were returning home, "the boy remained in Jerusalem and his parents did not know it."[8] Here you must understand something more sublime than human nature allows. For, he did not simply "remain," and his parents not know where he was. No! Scripture records in the Gospel According to John that the Jews were plotting against him, and he slipped away from their midst and disappeared.[9] Now, in this same way, I think, the boy remained in Jerusalem and his parents did not know where he had remained. We should not be surprised that they are called his "parents." They deserved the titles "mother" and "father," the one because she bore him, the other because he took care of him.

4. The passage continues, "We were seeking you, sorrowing."[10] I do not think they grieved because they thought the boy had gotten lost, or perished. Mary knew she had conceived of the Holy Spirit; she had heard the angel speaking, and the shepherds who ran to her, and Simeon prophesying. It was impossible for her to fear that the boy had wandered off and

5. Phil 2.7.
6. Lk 2.40.
7. Lk 2.41–42.
8. Lk 2.43.
9. Cf. Jn 8.59 and 10.39.
10. Lk 2.48.

perished. Most of all, dispel such a thought about Joseph. An angel had commanded him to take the boy and go to Egypt.[11] He had heard the words, "Do not fear to take Mary as your wife; for the child she has conceived is of the Holy Spirit."[12] It was impossible for him to fear that the child had perished, for he knew that he was divine. The sorrow, and the parents' search, mean something else than what the simple reader understands.

5. Sometimes you read the Scriptures and in them seek their meaning with a certain sorrow, and even pain. This is not because you think the Scriptures erred, or contain something wrong. Rather, they contain within themselves an expression and account[13] of the truth. You cannot discover what is true. In just this way his parents sought Jesus, lest perhaps he withdraw from them, or leave them and pass over to some other realm, or—what I consider more likely—lest he return to heaven to come down again when it pleased him. Therefore, they sought the Son of God "in sorrow." When they sought him, they did not find him "among their relatives." For, a human relationship could not contain the Son of God. They did not find him "among their acquaintances," because divine power is greater than mortal acquaintance and knowledge. Where, then, did they find him? "In the temple." For, it is there that the Son of God is found. If you ever seek the Son of God, look first in the temple; hasten thither. There you will find Christ, the Word and Wisdom—that is, the Son of God.

6. Because he was a small child, he is found "in the midst of the teachers," sanctifying and instructing them. Because he was a small child, he is found "in their midst," not teaching them but "asking questions." He did this because it suited his age, to teach us what befits boys, even if they are wise and learned. They should rather hear their teachers than want to teach them, and not show off with empty displays. As I was saying, he interrogated the teachers not to learn anything, but to teach them by his questions. From one fountain of doctrine,

11. Mt 2.13.
12. Mt 1.20.
13. *Sermo* and *ratio*, Jerome's expression for λόγος.

there flow both wise questions and wise answers. It is part of the same wisdom to know what you should ask and what you should answer. It was right for the Savior first to become a master of learned interrogation; later he would answer questions according to God's Reason and Word.[14] To him is glory and power for ages of ages. Amen.

14. Again Jerome expands Origen's expression, which would have been "according to God's Λόγος."

HOMILY 20

Luke 2.49–51

On the passage from, "But why were you seeking me?" up to the point where it says, "Mary kept all these words in her heart."

ARY AND JOSEPH kept seeking Jesus "among the relatives"[1] and did not find him. They looked "in the crowd"[2] and could not find him. They looked "in the temple"[3]—and not only "in the temple," but amid the teachers—and they find him "in the midst of the teachers."[4] Wherever there are teachers, Jesus is found "in their midst," provided that the teacher sits "in the temple" and never goes out of it. Jesus benefited his teachers, and as he spoke in their midst taught those of whom he appeared to be asking questions. In some way, too, he impelled them to seek what they did not know, and to search out what up until then they could not know whether they understood or not.

2. So Jesus is found "in the midst of the teachers." Once he is found, he says to those who seek him, "Why were you seeking me? Did you not know that I should be in my Father's house?"[5] First of all, we grasp the surface meaning of the passage. We should be armed against the impious heretics[6] who say that the Creator, the God of the Law and the prophets, is not the Father of Jesus Christ. See! Here the Father of Christ is called the God of the temple. Valentinians[7] should blush with shame when they hear Jesus say, "I should be in my Father's house."[8]

1. Lk 2.44.
2. Lk 2.44.
3. Lk 2.46.
4. Lk 2.46.
5. Lk 2.49.
6. Gnostics and Marcionites.
7. Gnostic heretics whom Irenaeus of Lyons refuted in his work *Against the Heresies.*
8. Lk 2.49.

All the heretics who accept the Gospel According to Luke and scorn what is written in it should blush. As I said, this is the simpler interpretation.

3. But, because the text adds, "Yet they did not understand what he said,"[9] we should consider the meaning of this passage more carefully. Were they so dense and foolish that they did not know what he was saying? Did they not understand that, when he said, "I should be in my Father's house," he meant "in the temple"? Or does it mean something else, something more profound, which would be more helpful to the hearers? Each one of us, if he is good and perfect, is the possession of God the Father. Therefore, in general terms, the Savior taught in regard to everything that he should be nowhere else than among those who are his Father's. If any one of you belongs to God the Father, he has Jesus in his midst. We should believe him when he says, "I should be in my Father's house." And I suspect that the believing Christian, rather than that structure, built by earthly labor as a type, is the rational temple of God, the living and true temple. Thus, just as he was in that temple as a type, so too he left it as a type. For "he went out of the" earthly "temple" saying, "Behold, your house will be left to you deserted."[10] He left that house and came to what belongs to God the Father, namely, the churches scattered throughout the whole world. He says, "I should be in my Father's house." So it was then that "they did not understand the word that he had spoken to them."[11]

4. At the same time, pay attention to this also. As long as he was in his Father's domain, he was above. Joseph and Mary did not yet have perfect faith. For this reason, they were unable to remain above with him. Scripture says that he went down with them. Jesus frequently goes down with his disciples. He does not always stay on a mountain. He does not always keep to the heights. He is on the mountain with Peter, James, and John, but with the rest of the disciples he is in another place. Because those who were troubled with various diseases were

9. Lk 2.50.
10. Mt 24.1 and 23.38.
11. Lk 2.50.

not strong enough to climb the mountain, he "went down and came"[12] to those who were below. Here too Scripture says, "He went down with them and came to Nazareth, and was subject to them."[13]

5. Children, we should learn to be subject to our parents. The greater is subject to the lesser. Jesus understood that Joseph was greater than he in age, and therefore he gave him the honor due a parent. He gave an example to every son. Sons should be subject to their fathers; and, if they have no fathers, they should be subject to those who serve as fathers. But why am I speaking about parents and children? If Jesus, the Son of God, is subject to Joseph and Mary, shall I not be subject to the bishop? God appointed him a father to me. Shall I not be subject to the presbyter, whom the Lord's choice set over me? I think Joseph understood that Jesus, who was subject to him, was greater than he. He knew that the one subject to him was greater than he and, out of reverence, restrained his authority. So each one should realize that often a lesser man is put in charge of better men. Sometimes it happens that he who is subject is better than he who appears to be in authority. Once someone who enjoys a higher position understands this, he will not be lifted up in pride by the fact that he is greater. He will know that a better one is subject to himself, just as Jesus was subject to Joseph.[14]

6. Then there follows, "But Mary kept all these words in her heart."[15] She suspected that they were something more than the words of a man. Hence, she "kept all his words in her heart," not as the words of a twelve-year-old boy, but as the words of him who had been conceived by the Holy Spirit, and whom she had seen "advancing in wisdom and grace before God and men."[16] Jesus "was advancing in wisdom," and seemed wiser with each stage of life. Is it possible that he was not wise,

12. Mt 8.1.

13. Lk 2.51.

14. Origen may have had his own relationship to the bishop of Alexandria in mind when he speaks about a lesser man put in charge of a greater, and, more generally, about the place of scholars and the learned in the Church with respect to bishops and presbyters.

15. Lk 2.51.

16. Lk 2.52.

so that he grew wise? Or is it because "he had emptied himself, taking the form of a slave"[17] that he took back what he had lost and was filled with those virtues that he had seemed to leave behind a little earlier, when he took on a body? Thus "he advanced" not only "in wisdom" but "in age." He advanced in age too.[18] Scripture speaks of two sorts of age. One is the age of the body, which is not subject to our power but to the law of nature. The other is the age of the soul, which is properly under our control. If we will it, we grow daily in this age.

7. And we come to its highest point, when "we are no longer little children, carried and tossed about by every wind of doctrine."[19] Instead, we should cease to be "little children" and begin to be grown men. We should say, "When I became a man, I destroyed the things of a small child."[20] Progress in this age—the one leading to growth of the soul—is, as I said, within our power. But, if this testimony is not enough, we can take another example from Paul. He says, ". . . until we all come to be a perfect man, according to the measure of the fullness of the age of Christ's body."[21] So it is within our power to "come to the measure of the age of Christ's body." And, if it is in our power, we should struggle with all our effort to put off the small child and destroy it, and to advance to the other stages of life, so that we too might hear the words, "But you will go to your fathers with peace, cared for in a good old age."[22] May we grow old in a spiritual old age, which is the truly good one, and come to our end in Christ Jesus, to whom is glory and power for ages of ages. Amen.

17. Phil 2.7.
18. Cf. *Homilies on Leviticus* 12.2.3 and *Commentary on Matthew* 13.26.
19. Eph 4.14.
20. 1 Cor 13.11.
21. Eph 4.13.
22. Gn 15.15.

HOMILY 21

Luke 3.1–4

On the passage from, "In the fifteenth year of the reign of Tiberius Caesar," up to the point where it says, "make his paths straight."

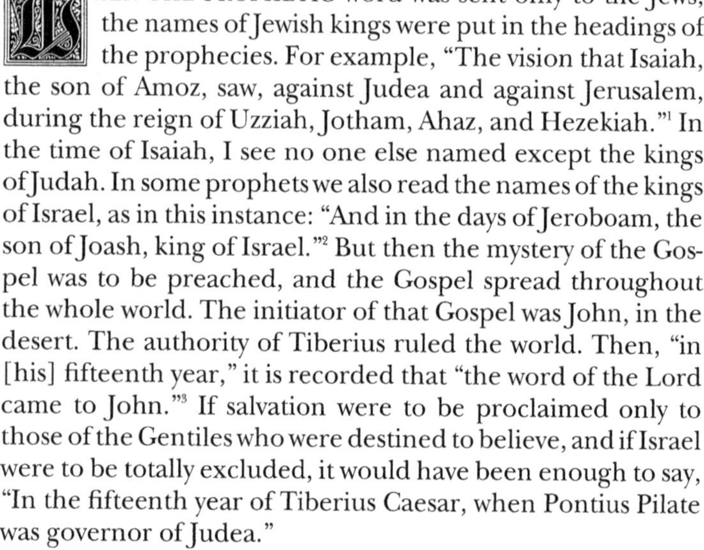

WHEN THE PROPHETIC word was sent only to the Jews, the names of Jewish kings were put in the headings of the prophecies. For example, "The vision that Isaiah, the son of Amoz, saw, against Judea and against Jerusalem, during the reign of Uzziah, Jotham, Ahaz, and Hezekiah."[1] In the time of Isaiah, I see no one else named except the kings of Judah. In some prophets we also read the names of the kings of Israel, as in this instance: "And in the days of Jeroboam, the son of Joash, king of Israel."[2] But then the mystery of the Gospel was to be preached, and the Gospel spread throughout the whole world. The initiator of that Gospel was John, in the desert. The authority of Tiberius ruled the world. Then, "in [his] fifteenth year," it is recorded that "the word of the Lord came to John."[3] If salvation were to be proclaimed only to those of the Gentiles who were destined to believe, and if Israel were to be totally excluded, it would have been enough to say, "In the fifteenth year of Tiberius Caesar, when Pontius Pilate was governor of Judea."

2. But, since many from Judea and Galilee were destined to believe, these kingdoms too were put in the heading. The passage reads, "Herod was tetrarch of Galilee, and his brother Philip was tetrarch of Iturea and the region of Trachonitis, and Lysanias was tetrarch of Abilene, under the high priests Annas and Caiaphas, and the word of the Lord came to John,

1. Is 1.1.
2. Am 1.1.
3. Lk 3.1–2.

the son of Zechariah, in the desert."[4] Once "the word of the Lord came to Jeremiah, the son of Hilkiah, who was one of the priests"[5] in the time of this or that king of Judah. Now "the word of the Lord comes to John, the son of Zechariah." It never came to prophets "in the desert." But "more sons of the deserted woman" were destined to believe "than of her who has a husband."[6] Hence, the word of God came to John, the son of Zechariah, in the desert.

3. But, at the same time, consider this. "Desert" is more intelligible if it is understood mystically, and not according to the simple letter. For, someone who preaches "in the desert" cries out to no purpose, since no one hears him speaking. Therefore, the precursor of Christ and "the voice of one crying out in the desert" is preaching in the desert of the soul that has no peace. Yet, not only then, but also now, "a burning and shining lamp"[7] comes first and "preaches a baptism of repentance for the remission of sins."[8] Then the "true light"[9] follows, when the lamp itself says, "He must increase, I must decrease."[10] The word of God comes to be in the desert, and "comes to the whole region lying along the Jordan."[11] For, what other places ought the Baptist have made the rounds of except the neighborhood of the Jordan? If anyone wanted to do penance, a bath of water was available.

4. Then, "Jordan" means "descending."[12] But the "descending" river of God, one running with a vigorous force, is the Lord our Savior. Into him we are baptized with true water, saving water. Baptism is also preached "for the remission of sins." Come, catechumens! Do penance, so that Baptism for the remission of sins will follow. He who stops sinning receives Baptism "for the remission of sins." For, if anyone comes sin-

4. Lk 3.1–2.
5. Jer 1.1.
6. Gal 4.27 quoting Is 54.1. Origen plays on the words "desert" and "deserted." This word-play was most effective in Greek, where ἐρῆμος is feminine in both its meanings, "desert" and "solitary woman."
7. Jn 5.35.
8. Lk 3.3.
9. Jn 1.9.
10. Jn 3.30.
11. Lk 3.3.
12. This explanation is frequent. Cf. *Commentary on John* 6.42; *Frag.* 76 on John (GCS Origenes 4.543); and Philo, *Allegorical Interpretation* 2.89.

ning to the washing, he does not receive forgiveness of sins. Therefore, I implore you, do not come to Baptism without caution and careful consideration. First show "results worthy of repentance."[13] Spend some time in good living. Keep yourselves clean of all stains and vices. Your sins will be forgiven when you yourselves begin to despise your own sins. Put aside your own offenses, and they will be forgiven you.

5. But we read this scriptural passage itself, which is quoted from the Old Testament, in Isaiah the prophet. For this Scripture says, "The voice of one crying in the desert, 'Prepare the way for the Lord. Make his paths straight.'"[14] The Lord wants to find in you a path by which he can enter into your souls and make his journey. Prepare for him the path of which it is said, "Make straight his paths." "The voice of one crying in the desert"—the voice cries, "prepare the way." For, first a voice comes to the ears. Then, after the voice—or rather, along with the voice—the word gains entrance to the sense of hearing.[15] In this manner was Christ proclaimed by John. Therefore, let us see what the voice proclaims about the Word. It says, "Prepare a way for the Lord." What way are we to prepare for the Lord? Surely not a material way? Or can the Word of God go on such a journey? Should not the way be prepared for the Lord within? Should not straight and level paths be built in our hearts? This is the way by which the Word of God has entered. That Word dwells in the spaces of the human heart.

6. If the human heart is pure, it is great and broad and spacious. Do you wish to know its size and its breadth? See what a great amount of divine thoughts it holds. The Lord himself says, "He gave me true knowledge of those things that are: to know the reason for the world, and the workings of the elements; the beginning and the end and the midpoint of the ages; the changing of the seasons and the passing of the months; the rotation of the years and the abode of the stars; the natures of animals and the fury of beasts; the power of

13. Lk 3.8.
14. Is 40.3–5.
15. On "voice" and "word," see *Hom.* 1.4.

spirits and the thoughts of men; the varieties of trees and the power of their roots."[16] You see that man's heart, which can grasp so much, is not small. Realize that its greatness is measured not by the size of the body but by the strength of its awareness. It can grasp such great knowledge of the truth!

7. But, to lead some simpler listeners through everyday examples to believe that the human heart is great, let us consider the following. Whatever cities we have traveled through, we have in our souls. Their qualities, and the plans of their streets and walls and buildings, are present in our hearts. We retain, in the picture and description of memory, the street we entered upon. In silent thought, we encompass the sea we sailed upon. As I said, man's heart, which can encompass such great things, is not small. But, if it is not small, and can encompass such great things, it follows that the way of the Lord is prepared in it and his path becomes straight, so that the Word of God and his Wisdom can walk in it. Prepare the way for the Lord by good living, and smooth out a path with outstanding works, so that the Word of God can walk in you without stumbling at all, and give you knowledge of his mysteries and his coming. To him is glory and power for ages of ages. Amen.

16. Wis 7.17–20.

HOMILY 22

Luke 3.5–8

On the passage from, "Every valley will be filled in," up to the point where it says, "God can raise up sons for Abraham from these stones."

ET US SEE what things are preached at Christ's coming. Among them, it is first written of John, "The voice of one crying in the desert, 'Prepare the way of the Lord. Make his paths straight.'"[1] What follows applies properly to the Lord and Savior. For, "every valley has been filled"[2] not by John, but by the Lord and Savior. Each one should reflect on himself, about who he was before he believed. Then he should observe that he has been a lowly valley, a steep valley, one that dropped down into the depths. But, when the Lord Jesus came, and sent the Holy Spirit as his deputy,[3] "every valley was filled." They were filled with good works and the fruits of the Holy Spirit. Love does not allow a valley to remain in you. If you possess peace and patience and goodness, not only will you cease to be a valley, but you will even begin to be God's mountain.

2. "Every valley will be filled." We see this done and fulfilled daily, both among the Gentiles and in the people of Israel, who have been cast down from on high. "Every mountain and hill will be made low."[4] Once that people was a mountain and a hill; now they are cast down and demolished. "Because of their sin, salvation has been given to the Gentiles, and they

1. Lk 3.4

2. Lk 3.5.

3. Tertullian calls the Holy Spirit Christ's deputy (*vicarius*) in *On the Veiling of Virgins* 1.4 and *On the Prescription of Heretics* 13.5; he calls Christ the Father's deputy in *Against Marcion* 3.6.7 and *Against Praxeas* 24.5.

4. Lk 3.5.

are to be jealous of the Gentiles."[5] But you will not err, either, if you say that opposing powers,[6] which were raised up against mortals, are the mountains and hills that were cast down. For, to fill in this sort of valley, the opposing powers—the mountains and hills—must be made low.

3. We also need to consider whether the next phrase, which was prophesied at Christ's coming, has been fulfilled. The passage reads, "And all that is crooked will be made straight."[7] Each of us was crooked. Or, if he was crooked once, but has not remained so up to the present day, this happened through the coming of Christ. His coming touched our souls; whatever was crooked is now straight. For, what profit is it to you, if Christ once came in the flesh, unless he also comes into your soul? We should pray that he will come to us each day so that we can say, "I live, now not I, but Christ lives in me."[8] For, if Christ lives in Paul and does not live in me, how does that benefit me? But, since he both comes to me and I profit by him, just as Paul profited, I too can speak like Paul: "I live, now not I, but Christ lives in me."

4. Let us also consider the other points that are proclaimed in Christ's coming. Nothing was rougher than you.[9] Consider your former actions. Look at your anger and the rest of your vices. If they have ceased to be what they were, you will realize that nothing was rougher than you, and—if I can say something even clearer—nothing was more uneven. Your morals and your speech were uneven, and your deeds were uneven. So my Lord Jesus came and leveled out your rough places and turned whatever was in disarray into level roads. Then there is a path in you with nothing to stumble on, level and very clear. God the Father can walk in you. Christ the Lord can make his dwelling in you and say, "My Father and I shall come and make our dwelling with him."[10]

5. Rom 11.11.
6. On the "opposing powers," cf. *Hom.* 6.5 and the note there.
7. Lk 3.5.
8. Gal 2.20.
9. Origen begins to comment on Lk 3.5: "And rough places will become level roads."
10. Jn 14.23.

5. There follows, "And all flesh will see God's salvation."[11] Once you were flesh. You who once were flesh—or rather, if I may say something more wonderful, who are still in the flesh—see "God's salvation." But what does Scripture mean when it says "all flesh"? No flesh is excepted that will not see "God's salvation." I leave it to be understood by those who understand the mysteries of the Scriptures, and can mine its veins.[12] But you should pay attention to what John says "to the people going out"[13] to baptism. If anyone wants to be baptized, let him go out. One who remains in his original state and does not leave behind his habits and his customs does not come to baptism properly. To understand what it is to go out to baptism, accept the testimony and listen to the words by which God speaks to Abraham: "Go out of your land,"[14] and so forth.

6. So John speaks the following words to the crowds that are going out to the baptismal washing—they have not gone out, but are only striving to go out. For, if they had already gone out, he would never call them "brood of vipers."[15] So, whatever he says to them, he also says to you, men and women, catechumens! You are arranging to come to Baptism. Take heed, lest perhaps it can be said to you, "Brood of vipers." For, if you have any similarity to sensual vipers and invisible serpents, "brood of vipers" will also be said to you. Unless you expel wickedness and the serpent's venom from your hearts, the words that follow will also be said to you: "Who showed you how to flee from the wrath to come?"[16]

7. Great wrath threatens this age. The entire world is going to suffer God's wrath. The wrath of God will overturn the great expanse of the heavens, and the breadth of the earth, and the choruses of the stars, and the splendor of the sun, and the nocturnal consolations of the moon. On account of men's

11. Lk 3.6.

12. Either Origen has no explanation for this phrase or he does not want to mention ἀποκατάστασις, or universal restoration, which he had taught earlier.

13. "To go out," for Origen, recalls the Exodus from slavery and sin. Cf. *Homilies on Exodus* 5.2.

14. Gn 12.1.

15. Lk 3.7.

16. Lk 3.7.

sins, all of these things will pass away. Once, indeed, God's wrath fell upon the earth alone, "because all flesh had left its life upon the earth."[17] But now the wrath of God is going to come both upon the heavens and upon the earth. "The heavens will pass away, but you will abide," Scripture says to God, "and all the heavens will grow old like a garment."[18] See what sort of wrath it is, and how great. It will consume the entire world and punish those who deserve punishment. And this wrath will find an object on which to exercise itself. Each of us has prepared an object for wrath by what he has done. The Epistle to the Romans reads, "For, according to your hardness and your impatient heart, you pile up for yourself wrath on the day of wrath and the revelation of God's just judgment."[19]

8. Then there follows, "Who showed you how to flee from the wrath to come? Produce fruits worthy of repentance."[20] To you, who are coming to Baptism, Scripture says, "Produce fruits worthy of repentance." Do you want to know which fruits are worthy of repentance? "Charity is a fruit of the Spirit; joy is a fruit of the Spirit; so are peace, patience, kindness, goodness, faith, gentleness, continence,"[21] and the others of this sort. If we have all of these virtues, we have produced "fruits worthy of repentance." Again it is said to those who were coming to John's baptism, "And do not begin to say among yourselves, 'We have Abraham for a father.' For, I say to you, God can raise up sons for Abraham from these stones."[22] John, the last of the prophets, prophesies the expulsion of the first nation[23] and the call of the Gentiles. To those who were boasting about Abraham he says, "And do not begin to say among yourselves, 'We have Abraham for a father.'" And again he speaks about the Gentiles, "For I say to you, that God can raise up sons for Abraham from these stones."

9. From which stones? Surely he was not pointing to irrational, material stones, but to men who were uncomprehending

17. Gn 6.12.
18. Ps 102.26–27.
19. Rom 2.5.
20. Lk 3.7–8.
21. Gal 5.22–23.
22. Lk 3.8.
23. That is, the Jews.

and sometimes hard.[24] They adored stones or wood. In them is fulfilled what the psalm sings about such men: "May they who make these idols, and all who trust in them, become like their idols."[25] Those who make idols and trust in them are like their gods: they are turned into stones and wood, without sensation, without any reason. For, when they merely see the order of creatures, their beauty, their function, and the great beauty of the world, they are unwilling to intuit the Creator from the creatures. Nor do they consider that there is some oversight, some Ruler of this great plan of salvation.[26] They are blind; they see the world only with those eyes with which irrational animals and beasts see it.

10. For they do not realize that, in these things they see ruled by reason, Reason is present. This is our explanation of what John said: "God can raise up sons for Abraham from these stones."[27] Therefore, we too should pray to God that we also might be made into "sons for Abraham," if once we were stones. May this happen in place of those sons who have been rejected, and who have lost the promise and their adoption by their own sin. I shall cite one more testimony about stones, since in the canticle of Exodus Scripture says, "Let them be turned into stones until your people, Lord, passes through, until that people of yours, which you possessed, passes through."[28] So God is asked that for a short while the Gentiles might be changed into stones—that is what the Greek word ἀπολιθοόντωσαν[29] really means—"until the" Jewish "people passes through." There is no doubt but that, after they have passed through, the Gentiles will cease to be stone, and will receive in place of their hard hearts a human and rational nature in Christ, to whom is glory and power for ages of ages. Amen.

24. Cf. Ambrose, *Exposition of the Gospel According to Luke* 2.75.
25. Ps 115.8.
26. Origen probably has the Epicureans in mind.
27. Lk 3.8.
28. Ex 15.16.
29. Ex 15.16(LXX). The Hebrew has "they are still as a stone"; Origen explains the more dramatic term of the LXX.

HOMILY 23

Luke 3.9–12

On the passage from, "Behold, the ax has been laid to the root of the trees," up to the point where it says, "But publicans also came to be baptized by him."

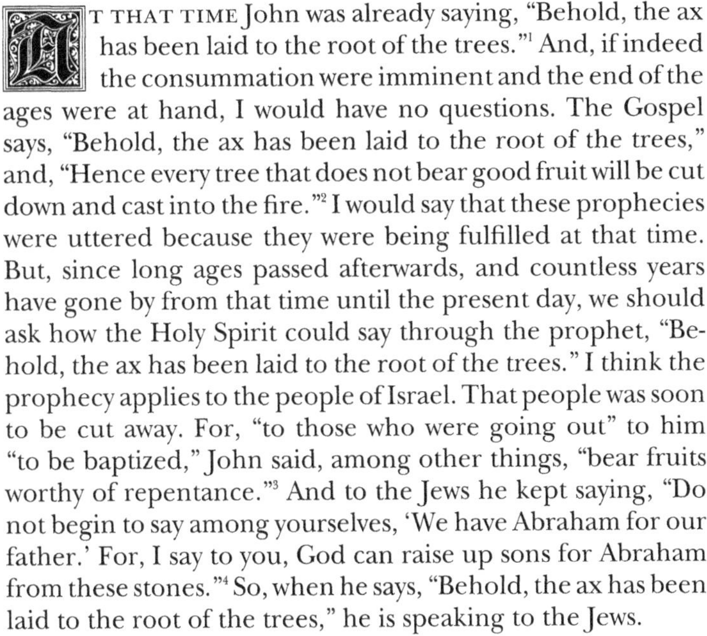

AT THAT TIME John was already saying, "Behold, the ax has been laid to the root of the trees."[1] And, if indeed the consummation were imminent and the end of the ages were at hand, I would have no questions. The Gospel says, "Behold, the ax has been laid to the root of the trees," and, "Hence every tree that does not bear good fruit will be cut down and cast into the fire."[2] I would say that these prophecies were uttered because they were being fulfilled at that time. But, since long ages passed afterwards, and countless years have gone by from that time until the present day, we should ask how the Holy Spirit could say through the prophet, "Behold, the ax has been laid to the root of the trees." I think the prophecy applies to the people of Israel. That people was soon to be cut away. For, "to those who were going out" to him "to be baptized," John said, among other things, "bear fruits worthy of repentance."[3] And to the Jews he kept saying, "Do not begin to say among yourselves, 'We have Abraham for our father.' For, I say to you, God can raise up sons for Abraham from these stones."[4] So, when he says, "Behold, the ax has been laid to the root of the trees," he is speaking to the Jews.

2. The apostolic word also fits this sense. The author says that the branches of infidelity have been broken off and cut down by this ax. The goal was to cut off from the tree, not the

1. Lk 3.9.
2. Lk 3.9.
3. Lk 3.7–8.
4. Lk 3.8.

root, but those shoots that had sprung up from the root. Thus, branches from the wild olive can be grafted onto the root of the original tree. "Therefore, every tree that does not bear good fruit will be cut down and thrown into the fire."[5] This is its end, to be burned in the fire. Then, three groups of people are mentioned who consult John about their salvation. Scripture calls the first group "people going out to baptism;" it names the second group "tax collectors," and the third is given the name "soldiers." "The crowds questioned him and said, 'What shall we do?' He answered them and said, 'If a man has two tunics, he should give one to someone who does not have one. If a man has food, he should do likewise.'"[6] I wonder whether it was appropriate to give the crowd this command.

3. For, to say that he who has two tunics should give one to someone who has none fits the apostles better than the crowd. To understand that this command fits the apostles more than the people, listen to what the Savior says to the apostles, "Do not take two tunics on a journey."[7] Therefore, there are two garments with which each one is clothed. He is commanded to give one "to him who does not have"; this denotes an alternate meaning. Just as we may not "serve two masters,"[8] the Savior does not wish us to have two tunics, or to be clothed with a double garment. Otherwise, one would be the garment of the old man, the other of the new man. On the contrary, he desires that "we strip ourselves of the old man and put on the new man."[9] Up to this point, the explanation is easy.

4. The next question is how, according to this interpretation, we are commanded to give a garment "to one who has none." Who is the man who does not have even one covering on his flesh, who is naked, who is covered with no garment at all? I do not mean by this that generosity, and pity towards the poor, and even extravagant clemency, are not commanded us, so that we should clothe the naked with our own spare tunic. I say this rather because this passage can be understood

5. Lk 3.9.
6. Lk 3.10–11.
7. Mt 10.10.
8. Lk 16.13.
9. Col 3.9–10.

more profoundly. We should give a tunic to him who has none at all. Who is the man who does not have a tunic? It is he who utterly lacks God. Therefore, we should divest ourselves and give to him who is naked. One has God; another does not have him at all; the latter is an opposing power.[10] Just as the Scripture says, "We should cast our sins into the depths of the sea,"[11] so we should cast away our vices and sins and throw them on him who was the cause of them for us. John continues, "He who has food should do likewise."[12] Whoever has food should give some to him who has none. He should generously give him not only clothing but also what he can eat.

5. "But the tax collectors also came to be baptized by him."[13] According to the simple interpretation, he teaches the tax collectors to seek "nothing more" than the law commands. Those who exact more transgress not John's commandment but that of the Holy Spirit, who spoke through John. I do not know whether, according to ἀναγωγή,[14] the passage signifies something else, something loftier. I do not know whether we should bring out such mystical things before this kind of an audience,[15] especially among those who do not examine the marrow of the Scriptures but are fascinated by the superficial sense alone. It is risky; but I have to touch on it cursorily and briefly. When we depart from the world and this life of ours has been transformed, some beings will be seated at the boundary of the world, as if they were exercising the office of tax collectors, very carefully searching to find something in us that is theirs.[16]

6. It seems to me that "the prince of this world" is like a tax collector. Hence, the Scripture says of him, "The prince of this world is coming, and he has no claim on me."[17] We should also understand in a reverent way what we read in the Apostle,

10. On the "opposing powers," cf. *Hom.* 6.5 and the note there.

11. Mi 7.19.

12. Lk 3.11.

13. Lk 3.12.

14. Jerome retains the Greek word, which means "lifting up" and, in Christian usage, the spiritual or "elevated" sense of Scripture.

15. Cf. *Homilies on Numbers* 13.7.

16. Cf. Clement of Alexandria, *Stromata* 4.18.117.2.

17. Jn 14.30.

namely, "Repay to all what is owed: tribute to whom tribute is due, taxes to whom taxes are due, honor to whom honor is due. You should owe nothing to anyone, except to love one another."[18] For this reason we should ponder what great dangers we are exposed to. Otherwise, when we do not have the means to pay the tax, we ourselves might be dragged off on account of the debt. This is what normally happens to those subject to worldly taxes, when someone is imprisoned for his debt and made a slave of the state. How many more of us are destined to be held by tax collectors of that sort! Jacob, the holy man, did not greatly dread them or fear that something that belonged to the tax collector's revenue should be found in him.

7. Jacob spoke boldly to that tax collector Laban, "See if any of your goods are in my possession."[19] Scripture gives testimony on this point and says, "And Laban did not recognize anything of his in Jacob's possession."[20] So our Savior, and the Holy Spirit who spoke in the prophets, teach not only men, but also angels and invisible powers. Why should I speak about the Savior? The prophets, too, and the apostles themselves, proclaim everything that they reecho not only to men, but even to angels. You know that it is true, for Scripture says, "Listen, o heaven, and I shall speak,"[21] and, "In the sight of the angels shall I sing to you,"[22] and, "Praise the Lord, you heavens of heavens; let the waters that are above the heavens praise the name of the Lord,"[23] and, "Let the angels praise him,"[24] and, "Bless the Lord, my soul, in every place of his power."[25] In many places, and especially in the psalms, you will find speech addressed to the angels. Power has been given to man—at least to him who has the Holy Spirit—to speak even to the angels. I shall give one example from these instances, so that we might realize that angels too can be taught by human

18. Rom 13.7–8.
19. Gn 31.32(LXX), which expands the Hebrew original.
20. Gn 31.34(LXX), again an expansion of the Hebrew.
21. Dt 32.1.
22. Ps 138.1.
23. Ps 148.4–5.
24. Ps 148.2.
25. Ps 103.22.

voices.[26] It has been written in the Apocalypse of John, "Write to the angel of the church of the Ephesians, 'I have something against you.'"[27] And again, "Write to the angel of the church of Pergamum, 'I have something against you.'"[28] Clearly it is a man who writes to angels and enjoins something.

8. I do not doubt that angels are even present in our assembly—not only generally, to every church, but even singly. The Savior says of them, "Their angels always see the face of my Father, who is in heaven."[29] Here a double church is present, one of men, the other of angels. If we say anything in accord with reason and according to the intent of the Scriptures, the angels rejoice and pray with us. And angels are present in the church—at least in that church that deserves them and belongs to Christ. This is the reason why women are commanded to have "a veil on their heads" when they pray, "because of the angels."[30] Which angels? Clearly those who aid the holy ones and rejoice in the church. Our eyes are closed by the stains of sins, and we do not see them. But the apostles of Jesus see them. He says to them, "Amen, amen, I say to you, you will see the heavens opened and the angels of God ascending and descending upon the Son of Man."[31]

9. If I had this grace, to see just as the apostles saw, and to behold, as Paul beheld, I would now see a multitude of angels. Elisha saw them. Gehazi, who stood with him, did not see them. Gehazi was fearful, lest he be captured by enemies. He saw only Elisha. But Elisha, as a prophet of the Lord, prays and says, "O Lord, open the eyes of this servant, and let him see that many more are with us than with them."[32] And, at the prayers of the holy man, Gehazi immediately perceived the angels which he had not seen before. We said all this to show how the tax collectors were taught by John—not only those who collected revenue for the state, but also those who were coming for repentance, and were not literally tax collectors. And others were soldiers who were going out to the baptism

26. On angels, cf. *Homilies on Numbers* 11.4 and *On First Principles* 1.8.1.
27. Rv 2.1 and 4.
28. Rv 2.12 and 14.
29. Mt 18.10.
30. 1 Cor 11.10.
31. Jn 1.51.
32. 2 Kgs 6.16–17.

of repentance. For, not only John and the prophets came, but even the Savior himself. They came to preach saving penance to men and angels and the rest of the powers, so that "at the name of Jesus every knee would bend, of those in heaven, those on earth, and those in the underworld; and every tongue confess that the Lord Jesus Christ is in the glory of God the Father,"[33] to whom is glory and power for ages of ages. Amen.

33. Phil 2.10–11.

HOMILY 24

Luke 3.15–16

On the passage from, "I indeed baptize you with water," up to the point where it says, "He will baptize you in the Holy Spirit and fire."

HE PEOPLE RECEIVED John, who was less than Christ. They reflected and thought, "Perhaps he is the Christ." But they did not receive him who had come, who was greater than John. Do you want to know the reason? Recognize this: John's baptism could be seen; the Baptism of Christ was invisible. John said, "For I baptize you in water, but he who comes after me is greater than I. He will baptize you in the Holy Spirit and in fire."[1] When does Jesus baptize "with the Holy Spirit"? And again, when does he baptize "with fire"? Does he baptize at one and the same time "with Spirit and fire," or at distinct and different times? He says, "But you will be baptized with the Holy Spirit not many days hence."[2] After his ascension into heaven, the apostles were baptized "with the Holy Spirit." But Scripture does not record that they were baptized "with fire."

2. At the Jordan river, John awaited those who came for baptism. Some he rejected, saying, "generation of vipers," and so on.[3] But those who confessed their faults and sins he received. In the same way, the Lord Jesus Christ will stand in the river of fire near the "flaming sword."[4] If anyone desires to pass over to paradise after departing this life, and needs cleansing, Christ will baptize him in this river and send him across to the place he longs for. But whoever does not have the sign of earlier baptisms, him Christ will not baptize in the fiery bath.

1. Lk 3.16.
2. Acts 1.5.
3. Lk 3.7.
4. Gn 3.24.

For, it is fitting that one should be baptized first in "water and the Spirit."[5] Then, when he comes to the fiery river, he can show that he preserved the bathing in water and the Spirit. Then he will deserve to receive in addition the baptism in Christ Jesus, to whom is glory and power for ages of ages. Amen.

5. Jn 3.5.

HOMILY 25

Luke 3.15

On the suspicion that the people had about John,
"that perhaps he was the Christ."

VEN LOVE ENTAILS a risk, if it is excessive. If someone loves another, he should consider the nature and the causes of his loving, and not love that person more than he deserves. For, if he goes beyond the measure and the limit of charity, then both he who loves and he who is loved will be in sin. To make this clearer, we can take John as an example. The people revered and loved him. And indeed he was a worthy object of wonder. More deference was paid to him than to the rest of men, for he had lived differently than all other mortals. None of us is content with simple food; we take pleasure in a variety of food. One kind of wine to drink does not suffice for us; we purchase wines with different tastes.

2. But John always ate locusts, and he always ate woodland honey.[1] He was content with simple and light food, lest his body grow fat on richer, savory dishes and be overpowered by exquisite banquets. This is the nature of our bodies; they are weighed down by excess food and, when the body is weighed down, the soul too is burdened. For, the soul is spread throughout the whole body and is subject to its passions. Hence, those who can observe it are rightly advised, "It is good not to eat meat or drink wine or do anything that scandalizes your brother."[2] So John's life was remarkable, and quite different than other men's way of living. He had no purse, no servant, not even an ordinary hut.

1. Cf. Mt 3.4.
2. Rom 14.21.

3. He dwelt in the desert, not only until "the day of his manifestation to Israel,"[3] but also at the time when he was preaching repentance to the people. He dwelt in the desert of Judea. He drank plain water; even in his drinking he was different from the rest. We live in cities; we are in the midst of people. We look for more elegant garments, food, and dwellings; but John lived in the desert. Notice what sort of garment he was clothed with: he had made a tunic "of camel's hair," and was girded with "a leather belt."[4] So everything about him was new. Because his life was so different, everyone who saw him admired him. And, because they admired him, more than anything else they revered him devoutly, especially because he was baptizing the penitents "for the remission of sins."[5]

4. For this reason, they loved him quite justly, but they did not keep their love within bounds; for they kept wondering "whether perhaps he was the Christ."[6] The apostle Paul warns against inordinate and irrational love when he says of himself, "I fear that someone might have an opinion of me above what he sees or hears from me, and that the greatness of the revelations might exalt me," and so on.[7] Paul feared that even he might fall into this error. So he was unwilling to state everything about himself that he knew. He wanted no one to think more of him than he saw or, going beyond the limits of honor, to say what had been said about John, that "he was the Christ." Some people said this even about Dositheus, the heresiarch of the Samaritans;[8] others said it also about Judas the Galilean.[9] Finally, some people burst forth into such great audacity of love that they invented new and unheard of exaggerations about Paul.

5. For, some say this, that the passage in Scripture that speaks

3. Lk 1.80.

4. Mt 3.4.

5. Lk 3.3

6. Lk 3.15.

7. 2 Cor 12.6–7. Jerome's Latin here differs from the Vulgate, and the clauses are collocated differently.

8. Dositheus of Samaria founded a Christian sect in the first century; cf. *Commentary on John* 13.27.162.

9. Judas the Galilean was a messianic pretender. Cf. Acts 5.37. Cf. also Josephus, *Jewish Antiquities* 18.1 and *Jewish War* 2.8.1.118.

of "sitting at the Savior's right and left"[10] applies to Paul and Marcion: Paul sits at his right hand and Marcion at his left. Others read the passage, "I shall send you an advocate, the Spirit of Truth,"[11] and are unwilling to understand a third person besides the Father and the Son, a divine and exalted nature. They take it to mean the apostle Paul. Do not all of these seem to you to have loved more than is fitting and, while they admired the virtue of each, to have lost moderation in love?

6. Even we in the church suffer this. Many people love us more than we deserve. They brag about it, and speak in praise of our sermons and our teaching. But our conscience cannot acquiesce in this. Others, however, criticize our homilies unfairly and reproach us with holding positions that we never knew we held.[12] But neither those who love too much, nor those who hate, abide by the rule of truth. The ones lie through love; the others lie through hatred. It is right to place a bridle even on charity and to permit it freedom to roam only insofar as it does not rush headlong over a cliff. Scripture says, in Ecclesiastes, "Do not be righteous in excess, nor think yourself more than you are, lest perhaps you should be struck dumb."[13] Following this, I can say something similar. Do not love a man "with your whole heart and with your whole soul and with all your strength."[14] Do not love an angel "with your whole heart and with your whole soul and with all your strength." In accord with the Savior's words, keep this command in respect to God alone. For, he says, "You shall love the Lord your God with your whole heart and with your whole soul and with all your strength."[15]

7. Someone might answer me and say, "The Savior teaches, 'You shall love the Lord your God with your whole heart and with your whole soul and with all your strength, and your neighbor as yourself.'[16] I wish to love Christ too. Therefore, teach me how I should love him. For, if I love him 'with my whole heart

10. Mt 20.21.
11. Jn 14.16–17.
12. Origen also complains about his critics in *Homilies on Genesis* 13.3.
13. Eccl 7.16.
14. Lk 10.27.
15. Lk 10.27.
16. Lk 10.27.

and with my whole soul and with all my strength,' I act against the commandment, insofar as I love another besides the one God thus. But, if I love him less than I do the Almighty Father, I fear that I might be found to be irreverent and contemptuous toward 'the firstborn of all creation.'[17] Teach me, and show me the way. Taking the middle path between the two, how should I love Christ?" Do you wish to know how Christ is to be loved?

8. Listen for a moment! "Love the Lord your God" in Christ, and do not think you can have a different love of the Father than of the Son. Love God and Christ at the same time. Love the Father in the Son, and the Son in the Father, "with your whole heart and with your whole soul and with all your strength." If anyone inquires and says, "Prove what you are asserting from the Scriptures," let him hear the apostle Paul. Paul had a rational love. He said, "I am certain that neither death nor life, neither angels nor powers, neither the present nor the future, neither power nor height nor depth nor any creature, will be able to separate us from the love of God, which is in Christ Jesus, our Lord and our Savior,"[18] to whom is glory and power for ages of ages. Amen.

17. Col 1.15.
18. Rom 8.38–39.

HOMILY 26

Luke 3.16–17

On the passage from, "His winnowing fan is in his hand, and he will cleanse his threshing floor," up to the point where it says, "And he will gather the grain into his barn."

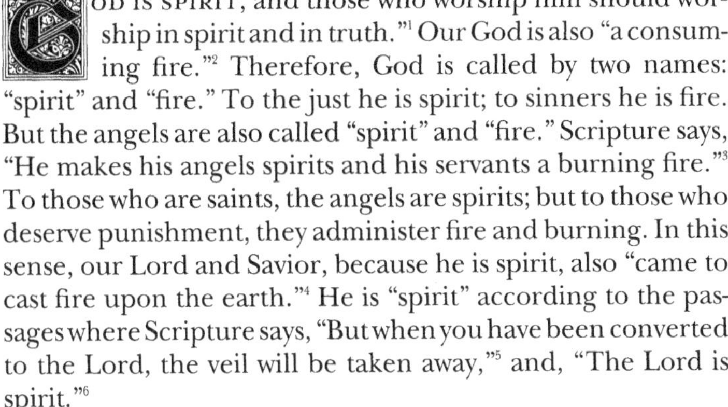

GOD IS SPIRIT, and those who worship him should worship in spirit and in truth."[1] Our God is also "a consuming fire."[2] Therefore, God is called by two names: "spirit" and "fire." To the just he is spirit; to sinners he is fire. But the angels are also called "spirit" and "fire." Scripture says, "He makes his angels spirits and his servants a burning fire."[3] To those who are saints, the angels are spirits; but to those who deserve punishment, they administer fire and burning. In this sense, our Lord and Savior, because he is spirit, also "came to cast fire upon the earth."[4] He is "spirit" according to the passages where Scripture says, "But when you have been converted to the Lord, the veil will be taken away,"[5] and, "The Lord is spirit."[6]

2. But "he came to cast fire" not upon the heavens, but "upon the earth." He himself shows that when he says, "I have come to cast fire upon the earth, and how I wish it were already burning."[7] For, if "you are converted to the Lord," who is spirit, Christ will be spirit for you, and has not "come to cast fire upon the earth." But, if you are not converted to him but cling to the earth and its fruits, "he comes to cast fire" upon the earth. Scripture also says something like this about God: "The fire of

1. Jn 4.24.
2. Dt 4.24.
3. Ps 104.4, cited in Heb 1.7.
4. Lk 12.49.
5. 2 Cor 3.16.
6. Jn 4.24 and 2 Cor 3.17.
7. Lk 12.49.

my wrath has been ignited"—not as high as heaven, but "all the way to the underworld below," and it will consume, not heaven, but "the earth and its vegetation."[8]

3. Why do I mention this? Because the baptism with which Jesus baptizes is "in the Holy Spirit and fire."[9] I am mindful of what I said before, and I have not forgotten my earlier explanation.[10] But I also wish to present something new. If you are holy, you will be baptized with the Holy Spirit. If you are a sinner, you will be plunged into fire. One and the same baptism will be turned into condemnation and fire for the unworthy and for sinners; but to those who are holy and have been turned to the Lord in total faith, the grace of the Holy Spirit, and salvation, will be given. Therefore, he who is said to baptize "in the Holy Spirit and fire" has "a winnowing fan in his hand, and he will cleanse his threshing floor. And he will gather his wheat into a barn, but the chaff he will burn in unquenchable fire."[11] I want to find the reason why our Lord has a winnowing fan, and what wind is blowing as the light husks are carried off this way or that, while the heavy grains of wheat are borne down into one place. For, wheat and chaff cannot be separated without wind.

4. I think that wind means temptations. Temptations show that, in the mixed heap of believers, some are husks and others are grains of wheat. For, when your soul is overcome by some temptation, the temptation does not turn you into chaff. Rather, since you are chaff—that is, light in weight and unbelieving—the temptation demonstrates that you are what you were concealing. But, in the opposite case, when you bear trials courageously, temptation does not make you faithful and patient; it rather brings into the open the virtues of patience and courage that were in you but hidden. The Lord says, "Do you think that I spoke to you for any other reason than that you might appear just?"[12] And in another place, "I afflicted you and visited you with penury, so that what was in your heart might

8. Dt 32.22.
9. Lk 3.16.
10. Cf. *Hom.* 24.1–2.
11. Lk 3.17.
12. Jb 40.8(LXX).

be made manifest."[13] In this way too, a storm does not let a house built on sand remain standing; if you wish to build, build on rock. When the storm has arisen, it will not destroy what is built on rock; but what is built on sand trembles and proves that it had no good foundation there.

5. Hence, before a storm arises, before the gusts of wind blow, before the rivers swell, while all things are still quiet, we should give all our attention to the foundations of our house. We should build our house out of the various solid stones of God's commandments. When persecution rages and a fearsome storm arises against Christians,[14] we should show that we have built on the rock, Christ Jesus. But, if anyone denies Christ—may this not happen to us—he should realize that he did not deny Christ at the time he seemed to do so. Rather, the seeds and the roots of his denial were already old. But then, what was in him came to light and was brought into the open. Hence, we should pray to the Lord that we might be a sound building, one that no storm can overturn, "founded on the rock," our Lord Jesus Christ, to whom is glory and power for ages of ages. Amen.

13. Dt 8.2–3 and 5.
14. Cf. *Homilies on Ezekiel* 10.5 and the *Exhortation to Martyrdom*.

HOMILY 27

Luke 3.18–22

On the passage from, "He was also proclaiming many other things [to the people] and encouraging them," up to the point where it says, "The Holy Spirit came down upon him."

NE WHO TEACHES the word of the Gospel proclaims not one thing, but many. Scripture indicates this when it says, "He was also proclaiming many other things [to the people] and encouraging [them]."[1] Therefore, John also preached "other things" to the people, which have not been recorded. But consider how many things there are that have been recorded. He proclaimed Christ. He pointed him out. He preached the baptism of the Holy Spirit. He taught the tax collectors salvation and the soldiers discipline. He taught that the threshing floor was being cleansed, trees cut down, and the rest, which the account in the Gospel narrates. Hence, apart from these things that have been written down, he is shown to have proclaimed other things, which are not written down. For the Scripture says, "He was also proclaiming many other things to the people and encouraging them."[2]

2. The Gospel According to John reports about Christ that he said many other things "that are not written in this book";[3] "if they were written down, I do not think that the world itself would be able to hold the books that would have to be written."[4] Thus too, in the present instance, understand that perhaps Luke was unwilling to record those things explicitly, because John proclaimed some things that were too great to be committed to writing. He only indicated that they were said. For this reason he wrote, "He was also proclaiming many other things

1. Lk 3.18.
2. Lk 3.18.
3. Jn 20.30.
4. Jn 21.25.

to the people and encouraging them."[5] We should also admire John because of those words that come later, especially because there was "no one among the sons of women greater than John the Baptist."[6] By merit of his virtue, he rose to such a high estimate that many thought he was the Christ.[7]

3. But this is even more remarkable: Herod the Tetrarch had royal power and was enabled to kill him when he wished. Herod had committed an unjust act and, against the law of Moses, taken his brother's wife. She had a daughter from her previous husband. John did not fear Herod nor respect his person. He did not think, as I said, of his royal power. He did not fear death. For, he knew, even if he were not a prophet, that if Herod were provoked he could kill him. He knew all of this. But with prophetic freedom[8] he rebuked Herod and condemned his incestuous marriage. For this reason he was confined in prison. John was not anxious about death or about an uncertain sentence. When he was in chains, he was thinking about Christ, whom he had proclaimed. He himself could not go to Christ, so he sent his disciples to ask a question: "Are you he who is to come, or do we wait for another?"[9]

4. Notice that even while in prison he is teaching. For, he also had his disciples in that place. Why did they stay there, unless John exercised the office of teacher even in prison and taught them with divine words? In the course of these words, a question about Jesus arose. John sends some of his disciples and asks, "Are you he who is to come or do we wait for another?" The disciples return and announce to the teacher what the Savior had bidden them to say. With Jesus' words, John was armed for battle. He died confidently, and was beheaded without resistance, strengthened by the words of the Lord himself and believing that he in whom he believed was truly the Son of God. This is what we have to say about John, and his freedom, and about Herod's madness. To his many other crimes he also added this one: he first shut John up in prison and afterwards beheaded him.

5. Lk 3.18.
6. Lk 7.28.
7. Lk 3.15.
8. Cf. *Commentary on Matthew* 10.22.
9. Mt 11.3.

5. The Lord was baptized. The heavens were opened and "the Holy Spirit came down upon him." A voice from the heavens thundered and said, "This is my beloved Son, in whom I am pleased."[10] We should say that heaven was opened at the baptism of Jesus and for the plan of forgiving sins. These are not the sins of him "who had committed no sin, nor was deceit found in his mouth."[11] The heavens were opened and the Holy Spirit came down for the forgiveness of the whole world's sins. After the Lord "ascended on high, leading captivity captive,"[12] he gave us the Spirit. The Spirit had come to him, and he gave the Spirit at the time of his Resurrection when he said, "Receive the Holy Spirit. If you forgive anyone's sins, they will be forgiven him. If you retain them for anyone, they will be retained."[13] But "the Holy Spirit came down upon" the Savior "in the form of a dove."[14] The dove is a gentle bird, innocent and simple. Hence, we too are commanded to imitate the innocence of doves.[15] Such is the Holy Spirit: pure and swift, and rising up to the heights.

6. For this reason, we say in prayer, "Who will give me wings like those of a dove? I shall fly and take rest"[16]—that is, "who will give the wings of the Holy Spirit?" In another place the prophetic word promises, "If you sleep between the plots of land, the wings of a dove are of silver, and the pinions of its tail are made of gleaming gold."[17] For, if we rest "between the plots" of the Old and New Testaments, "silver wings of a dove" will be given to us, that is, the words of God, and the pinions of its tail, radiant with the gleam of gold, so that our senses might be filled with perceptions of the Holy Spirit—that is, our speech and our mind filled by his coming, and we would neither speak nor understand anything besides what he suggests. That way, all sanctification, both in our hearts and in our words and deeds, might come from the Holy Spirit in Christ Jesus, to whom is glory and power for ages of ages. Amen.

10. Lk 3.22.
11. 1 Pt 2.22.
12. Ps 68.18 and Eph 4.8.
13. Jn 20.22–23.
14. Lk 3.22.
15. Cf. Mt 10.16.
16. Ps 55.6–7.
17. Ps 68.13 (LXX), which appears to make little sense.

HOMILY 28

Luke 3.23–38

On the Savior's genealogy, and on the fact that in Matthew and Luke different ancestors are recorded for him.

UR LORD and Savior was greater than Melchizedek, whose genealogy Scripture does not trace. Now, the Lord is described as being born according to the order of his ancestors. Although his divinity has no human origin, for your sake he willed to be born, since you have your origin in flesh. But the evangelists do not give the same account of his genealogy. This fact has disquieted some people very much. Matthew begins to construct his genealogy from Abraham, and reaches the point at which he says, "But the birth of Jesus Christ was thus,"[1] and describes him not at the time of his baptism but at the time at which he came into the world. Luke, in contrast, when he explains his genealogy, does not proceed from the earlier to the later; instead, after he had already said that Jesus was baptized, he traces his ancestry all the way back to God himself.

2. Nor are the same persons mentioned in his genealogy when his descent and his ascent are traced.[2] Matthew, who makes him descend from the heavenly regions, mentions women—not any women at all, but sinners, and those whom Scripture had reproved. But Luke, who tells of Jesus at his baptism, makes mention of no woman. Matthew, as we said, names Tamar who, by deception, lay with her father-in-law; and Ruth, the Moabite, who was not from the race of Israel; and Rahab—

1. Mt 1.18.

2. Cf. Julius Africanus, *Letter to Aristides* (PG 10.52–64). Aristides was a friend of Origen who also explained the two genealogies of Jesus.

I cannot learn where she was taken from;[3] and the wife of Uriah, who violated her husband's bed. For, our Lord and Savior had come for this end, to take upon himself men's sins. God "made him who had committed no sin to be sin for our sake."[4] For this reason, he came down into the world and took on the person of sinners and depraved men. He willed to be born from the stock of Solomon, whose sins have been recorded,[5] and from Rehoboam, whose transgressions are reported,[6] and from the rest of them, many of whom "did evil in the sight of the Lord."[7]

3. But, when he rises up from the washing and his ancestry is described for a second time, he is born not through Solomon but through Nathan.[8] Nathan reproached his father for the death of Uriah and the birth of Solomon. But in Matthew the word "begot" is always added, whereas Luke is completely silent on the matter. In Matthew it is written, "Abraham begot Isaac; Isaac begot Jacob; Jacob begot Judah and his brothers; Judah begot Perez and Zerah by Tamar."[9] Right up to the end, "begot" is always added. But in Luke, when Jesus comes up from baptism, the passage says, "The son, as it was believed, of Joseph."[10] And, in such a long series of names the word for "begetting" is never recorded, except that "he was thought to be the son of Joseph."

4. In Matthew's Gospel, the words "he began"[11] are not included. But in Luke, because Jesus was about to come up from his baptism, we read "he began." The Scripture records, "And Jesus himself was beginning."[12] For, when he has been baptized and has taken on the mystery of the second birth,[13] he is said

3. Elsewhere, however, Origen praises Rahab.
4. 2 Cor 5.21.
5. Cf. 1 Kgs 11.6–8.
6. Cf. 1 Kgs 14.21–31.
7. Cf. 1 Kgs 15.26 and 34.
8. Origen here erroneously identifies the Nathan who, according to Lk 3.31, was David's son, with the prophet Nathan, and refers to 2 Sm 12. Cf. *Frag.* 16 on 2 Sm 5.14 (GCS Origenes 3.300).
9. Mt 1.2–3.
10. Lk 3.23.
11. That is, his ministry. Lk 3.23.
12. Jerome varies the translation; "he was beginning" represents the awkward Greek expression more exactly than "he began."
13. Cf. Clement of Alexandria, *Christ the Educator* 1.6.25.2.

"to have begun." He did this so that you too could wipe away your former birth and be born in a second rebirth.[14] The people of the Jews, as long as they were in Egypt, did not have any beginning of their months. But, when they went out of Egypt, God said to them, "This month, the beginning of months, will be for you the first of the months of the year."[15] Thus too, when Jesus is not yet baptized, he is not said "to have begun." For, we should not think that the words "was beginning" were added to "and Jesus himself" without any purpose.

5. But we also have to consider the passage that reads, "about thirty years old." "Joseph was about thirty years old"[16] when he was released from his chains and interpreted Pharaoh's dream. He was made the governor of Egypt. During the time of plenty, he gathered in the wheat, so that during the time of famine he would have some to distribute. I think that Joseph's age of thirty came before as a type of the Savior's thirty years.[17] For, this second Joseph did not gather in the kind of wheat that the first Joseph did in Egypt. He, Jesus, gathers in true and heavenly wheat, so that in the time of abundance he might gather in the wheat that he will give out when famine is sent upon Egypt, "not hunger for bread or thirst for water, but hunger to hear the word of God."[18]

6. So, during time of plenty, Jesus gathers in words from the prophets, the Law, and the apostles. Scripture is now no longer being written, and no other New Testament is being put together, and no apostles are being sent. But Jesus has gathered the crop into the grain-barns of the apostles, that is, into their souls and the souls of all the saints. May he then distribute it and nourish Egypt, which is threatened by famine, and especially his brothers, of whom Scripture says, "I shall tell your name to my brothers, and in the midst of the church I will sing of you."[19] Other men, too, have words about patience, and words about justice, and words about the other virtues. This is the wheat that Joseph distributed to the Egyptians. But there

14. The redundancy is Jerome's.
15. Ex 12.2.
16. Gn 41.46.
17. Cf. *Homilies on Exodus* 1.4.
18. Am 8.11.
19. Ps 22.22.

is another sort of grain that he gives to his brethren (that is, to his disciples) from that land of Goshen (that is, from the land that looks to the East). This is evangelical grain, apostolic grain. We should make loaves of this grain, but in such a way that they are not mixed with the "old leaven."[20] We can have new bread made from the wheat of the Scriptures, and of flour ground in Christ Jesus, to whom is glory and power for ages of ages. Amen.

20. 1 Cor 5.7.

HOMILY 29

Luke 4.1–4

On the passage, "But Jesus, full of the Holy Spirit, returned"; and about his first temptation.

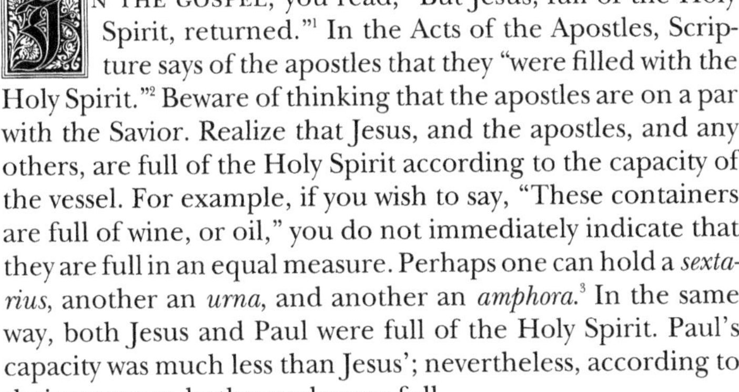

IN THE GOSPEL, you read, "But Jesus, full of the Holy Spirit, returned."[1] In the Acts of the Apostles, Scripture says of the apostles that they "were filled with the Holy Spirit."[2] Beware of thinking that the apostles are on a par with the Savior. Realize that Jesus, and the apostles, and any others, are full of the Holy Spirit according to the capacity of the vessel. For example, if you wish to say, "These containers are full of wine, or oil," you do not immediately indicate that they are full in an equal measure. Perhaps one can hold a *sextarius*, another an *urna*, and another an *amphora*.[3] In the same way, both Jesus and Paul were full of the Holy Spirit. Paul's capacity was much less than Jesus'; nevertheless, according to their measure, both vessels were full.

2. After he had received baptism, the Savior was "full of the Holy Spirit," who had come upon him from heaven "in the form of a dove";[4] and "he was led by the Spirit."[5] For, "as many as are led by the Spirit of God are sons of God."[6] But he was the Son of God in the proper sense, distinct from all others, so it was fitting for him to be led by the Holy Spirit. Thus Scripture says, "But he was led into the desert by the Spirit for forty days and he was tempted by the devil."[7] Jesus was tempted for forty

1. Lk 4.1.
2. Acts 2.4.
3. Roman measures: 48 *sextarii* = 2 *urnae* = 1 *amphora*. An *amphora* was a little less than 7 gallons, a *sextarius* a little more than a pint.
4. Lk 3.22.
5. Lk 4.1.
6. Rom 8.14.
7. Lk 4.1–2.

days. We do not know what the temptations were. Perhaps they have been omitted because they were too great to be entrusted to writing. It is right to say that "the world could not hold all the books"[8] of what Jesus taught and did, if they had been written. Thus too, the world could not have born the forty days of temptations with which the Lord was tempted by the devil, if Scripture had related them. It is enough for us to know only this: "For forty days he was in the desert and was tempted by the devil. And he did not eat anything during those days."[9] He was mortifying the sensations of the flesh by an unbroken and unremitting fast.

3. "And, when the days were finished, he was hungry. But the devil said to him, 'If you are the Son of God, say to this stone that it should become bread.'"[10] "Say to this stone," he says. To which stone? Exactly which stone did the devil point out, which he wants to become bread? What kind of temptation is that? When a son asks his father for bread, he does not give him a stone.[11] But the adversary, fickle and deceptive as he is, gives a stone instead of bread. Is this all that the devil wanted, that a stone should become bread? That men should eat not bread, but a stone that the devil pointed out instead of bread? I think that even to the present day the devil points out a stone and urges each individual to speak, "Say that this stone should become bread." Since he had taken on flesh, the Lord was tempted first with every temptation that men were to be tempted with. He is tempted for this reason, that once he conquers, we might also conquer.

4. Perhaps what I am saying is unclear, unless it is made more understandable by an example. If you should see the heretics eating the falsehood of their doctrines in place of bread, know that their speech is the stone that the devil pointed out. And do not think that the devil has one stone; he has many stones. Matthew raises this point when he says, "Say that these stones should become bread."[12] Marcion spoke, and the devil's stone

8. Jn 21.25.
9. Lk 4.1–2.
10. Lk 4.2–3.
11. Cf. Mt 7.9 and Lk 11.11.
12. Mt 4.3.

became his bread. Valentinus spoke, and another stone is turned into bread for him. Basilides also had bread of this sort; so did the rest of the heretics. Hence, we should carefully take precautions, lest perhaps we eat the devil's stone and think we are eating God's bread. Otherwise, why was it a temptation for the Savior to consider making bread from a stone and eating it? Let us imagine that, at the devil's suggestion, the Lord had turned a stone into bread, eaten what he had made by his own power, and satisfied his hunger. What is the temptation, what is the devil's victory, if Scripture had simply recorded this as a fact?

5. As we have said, once the account is examined, the details show both that the Lord was really tempted to do the devil's bidding, and that a real victory took place, because he refused him. At the same time, we are shown that bread made from a stone is not the word of God that nourishes men. Scripture says of that word, "Man will not live by bread alone, but by every word that will go forth from God's mouth will man live."[13] "To you, o fickle and depraved one, who do not fear to tempt me, I answer that the bread of God's word, which gives life to man, is a different bread." And let us see at the same time that it is not the Son of God who says this, but the man whom the Son of God deigned to assume.[14] For, it is as a man that he answers and says, "Scripture says, 'Man will not live by bread alone.'"[15] This makes it clear that not God, but man, was tempted.

6. After carefully winnowing through the meaning of the Scriptures, I believe I have found the reason why only Matthew, Luke, and Mark, but not John, described the temptation of the Lord. John made God his starting point. He said, "In the beginning was the Word, and the Word was with God, and the Word was God."[16] He could not construct a sequence of divine generation. He only stated that the Word was from God and with God. He added, "And the Word was made flesh."[17] John

13. Dt 8.3 and Mt 4.4.

14. The phrase Jerome uses, *hominem assumere,* was one of the classical expressions of Antiochene christology.

15. Lk 4.4.

16. Jn 1.1.

17. Jn 1.14.

was speaking about God, and God cannot be tempted. Thus, he does not mention his being tempted by the devil. But the "Book of the Generation of Jesus Christ"[18] in the Gospel According to Matthew tells of him as a man who was born of Mary. Luke, too, describes his ancestry. And in Mark, he is also tempted as a man. So in each case he gives the same answer: "Man will not live by bread alone." If the Son of God is God made man for you, and is tempted, then you, who are man by nature, should not complain if perhaps you are tempted.

7. If you are tempted, you imitate him as man, who was tempted for your sake. And, if you overcome every temptation, you will have hope with him, who was man then, but now has ceased to be man.[19] Once he was man; after he was tempted, "the devil left him until the time"[20] of his death. "Rising from the dead, he dies no more."[21] Every man is subject to death. Therefore, he who never dies is now not man but God. But, if he who once was man is God, then you should become like him. "We shall be like him, and see him as he is."[22] It will be necessary for you, too, to become God[23] in Christ Jesus, to whom is glory and power for ages of ages. Amen.

18. Mt 1.1.

19. The explanation of this odd statement follows. Origen makes mortality a necessary quality of humanity. If Christ now dies no more, he is no longer (in that sense) "a man."

20. Lk 4.13.

21. Rom 6.9.

22. 1 Jn 3.2.

23. Divinization, or θέωσις, is a common expression for "salvation" in the Greek Fathers, who saw the misery of the human condition primarily in death rather than in sin and guilt.

HOMILY 30

Luke 4.5–8

On the Savior's second temptation.

BOTH THE SON of God and the Antichrist are eager to reign. But the Antichrist wants to kill those he has subjected to himself. Christ reigns to save. And, if we are faithful, Christ, who is Word, Wisdom, Justice, and Truth, reigns over each of us. But, if we are lovers of pleasure rather than lovers of God, then sin reigns over us. The Apostle says of it, "Therefore, let not sin reign in your mortal body."[1] Hence, two rival kings eagerly strive to reign: the devil, the king of sin, over sinners; and Christ, the King of Justice, over the just. The devil knew that Christ had come to take away his kingdom and to begin to subject those who had been under him to Christ. Therefore, "he showed him all the kingdoms of the world"[2] and of the men of this world. Some are ruled by fornication, others by avarice; some are transported by popularity, others are captivated by the allure of beauty.

2. And we should not think that, when the devil showed Jesus the kingdoms of the world, he showed him, for example, the kingdom of the Persians, and of the Indians. "He showed him all the kingdoms of the world," that is, his own kingdom, how he reigned in the world. The devil urged Christ to do what he willed, so that he would have even Christ as his subject. The devil says, "Do you want to reign over all of these?" He shows him countless multitudes of people whom he holds under his power. And indeed, if we want to confess our wretchedness and our unhappiness openly, the devil is king of almost the entire world. This is why the Savior calls him "the prince of this

1. Rom 6.12.

2. Lk 4.5–6.

world."[3] What he is saying is this: "Do you see these people who are under my reign?" And "he shows [them] to him in a moment of time," that is, in the present course of the ages, which in comparison with eternity lasts the equivalent of a moment.

3. And the Savior had no need of having the activities of this world shown to him any longer. As soon as he turns the glance of his eyes to consider it, he beholds both sin reigning and those who are ruled by vices. He also sees the very "prince of this world,"[4] the devil, vaunting himself and rejoicing in his own destruction, because he has such great men under his power. So the devil says to the Lord, "Have you come to do battle against me and to take from my kingdom those whom I now hold subject? I do not want you to contend. I do not want you to struggle, lest you be afflicted during the contest. There is only one thing I ask of you: 'Fall down and adore me,'[5] and then take the whole kingdom that I possess." Our Lord and Savior does indeed wish to reign, and to have all nations subject to himself, so that they will devote themselves to justice, truth, and the rest of the virtues. But he wills to reign as Justice, so that he would reign without sin, and do nothing dishonorable. He does not will to be crowned without toil, as the devil's subject, or to reign over others when he himself is ruled by the devil.

4. So Jesus says to him, "Scripture says, 'You shall adore the Lord your God, and him alone shall you serve.'"[6] He says, "I want all of these to be subject to me, so that they might adore the Lord God and serve him alone. This is what my kingdom longs for. Yet you want to begin sin with me. But I have come here to absolve it, and I long to take it away from others also. Know and recognize that I abide by what I said. The Lord God alone is to be adored. And I shall put all of these under my power, and subject them to my reign." And we, too, rejoice because we are his subjects. Let us pray God that Christ Jesus will put to death "sin reigning over our bodies"[7] and reign alone in us, to whom is glory and power for ages of ages. Amen.

3. Jn 12.31 and 16.11.
4. Jn 12.31.
5. Lk 4.7.
6. Dt 6.13 and Lk 4.8.
7. Cf. Rom 6.12.

HOMILY 31

Luke 4.9–12

On the Savior's third temptation.

EARCH THE SCRIPTURES,[1] and even on points that are thought to be simple you will find no small mysteries. We can search the beginning of the Gospel reading that we heard today and let what was hidden come forth into open view. The passage says that the devil "led" Jesus "into Jerusalem."[2] This is unbelievable—that the devil should lead the Son of God and he should follow. Obviously, he followed like an athlete who freely sets out for a competition. He was not afraid of his competitor, nor did he dread the deceits of his extremely cunning enemy. He was basically saying, "Lead on where you will. Test me as it pleases you. I give myself willingly to be tried. I endure what you bring against me. I offer myself for any of your temptations. You will find that I am stronger in every way."

2. "So the devil led him into Jerusalem, placed him upon the parapet of the temple, and said to him, 'If you are the Son of God, cast yourself down from here.'"[3] He led him onto the roof, to the highest point of the temple, and urged him to throw himself headlong from there. The devil proposed this dishonestly and, under the pretext of having Christ display his glory, strove for a different end. So the Savior stated, "Scripture says, 'You shall not tempt the Lord your God.'"[4] Consider, too, how the devil tempts. He does not dare to tempt with any means other than the Divine Books. He takes his text from the Psalms

1. Cf. Jn 7.52.
2. Lk 4.9.
3. Lk 4.9.
4. Lk 4.12.

and says, "If you are the Son of God, cast yourself down. For Scripture says, 'He gave his angels a command concerning you, that they should raise you up in their hands, lest perhaps you strike your foot against a stone.'"[5] How can you, o devil, know that these words have been written? Have you read the prophets, or do you know the divine utterances? Even though you remain silent, I shall answer for you. You read, not to become better through reading the holy books, but to use the simple, literal sense for killing those who are the friends of the letter.[6] You know that, if you wish to speak to him from other books,[7] you will not deceive him, nor will your assertions have any authority.

3. Marcion reads the Scriptures as the devil does. So do Basilides and Valentinus. Along with the devil they say to the Savior, "Scripture says, 'He gave his angels a command concerning you, that they should raise you up in their hands, lest perhaps you strike your foot against a stone.'"[8] Whenever you hear quotations from the Scriptures, be careful of trusting the speaker immediately. Consider the person: what sort of a life he leads, what sort of opinions he holds, what sort of intention he has. Otherwise, he might pretend that he is holy and not be holy, and, infected with the poisons of heresy, he might be a wolf concealed in a sheep's skin. The devil might even be in him, citing the Scriptures. When an opportune moment arises, the devil cites the Scriptures. For the benefit of those who hear him, Paul does the opposite. He quotes passages not only from the Scriptures, but even from secular books. He says, "Cretans are always liars, evil beasts, lazy bellies."[9] And again from another author, "For, we are also his offspring."[10] And once more, from a comic playwright, "Evil conversations corrupt good

5. Lk 4.9–11, citing Ps 91.11–12.

6. The devil encourages strictly literal interpretation, to corrupt the simple.

7. Origen here means secular books, as his argument will make clear.

8. Lk 4.9–11.

9. Ti 1.12, quoting Epimenides (a philosopher of the sixth century B.C.), *On Oracles.* With this and the next two phrases, Origen identifies the three quotations from pagan authors found in the New Testament.

10. Acts 17.28, quoting Aratus (an epic poet of the fourth and third centuries B.C.), *Phaenomena* 5.

morals."[11] But, even if the devil speaks from the Scriptures, he could not deceive me by this action, nor, if Paul takes an illustration from Gentile literature, will he turn me against his eloquence. For, Paul takes words even from what is foreign to us to sanctify them.

4. Therefore, let us see what the devil says to the Lord from the Scriptures: "Scripture says, 'He gave his angels a command concerning you, that they should raise you up in their hands, lest perhaps you strike your foot against a stone.'"[12] See how crafty he is, even in the texts he quotes. For, he wishes to diminish the Savior's glory, as if the Savior needed the help of angels. It is as if he would strike his foot unless he were supported by their hands. The devil takes his verse from Scripture and applies it to Christ.[13] Yet it is written not of Christ, but about the saints in general. Freely and in total confidence I contradict the devil. This passage cannot be applied to the person of Christ, for Christ does not need the help of angels. He is greater than the angels and obtained a better name than they by inheritance. For, God never said to any of the angels, "You are my Son; today I have begotten you."[14] He has spoken to none of them as to a son. "He makes his angels spirits, and his servants a burning fire."[15] But to his own Son he speaks properly, and says countless things about him in the prophets.

5. As I say, the Son of God does not need the help of angels. No, devil; learn, rather, that, unless Jesus helps the angels, they strike their feet. We have just heard a passage about the angels, "That we shall judge the angels."[16] If any of the angels is seen to stumble, he stumbles because he did not reach out his hand to Jesus. If Jesus had taken his hand, he would not have stumbled. For, when someone trusts in his own strength and does not call upon the help of Jesus, he stumbles and falls. And

11. 1 Cor 15.33, quoting Menander (a writer of comedies of the fourth and third centuries B.C.), *Thais.*

12. Lk 4.9–11.

13. Cf. Jerome, *Commentary on Matthew* 1, on Mt 4.6.

14. Ps 2.7, quoted in Lk 3.22; cf. Heb 1.5–7.

15. Ps 104.4, quoted in Heb 1.7.

16. 1 Cor 6.3. A passage from 1 Corinthians had been read in the same service; cf. *Hom.* 12.2.

you, o devil, fell "like lightning from heaven,"[17] because you were unwilling to believe in Jesus Christ, the Son of God. But, to understand why your interpretation is wrong, listen. What follows concerns the saints. God frees "from ruin and the mid-day devil"[18] not Jesus Christ but the saints. Read the ninetieth psalm,[19] which begins, "He who dwells in the help of the Most High will remain in the protection of the God of heaven"[20] and you will find that this fits the just man more than the Son of God. "A thousand will fall at your side, and ten thousand at your right hand, but he will not come near to you. But you will see with your eyes, and you will behold the retribution of sinners,"[21] and the rest; you should interpret these words as applying to the person of the just man.

6. Likewise, the devil adduces texts from Scripture so perversely as to assert that passages applying to the just should be applied to the Savior.[22] Meanwhile, he remains silent about and passes over verses that have been written against him. For, when he quoted, "He has given his angels a command concerning you, that they should raise you up in their hands, lest perhaps you strike your foot against a stone," he was silent about what follows: "You will walk on the asp and the basilisk, and you will tread the lion and the dragon underfoot."[23] Why do you keep silence about these words, o devil, unless you are the basilisk and the petty ruler of all serpents?[24] Your poisons are more harmful than those of other snakes, for, as soon as you see someone, you kill him.[25] You also know that another opposing power[26] exists that is allied with you. It is called the "asp," and is subjected to the just man. For this reason you keep silent about all these matters.

17. Lk 10.18.
18. Ps 91.6.
19. In the numbering of the LXX; in the Hebrew numbering, Ps 91.
20. Ps 91.1.
21. Ps 91.7–8.
22. Cf. Jerome, *Commentary on Matthew* 1, on Mt 4.6.
23. Ps 91.13.
24. Origen puns: βασιλίσκος in Greek means "serpent," and is also the diminutive form of βασιλεύς, "king."
25. Basilisks, according to legend, killed their victims merely by looking at them.
26. On the "opposing power," cf. *Hom.* 6.5 and the note there.

7. You are the "dragon" and you are the "lion" of which Scripture says, "You will walk on the asp and the basilisk, and you will tread the lion and the dragon underfoot."[27] Go ahead and keep silent. We, however, read the Scriptures more correctly. We know we have the power to tread you underfoot; we know that this word has been given to us. For, I say, it was given not only in the Old Testament, as this psalm states, but also in the New Testament. For, the Savior says, "Behold, I give you power to tread upon serpents and scorpions and every power of the enemy, and nothing will harm you."[28] Encouraged by this power, we should take up these great weapons and accomplish everything. Through our lives we should tread the lion and the dragon underfoot. And, to know how a lion is tread underfoot and a dragon crushed, read the letter of Paul in which he says that the sinner treads the Son of God underfoot.[29] So, just as the sinner treads the Son of God underfoot, so, in the opposite way, the just man "treads the lion and the dragon underfoot,"[30] and he treads on "every power of the enemy"[31] in the name of Jesus Christ, to whom is glory and power for ages of ages. Amen.

27. Ps 91.13.
28. Lk 10.19.
29. Cf. Heb 10.29.
30. Ps 91.13.
31. Lk 10.19.

HOMILY 32

Luke 4.14–20

On the passage from, "Jesus returned in the power of the Spirit," up to the point where it says, "And the eyes of all in the synagogue were fixed on him."

IRST OF ALL, "Jesus, full of the Holy Spirit, returned from the Jordan and was led by the Spirit into the desert for forty days."[1] When he was being tempted by the devil, since he was still to struggle against him, the word "spirit" is put down twice without any qualification. But, when he has fought and overcome the three temptations that Scripture mentions, then see what is written of the Spirit, emphatically and carefully. The passage says, "Jesus returned in the power of the Spirit." "Power" has been added, because he had trodden down the dragon and conquered the tempter in hand-to-hand combat. So "Jesus returned in the power of the Spirit to the land of Galilee, and reports about him went out to the whole surrounding region. And he was teaching in their synagogues, and was glorified by all."[2]

2. When you read, "He was teaching in their synagogues and was glorified by all," beware of thinking that only they are blessed, and of believing that you have been deprived of his teaching. If the Scriptures are true, then the Lord speaks not only there, in the congregations of the Jews, but today too, in this congregation. And Jesus teaches not only in this congregation, but in other gatherings, and in the whole world. He seeks instruments through whom he can teach. Pray that he will find me, too, well tempered and fit for singing! At the time when

1. Lk 4.1–2.
2. Lk 4.14–15.

mortal men need prophecy, Almighty God seeks prophets, and finds them—for example Isaiah, Jeremiah, Ezekiel, and Daniel. So Jesus seeks instruments through which he can teach his word or instruct the people in the synagogues and be glorified by all. Jesus is "glorified by all" more now than at that time when he was known in only one province.

3. Thereupon, "he came to Nazareth, when he had been reared, and, according to custom, he entered the synagogue on the Sabbath day, and stood up to read. And the book of the prophet Isaiah was given to him. And he opened the scroll and found the place where it is written, 'The Spirit of the Lord is upon me. For this reason he anointed me.' "[3] It was no accident that he opens the scroll and finds the chapter of the reading that prophesies about him. This too was an act of God's providence. For Scripture says, "A sparrow does not fall into a net without the Father's willing it,"[4] and, "The hairs of the head" of the apostles "have all been counted."[5] So perhaps this too should be thought to have happened not by accident or by chance, but by the providence and disposition of God. Precisely the book of Isaiah was found, and the reading was no other but this one, which spoke about the mystery of Christ: "The Spirit of the Lord is upon me; for this reason he anointed me." For it is Christ who says these words.

4. So we should consider what those things are that he spoke through the prophet and later proclaims about himself in a synagogue. He says, "He sent me to preach the Gospel to the poor."[6] The "poor" stand for the Gentiles, for they are indeed poor. They possess nothing at all: neither God, nor the law, nor the prophets, nor justice and the rest of the virtues. For what reason did God send him to preach to the poor? "To preach release to captives."[7] We were the captives. For many years Satan had bound us and held us captive, and subject to himself. Jesus has come "to proclaim release to captives, and

3. Lk 4.16–18.
4. Mt 10.29; Lk 12.6; cf. *Commentary on John* 20.36.333.
5. Lk 12.6–7.
6. Lk 4.18.
7. Lk 4.18.

sight to the blind."[8] By his word and the proclamation of his teaching the blind see. Therefore, his "proclamation" should be understood ἀπὸ κοινοῦ[9] not only of the "captives" but also of the "blind."

5. "To send broken men forth into freedom. . . ."[10] What being was so broken and crushed as man, whom Jesus healed and sent away? "To preach an acceptable year to the Lord. . . ."[11] Following the simple sense of the text, some say that the Savior preached the Gospel in Judea for only one year,[12] and that this is what the passage "to preach an acceptable year of the Lord and a day of retribution" means. But perhaps the divine word has concealed some mystery in the preaching of a year of the Lord. For, other days are to come, not days like those we now see in the world; there will be other months, and a different order of Kalends.[13] Just as those will be different, so too will there be a year pleasing to the Lord. But all of this has been proclaimed so that we may come to "the acceptable year of the Lord," when we see after blindness, when we are free from our chains, and when we have been healed of our wounds.

6. But, when Jesus had read this passage, he rolled up "the scroll, gave it to the servant, and sat down. And the eyes of all in the synagogue were fixed on him."[14] Now too, if you want it, your eyes can be fixed on the Savior in this synagogue, here in this assembly. For, when you direct the principal power of seeing in your heart to wisdom and truth, and to contemplating

8. Lk 4.18.

9. Jerome keeps the Greek expression, which is the name of a figure of speech. It means "from the common attribution"; that is, the modifier of one word of a pair is intended to modify the other also. Thus, as Origen interprets the passage, Jesus' proclamation is addressed both to captives and to the blind: that is, he proclaims both release and sight. Jerome liked the Greek expression. Pierre Courcelle, *Late Latin Writers and Their Greek Sources*, trans. Harry E. Wedeck (Cambridge: Harvard University Press, 1969), p. 51, lists the places where Jerome retains this Greek technical literary term and others like it. Cf. *Frag.* 209.

10. Lk 4.18.

11. Lk 4.19.

12. A Gnostic interpretation of Lk 4.19, which Irenaeus had already refuted; cf. *Against the Heresies* 2.22.1.

13. The Kalends were the first day of each month in the Roman calendar. Origen does not explain here what this future calendar is.

14. Lk 4.20.

God's Only-Begotten, your eyes gaze on Jesus. Blessed is that congregation of which Scripture testifies that "the eyes of all were fixed on him"! How much would I wish that this assembly gave such testimony. I wish that the eyes of all (of catechumens and faithful, of women, men, and children)—not the eyes of the body, but the eyes of the soul—would gaze upon Jesus. For, when you look to him, your faces will be shining from the light of his gaze. You will be able to say, "The light of your face, o Lord, has made its mark upon us."[15] To him is glory and power for ages of ages. Amen.

15. Ps 4.6–7.

HOMILY 33

Luke 4.23–27

On the passage from, "Doubtless you will quote me this saying," and so on, up to the point where it says, "But none of them was cleansed except Naaman the Syrian."

NSOFAR AS LUKE'S narrative is concerned, Jesus has not yet stayed in Capernaum. Nor is he said to have performed any sign in that place, because he had not been there. Before he comes to Capernaum, it is recorded that he was in his native territory, that is, in Nazareth. He says to his fellow-citizens, "Doubtless you will quote me this saying: 'Physician, cure yourself. Do here, too, in your native territory, whatever we heard was done in Capernaum.'"[1] For this reason, I think that some mystery is hidden in this passage before us. Capernaum, a type of the Gentiles, takes precedence over Nazareth, a type of the Jews. Jesus knew that he had no honor in his own native territory—neither he, nor the prophets, nor the apostles. So he was unwilling to preach there. Instead, he preached among the Gentiles, so that the people of his native territory would not say to him, "Doubtless you will quote me this saying: 'Physician, cure yourself.'"

2. There will be a time when the people of the Jews will say, "'Whatever we have heard was done in Capernaum'"—that is, signs and wonders among the Gentiles—"'do among us, too, in your native territory.'[2] What you have shown to the whole world, show to us as well. Preach your word to the people of Israel, so that at least 'when the full number of the Gentiles has entered in, then all of Israel will be saved.'"[3] For this reason, it

1. Lk 4.23.
2. Lk 4.23.
3. Rom 11.25–26.

seems to me that the Savior answered the Nazarenes' question logically and correctly: "No prophet is accepted in his native country."[4] And I think this word he speaks is truer according to the mystery than according to the letter.

3. It is true that Jeremiah was not accepted in Anathoth, his native land; nor was Isaiah, whatever his native land was, nor the rest of the prophets. But it seems to me that the passage should be understood this way: we say that the native land of all the prophets was the people of the circumcision. This people received neither the prophets nor their prophecies. But, then, the Gentiles, who had been far from the prophets and had no knowledge of them, received the prophecy of Jesus Christ. So, "no prophet is accepted in his native country," that is, among the people of the Jews. We were foreign to the covenant and alien to the promises. But we received the prophets with all our hearts. We "have Moses and the prophets,"[5] who preached about Christ much more than they do. Since they did not receive Jesus, they did not receive those men, either, who proclaimed him.

4. This is why he adds something else to what he said. After, "No prophet is accepted in his native country," he adds, "For, in truth I say to you, that in the days of Elijah there were many widows in Israel, when the heavens were closed for three years and six months."[6] What he is saying is this. Elijah was a prophet, and he was among the people of the Jews. But, when he was about to do something miraculous, although there were many widows in Israel, he left them and went "to a widow in Sarepta of Sidonia"[7]—that is, to a little Gentile woman. Elijah was revealing the form of a future reality. "It was not hunger for bread or thirst for water, but hunger for hearing the word of God"[8] that occupied the people of Israel. Elijah comes to a widow, about whom a prophet says, "The sons of the deserted woman are more numerous than those of her who has a husband."[9] When he comes, he multiplies her bread and her foodstuffs.

4. Lk 4.24.
5. Lk 16.29.
6. Lk 4.25.
7. Lk 4.26; cf. 1 Kgs 17.9.
8. Am 8.11.
9. Is 54.1.

You were a widow in Sarepta of Sidonia. The "Canaanite woman comes"[10] from that territory and wants her daughter to be cured. Because of her faith she deserved to receive what she was asking for. "So there were many widows in the people of Israel, but Elijah was sent to none of them, but to a widowed woman in Sarepta."[11]

5. He also says something else which pertains to the same meaning: "There were many lepers in Israel in the days of Elijah the prophet, and not one of them was made clean, but only Naaman the Syrian."[12] He too was not from Israel. Consider that right up to the present day there are many lepers in "Israel according to the flesh."[13] Realize, in contrast, that men covered with the filth of leprosy are cleansed in the mystery of Baptism by the spiritual Elijah, our Lord and Savior. To you he says, "Get up and go into the Jordan and wash, and your flesh will be restored to you."[14] Naaman got up and went. When he washed, he fulfilled the mystery of baptism, "and his flesh became like the flesh of a child."[15] Which child? The one that is born "in the washing of rebirth"[16] in Christ Jesus, to whom is glory and power for ages of ages. Amen.

10. Mt 15.22.
11. Lk 4.26.
12. Lk 4.27.
13. 1 Cor 10.18.
14. 2 Kgs 5.10.
15. 2 Kgs 5.14.
16. Ti 3.5.

HOMILY 34

Luke 10.25–37

On the passage from, "Master, what shall I do to possess eternal life?" up to the point where it says, "Go and do likewise."

HILE IN THE LAW there are many precepts, in the Gospel the Savior laid down only two. By a kind of short cut, they lead those who obey them to eternal life. In this regard, the teacher of the Law had questioned Jesus and said, "Master, what shall I do to possess eternal life?"[1] This passage, from the Gospel According to Luke, was read to you today. Jesus responded to this as follows: "What is written in the Law? How do you read it?" [The teacher replied,] "You shall love the Lord your God with your whole heart and with your whole soul and with all your strength and with your whole mind; and your neighbor as yourself."[2] Then Jesus said, "You have answered well. Do this, and you shall live."[3] Without any doubt it is eternal life about which the teacher of the Law had questioned Jesus, and with which the Savior's words dealt. At the same time, a precept in the Law clearly teaches us to love God. In Deuteronomy the Law says, "Israel, the Lord your God is one God," and, "You shall love the Lord your God with your whole mind,"[4] and so forth, and "your neighbor as yourself."[5] The Savior bore witness about these commands and said, "On these two commandments depend the whole Law and the prophets."[6]

2. But the teacher of the Law "wanted to justify himself" and show that no one was a neighbor to him. He said, "Who is my

1. Lk 10.25.
2. Lk 10.27.
3. Lk 10.28.
4. Dt 6.4–5.
5. Lv 19.18.
6. Mt 22.40.

neighbor?" The Lord adduced a parable, which begins, "A certain man was going down from Jerusalem into Jericho," and so on.[7] And he teaches that the man going down was the neighbor of no one except of him who willed to keep the commandments and prepare himself to be a neighbor to every one who needs help. For, this is what is found after the parable, at its end: "Which of these three does it seem to you is the neighbor of the man who fell among robbers?" Neither the priest nor the Levite was his neighbor, but—as the teacher of the Law himself answered—"he who showed pity" was his neighbor. Hence, the Savior says, "Go and do likewise."[8]

3. One of the elders[9] wanted to interpret the parable as follows. The man who was going down is Adam. Jerusalem is paradise, and Jericho is the world. The robbers are hostile powers. The priest is the Law, the Levite is the prophets, and the Samaritan is Christ. The wounds are disobedience, the beast is the Lord's body, the *pandochium* (that is, the stable),[10] which accepts all who wish to enter,[11] is the Church. And further, the two *denarii* mean the Father and the Son. The manager of the stable is the head of the Church, to whom its care has been entrusted. And the fact that the Samaritan promises he will return represents the Savior's second coming.

4. All of this has been said reasonably and beautifully. But we should not think that it applies to every man. For, not every man "goes down from Jerusalem into Jericho," nor do all dwell in this present world for that reason, even if he who "was sent on account of the lost sheep of the house of Israel"[12] went down. Hence, the man who "went down from Jerusalem into Jericho" "fell among robbers" because he himself wished to go down. But the robbers are none other than they of whom the Savior says, "All who came before me were thieves and robbers."[13] But still, he does not fall among thieves, but among robbers, who

7. Lk 10.30.
8. Lk 10.36–37.
9. Cf. *Commentary on Matthew* 16.9.
10. Jerome keeps the Greek word, which means "inn," and glosses it as "stable."
11. This is the sense of the Greek word πανδοχεῖον, which is compounded from the words for "all" and "receiving."
12. Mt 15.24.
13. Jn 10.8.

are far worse than thieves. He fell among them when he was going down from Jerusalem. "They robbed him and inflicted blows on him."[14] What are the blows? What are the wounds that have wounded a man? They are vices and sins.

5. Then the robbers, who had stripped and wounded him, do not help the naked man, but they strike him again with blows and leave him. Hence, Scripture says, "They robbed him and inflicted wounds on him; and they went away and left him"—not dead, but "half-dead."[15] But it happened that first a priest, and then a Levite, were going down on the same road. Perhaps they had done some good to other men, but not to this man, who had gone down "from Jerusalem to Jericho." For, the priest saw him—I think this means the Law. And the Levite saw him—that is, in my view, the prophetic word. When they had seen him, they passed by and left him. Providence was saving the half-dead man for him who was stronger than the Law and the prophets, namely for the Samaritan. The name means "guardian."[16] He is the one who "neither grows drowsy nor sleeps as he guards Israel."[17] On account of the half-dead man, this Samaritan set out not "from Jerusalem into Jericho," like the priest and the Levite who went down. Or, if he did go down, he went down to rescue and care for the dying man. The Jews had said to him, "You are a Samaritan and you have a demon."[18] Though he denied having a demon, he was unwilling to deny that he was a Samaritan, for he knew that he was a guardian.

6. So, when he had come to the half-dead man and seen him rolling about in his own blood, he had pity on him. He drew near to him, in order to become his neighbor. "He bound his wounds, poured in oil mixed with wine,"[19] and did not say what the prophet records: "There is no poultice to put on, neither oil nor bandages."[20] The Samaritan is that man whose care and help all who are badly off need. The man who was going down from Jerusalem and fell among thieves, who was wounded and

14. Lk 10.30.
15. Lk 10.30.
16. Origen gives the same explanation in *Commentary on John* 20.35.320.
17. Ps 121.4.
18. Jn 8.48.
19. Lk 10.34.
20. Is 1.6.

left by them half-alive, needed the help of this Samaritan most of all. You should know that, according to God's providence, this Samaritan was going down to care for the man who had fallen among thieves. You learn that clearly from the fact that he had bandages, oil, and wine with him. I do not think that the Samaritan carried these things with him only on behalf of that one, half-dead man, but also on behalf of others who, for various reasons, had been wounded and needed bandages, oil, and wine.

7. He had oil. Scripture says of it, "to gladden one's face with oil"[21]—without doubt, it means the face of him who was healed. He cleans the wounds with oil, to reduce the swelling of the wounds, but also with wine, adding in something that stings. And the man who had been wounded "he placed on his own beast," that is, on his own body, since he deigned to assume a man.[22] This Samaritan "bears our sins"[23] and grieves for us. He carries the half-dead man, and brings him to the *pandochium*—that is, the Church, which accepts everyone[24] and denies its help to no one. Jesus calls everyone to the Church when he says, "Come to me, all you who labor and are burdened, and I shall refresh you."[25]

8. After he has brought him in, he does not depart immediately. He remains for a day at the inn with the half-dead man. He cares for his wounds not only during the day, but also at night. He devotes all his attention and activity to him. And, when he wants to set out in the morning, "he takes two *denarii*" from his tested silver, from his tested money, and pays the inn-keeper. Without a doubt the inn-keeper was the angel of the Church, whom the Samaritan bade to care for the man diligently and bring him back to health. For a short time he himself cared for the man. "Two *denarii*" appear to me to be knowledge of the Father and the Son, and understanding of how the Father is in the Son and the Son is in the Father. An angel is given this knowledge as if it were a payment. He is to care diligently

21. Ps 104.15.

22. *Hominem assumere*; see *Hom.* 29.5.

23. Mt 8.17.

24. See note 11 above.

25. Mt 11.28.

for the man entrusted to him. The promise is made to him that whatever of his own money he spends on healing the half-dead man will be repaid directly to him.

9. The Samaritan, "who took pity on the man who had fallen among thieves," is truly a "guardian,"[26] and a closer neighbor than the Law and the prophets. He showed that he was the man's neighbor more by deed than by word. According to the passage that says, "Be imitators of me, as I too am of Christ,"[27] it is possible for us to imitate Christ and to pity those who "have fallen among thieves." We can go to them, bind their wounds, pour in oil and wine, put them on our own beasts, and bear their burdens. The Son of God encourages us to do things like this. He is speaking not so much to the teacher of the Law as to us and to all men when he says, "Go and do likewise."[28] If we do, we shall obtain eternal life in Christ Jesus, to whom is glory and power for ages of ages. Amen.

26. Cf. note 16 above.
27. 1 Cor 4.16.
28. Lk 10.37.

HOMILY 35

Luke 12.57–59

On the passage from, "When you go with your adversary," up to the point where it says, "And you will repay the last farthing."

UNLESS WE WERE by nature suited to judge what is just, the Savior would never have said, "But why do you not judge for yourselves what is just?"[1] We should not digress too long on the examination of this sentence, since much more difficult verses follow in this chapter. Let it suffice to have said this much about it. We should rather spread out the sails of our souls to God and pray for the coming of his Word.[2] Then God's Word could interpret the parable in Scripture which reads, "When you go on your way to a ruler with your adversary, make an effort to be freed from him, lest perhaps he should hand you over to the judge, and the judge hand you over to the debt collector, and you be sent to prison. Amen, I say to you, you will not get out of there until you pay back the last farthing."[3] I see four persons mentioned here: the adversary, the ruler, the judge, and the debt collector. The evangelist Matthew seems to have said something similar when he wrote, "Be gracious to your adversary while you are on your way with him."[4] Hence, I ask whether this passage has the same sense as Luke's or whether there is merely some similarity. In Matthew's version, one person is omitted and another is changed.

2. The "ruler" is omitted. For the "debt collector," Matthew has "servant." Both Matthew and Luke include the "adversary"

1. Lk 12.57.

2. Origen also asks for prayers to understand the Scripture elsewhere, for example in *Homilies on Ezekiel* 4.3 and 11.2.

3. Lk 12.58–59.

4. Mt 5.25–26.

and the "judge." Therefore, we go with our adversary to a ruler. While we are still on the way, we should work courageously to be freed from him. From whom? The word is ambiguous, and could refer either to the ruler or to the adversary. "Lest perhaps he"—either the adversary or the ruler—"should hand you over to the judge, and the judge hand you over to the debt collector," and "you will not get out of there until you pay back the last farthing." Matthew says for this "until you pay back the last penny."[5] Each of them kept the word "last." But they seem to diverge, insofar as Matthew says "penny" whereas Luke wrote "farthing."

3. I have to touch on some more hidden matters,[6] that we might understand that the adversary is of one sort, while the three other persons—that is, the ruler, the judge, and the debt collector—are of another sort. We read that the angel of justice and the angel of iniquity argued about Abraham's salvation and his loss, as each of the camps wished to claim him for itself. The condition is, of course, that someone should be willing to accept a writing of this kind.[7] But, if it displeases anyone, he should go to the book entitled *The Shepherd.* There he will find that two angels are present to every man: a wicked angel, who exhorts him to wrongdoing; and a good angel, who urges him to do everything good.[8] Elsewhere, too, it is recorded that two angels attend a man, for good and for evil. The Savior, too, mentions the good angels when he says, "Their angels always see the face of my Father, who is in heaven."[9] You should also ask whether the angels of those who are little children in the Church "always see the Father's face," while others' angels do not have the liberty to behold the Father's face. For, we cannot

5. Mt 5.26.

6. On the Gnostic interpretation of Lk 12.58–59, see Irenaeus, *Against the Heresies* 1.25.4.

7. See J. T. Milik, "4 Q Visions de ʿAmram et une citation d'Origène," *Revue Biblique* 79(1972) 77–97, who studied an apocryphal writing from Qumran on Amram, the father of Moses and Aaron. Milik believes that the text was translated into Greek and read by Origen, who alludes to it here. Hence "Abraham" is an incorrect reading for "Amram."

8. Cf. *Hom.* 12.4–6 and Hermas, *Shepherd* 36.2–10.

9. Mt 18.10.

hope that everyone's angel always sees "the face of the Father, who is in heaven." If I am in the Church, no matter how very little I am, my angel enjoys the liberty and the trust always to see "the face of the Father, who is in heaven."[10]

4. But, if I am an outsider, and not a member of that Church "that has neither spot nor wrinkle, nor anything of that sort,"[11] and the facts prove that I am not a member of such a congregation, then my angel does not enjoy the trust of beholding "the face of the Father, who is in heaven." For this reason the angels care for good people. They know that, if they guide us well and lead us to salvation, they too will enjoy the trust of seeing the Father's face. If salvation is secured for men by their care and diligence, they always behold the Father's face. So too, if someone perishes through their negligence, they realize that the matter is a danger to them. A good bishop, the best steward of a church, knows that, if the sheep of the flock entrusted to him are kept guarded, it is because of his meritorious service and virtue. Realize that the same is true of the angels. If someone who was entrusted to an angel sins, the angel is disgraced. And the opposite is also true. If someone entrusted to an angel, even the least person in the Church, makes progress, it redounds to the angel's glory. For, they will see "the face of the Father, who is in heaven," not sometimes, but "always." Other angels never see it. For, according to the merit of those whose angels they are, the angels will contemplate the face of God either always or never, little or much. God has clear and certain knowledge of this matter. So does someone found to be instructed by Christ, rare as that is.

5. So we should first see who the adversary is with whom we are making the journey. The adversary is always with us. How unhappy and wretched we are! As often as we sin, our adversary rejoices. He knows that he has an opportunity to rejoice and to boast before the ruler of this age, who sent him. The adversary of—for example—this or that person subjects him to the ruler of this age through such, and so many, sins, through this

10. Cf. *Homilies on Numbers* 20.3.
11. Eph 5.27.

or that offense. But sometimes it happens that someone has prepared himself with God's armor and covered himself completely with it. The adversary tries to inflict a wound, but he does not have the ability to strike. The adversary always accompanies us, and never deserts us. He seeks the chance to lay a trap, to see if he can somehow cause our downfall and put an evil thought into the ruling part of our minds.

6. "When you go to the ruler. . . ."[12] Who is this ruler? "When the Most High divided the nations, when he distributed the sons of Adam, he fixed the boundaries of the nations according to the number of the angels of God. And his people Jacob became the Lord's portion, Israel the cord of his inheritance."[13] Therefore, the earth was divided up among rulers—that is, angels—from the beginning. Daniel attests more clearly that those whom Moses calls "angels" are "rulers" when he writes, "the ruler of the kingdom of the Persians," and, "the ruler of the kingdom of the Greeks," and, "Michael, you ruler."[14] Thus, there are rulers of the nations.[15] And each of us has an adversary close by him. The adversary's task is to lead us to the ruler and say, "O ruler"—for example, ruler of the kingdom of the Persians—"this is the one who was under you. I have preserved him for you, just as he was. None of the rest of the rulers was able to bring him under himself—not even the one who boasted that he came for that purpose,[16] to take the men from all the lands of the Persians and the Greeks and all the other nations and make them subjects of God's inheritance."

7. Christ our Lord conquers all the rulers. He crosses their borders and brings captive peoples over to himself for salvation. You, too, belonged to the party of some ruler. Christ came, snatched you from the perverse power, and offered you to God the Father. Hence, our adversary walks along, leading us to his ruler. I believe that every word of the Scriptures has its meaning. So I do not think it is pointless that, in Greek, the word

12. Lk 12.58.

13. Dt 32.8–9.

14. Dn 10.20–21.

15. Cf. *Homilies on Numbers* 11.4; and *Hom.* 12.3, where the rulers are good angels.

16. That is, Christ.

"judge" is written with the definite article.[17] The article signifies singularity. But "ruler" is written simply, without the article.[18] The passage says, "when you go with your adversary." The word "your" is significant. For, all are not the adversaries of all, but specific people have specific adversaries. They follow them everywhere and are their companions. "When you go with your adversary to a ruler. . . ." Luke did not add the article to "ruler," so that it would not seem to indicate a specific ruler. He wrote it without an article, to point out one from among many. The Greeks understand this better.

8. Each individual does not have his own ruler. If someone is an Egyptian, he is under the ruler of Egypt. A Syrian is under the ruler of the Syrians. Each one is under the ruler of his nation. It should suffice that I have gone this far; I do not need to pass from this point to another, longer one, and mention all the rest of the nations too. Scripture says, "See Israel according to the flesh."[19] For a prudent man, to have begun is to have spoken.[20] Even to begin the explanation of such a matter before the people might be foolhardy. Scripture says, "When you are on the way to a ruler with your adversary—who wants to draw you away from another ruler and lead to his ruler—make an effort to be freed from [the adversary]."[21] You must strive with all your effort to be freed while you are still on the way, before you get to the ruler. Do it before the ruler hands you over to the judge, once the adversary has prepared you for this; later, you will try in vain.

9. So, "make an effort to be freed" from your adversary and from the ruler to whom your adversary brings you. "Make an effort" to possess wisdom, justice, courage, and temperance,[22] and then the saying will be fulfilled, "Behold the man, and his works before his face."[23] Unless you make an effort, you will be

17. Lk 12.58. Jerome expands what Origen wrote to make it clear to his Latin readers. The article indicates, to Origen, that the judge is Christ.

18. Lk 12.58.

19. 1 Cor 10.18.

20. *Prudenti coepisse dixisse est.* Jerome uses a Latin aphorism.

21. Lk 12.58.

22. The four cardinal virtues, with "wisdom" substituted for "prudence"; see *Hom.* 8.4.

23. Cf. Is 62.11 (Hebrew and LXX); Origen's text represents neither exactly.

unable to annul your adversary's compact. His "friendship is enmity against God."[24] "When you go on the way to the ruler with your adversary, make an effort." Some mystery or some secret lies hidden in the phrase, "on the way, make an effort." The Savior says, "I am the Way, and the Truth, and the Life."[25] If you make an effort to be freed from your enemy, then you are on the way. And, when you stand on him who says, "I am the Way," it is not enough simply to stand. Rather, "make an effort to be freed" from your adversary. For, unless you make an effort to be freed from your adversary, listen to what will follow for you. The adversary "brings you to the judge";[26] or rather, when the ruler receives you from the adversary, he takes—actually, "drags"—you to the judge. What a fine word, "drags." It shows that they are in a sense dragged reluctantly and unwillingly, and forced to be condemned. For, what murderer goes to the judge at a rapid pace? Who hastens to go joyfully to his condemnation, and is not dragged unwillingly and with resistance? For, he knows that he is going to hear a sentence of death.

10. "Lest perhaps he should drag you before the judge."[27] Who do you think that judge is? I do not know any other judge besides our Lord Jesus Christ. Of him the Scripture says elsewhere, "He will put the sheep on the right, but the goats on the left."[28] And again, "Whoever confesses me before men, him shall I also confess before my Father who is in heaven. But, whoever denies me before men, him shall I deny before my Father who is in heaven."[29] ". . . lest perhaps he should drag you to the judge, and the judge hand you over to the debt collector."[30] Each one of us incurs a penalty for each single sin, and the size of the penalty is reckoned according to the quality and nature of the offense.[31] I ought to adduce some testimony from the Scriptures about the penalty, and about monetary fines.

24. Jas 4.4.
25. Jn 14.6.
26. Lk 12.58.
27. Lk 12.58.
28. Mt 25.33.
29. Mt 10.32–33.
30. Lk 12.58.
31. Cf. *Homilies on Numbers* 8.1. Here and elsewhere, Origen collects and compares debts mentioned in Mt and Lk. Cf. *Hom.* 35.13–15 and *Frag.* 228.

One man incurs a debt of five hundred *denarii*, and owes that much. Another is obliged to pay fifty *denarii*.[32] The creditor cancels these debts for both debtors. Another one, as the Scripture says, "is brought forward, who owed ten thousand *talents*."[33] He is obliged to pay ten thousand *talents*. Why should I have to search out more examples?

11. Each one receives a sentence with a different fine, according to the quality and quantity of his sin. If your sin is small, a fine of a farthing is inflicted on you, as Luke writes, or a penny, as Matthew has it.[34] But you must pay even this debt, because it makes you a debtor. For, "you will not get out of prison unless you have repaid even the smallest debts." Whoever is faithful receives no penalty, however, but is enriched daily. "For, the whole world of riches is his; but the unfaithful man does not have even an *obol*."[35] One is sentenced to pay a *denarius*, another a *mina*, another a *talent*. There is one who investigates this transaction. He knows the measure of every sin and says, "This offense entails a fine of one *talent*; that sin merits a penalty of this or that sort." Scripture says, "But, when he began to draw up an account, ..."[36] An account is to be drawn up for each of us. There is no other time to give an account except the time of judgment. Then, what has been entrusted to us, and what gains and losses we have made, will be clearly known. We shall know which one of us received a *mina*, or one *talent*, or two, or five.[37] Why is it necessary to go over more examples? It is enough to have said this, in general. We are going to have to give an account and, if we are found to be debtors, we shall be dragged to the judge, and the judge will hand us over to the debt collector.

12. Each of us has his own debt collector. But the whole multitude is handed over to many debt collectors, as is written in Isaiah: "My people, your debt collectors despoil you, and those who are powerful are your masters."[38] The debt collectors

32. See Lk 7.41–42.
33. Mt 18.24.
34. See above, *Hom.* 35.2.
35. Prv 17.6(LXX).
36. Mt 18.24.
37. Cf. Mt 25.14–30 and Lk 19.11–27. A *mina* [μνᾶ in Greek] was both a unit of weight, equivalent to about one pound, and a unit of currency, one-sixtieth of a *talent*. Cf. *Hom.* 39.7; *Frags.* 200, 227, 228, and 231.
38. Is 3.12(LXX).

are our masters, if we owe something. But, if we enjoy trust and say with an untroubled countenance, "I have kept the precept that commands, 'Return to all what you owe: tribute to those to whom tribute is due, reverence to whom reverence is due, taxes to whom taxes are due, honor to whom honor is due.'"[39] If I render all things due to everyone, then I shall come to the debt collector and answer with an untroubled heart, "I owe you nothing."

13. The debt collector comes to claim his due. I resist him. I know that, if I owe nothing, he has no power over me. But, if I am a debtor, the debt collector will send me to prison, following the order we have spoken of. For, the adversary brings me to the ruler, and the ruler to the judge; the judge will hand me over to the debt collector, and the debt collector will put me in prison. What law governs that prison? I shall not come out of it, nor will the debt collector allow me to go out, unless I have paid every debt. The debt collector does not have the power to cancel even a penny of the debt, or the smallest portion of it, for me. There is only one who can cancel a debt when the debtors are unable to pay their debts. Scripture says, "One man came to him who owed five hundred *denarii*, and another who owed fifty. Since they did not have the money to pay him, he forgave both of them."[40] He who forgave was the Lord. But he who collects debts is not the Lord, but one whom the Lord assigns to collect debts.

14. You were not worthy to have a debt of five hundred *denarii*, or fifty, canceled. Nor did you deserve to hear, "Your offenses are forgiven you."[41] You will be sent to prison, and there you will have payment exacted by labor and work, or by punishments and torture; and you will not get out, unless you have paid the penny and the "last farthing," which in Greek means "meager."[42] Our sins are either heavy—for Scripture says, "This people's heart is grown heavy"[43]—or, in comparison with greater sins, they are meager and fine. Therefore, first of

39. Rom 13.7.
40. Lk 7.41–42.
41. Lk 7.48.
42. Jerome glosses the Greek word.
43. Is 6.10.

all, he is blessed who does not sin, and, secondly, he who, by comparison, has only a meager sin.

15. And even among meager and fine sins there is a difference. For, unless there were something else between a light sin and a fine sin, Scripture would never have said, "You will not come out from there unless you pay the last penny."[44] By the "last farthing" Scripture may mean a sum of money; a farthing is a small sum, a *denarius*, or a *drachma*, or an *obol*, or a *stater*.[45] You might owe a great sum, like the man who, Scripture says, owed ten thousand *talents*. I cannot clearly state how long a time we are shut up in the prison, until we pay the debt. For, if he who owes a little debt does not come out until he pays the last penny, then surely for him who owed such a great debt infinite ages will be counted off for paying what he owes. For this reason, "we should make an effort to be freed from our adversary"[46] while we are on the way. Then we can be joined to the Lord Jesus, to whom is glory and power for ages of ages. Amen.

44. Mt 5.26.

45. The *denarius* was a Roman silver coin, the *drachma* a Greek silver coin (6,000 of which made a *talent*), the *obol* another Greek coin (one-sixth of a *drachma*), and the *stater* a small silver coin of the Jews, worth four *drachmas*.

46. Lk 12.58.

HOMILY 36

Luke 17.20–21, 33

On the passage from, "Whoever wishes to save his life will lose it," up to the point where it says, "The Kingdom of God is within you."

ESUS SAYS, "Whoever seeks to save his life will lose it. And, whoever loses it will save it."[1] The martyrs seek "to save their souls."[2] They lose their lives to save their souls. But those who wish to save their souls without losing their lives lose "both their bodies and their souls in Gehenna."[3] Hence, Jesus says, "Do not fear those who can kill the body, but fear rather him who can destroy soul and body in Gehenna."[4] We can say something on this topic, according to the ability of our intelligence. "But the animal man does not receive things that are spiritual,"[5] and hence cannot be saved. "The animal body is sown; the spiritual body rises."[6] Moreover, "one who clings to the Lord" is made "one spirit."[7] Hence, if "one who is joined to the Lord"[8] when he was animal, is turned thereby into a spiritual being and "is one spirit,"[9] we too should lose our lives, to adhere to the Lord and be transformed into one spirit.

2. But the Pharisees also asked the Savior about the Kingdom of God, "when it would come."[10] He answered, "The Kingdom of God does not come through watching. And they do not say, 'See, here!' or 'See, there!' For the Kingdom of God is within you."[11] The Savior does not say to everyone, "The Kingdom of

1. Lk 17.33.
2. The meaning of the word Origen uses shifts between "soul" in the philosophical sense (i.e., as distinct from "body") and "life," a more Biblical sense.
3. Mt 10.28.
4. Mt 10.28.
5. 1 Cor 2.14.
6. 1 Cor 15.44.
7. 1 Cor 6.17.
8. 1 Cor 6.17.
9. 1 Cor 6.17.
10. Lk 17.20.
11. Lk 17.20–21.

God is within you." For, in sinners, the kingdom of sin exists. Without any ambiguity, either the Kingdom of God reigns in our hearts, or the kingdom of sin. For this reason, we should attentively ponder what we do and speak and think. Then we shall see whether the Kingdom of God or the kingdom of sin reigns in us. The Apostle knew that this difference existed. He warns some people and says, "Let sin not reign in your mortal bodies."[12]

3. If any of us longs for the Kingdom of God, God reigns over him. If anyone is tortured by the passion of avarice, avarice reigns over him. One who is just has justice as his ruler. One who is carried along by desire for empty glory has the fickle breeze of popularity reigning over him. Grief, fear, passion, and desire[13] each reign over him, as he is in the grips of different agitations of the mind. Knowing those things, and knowing how many sorts of kingdoms there are, let us rise up[14] and pray to God that he might take from us the kingdom of the enemy. May we be able to live under the reign of Almighty God—that is, under the reign of wisdom, peace, justice, and truth.[15] All of these are comprehended in the Only-Begotten Son of God, to whom is glory and power for ages of ages. Amen.

12. Rom 6.12.

13. Plato's four affections.

14. Cf. *Homs.* 12.6 and 39.7.

15. See *Hom.* 8.3. These are four titles (ἐπίνοιαι) of Christ.

HOMILY 37

Luke 19.29–40

On the passage where the foal of an ass is untied by the disciples.

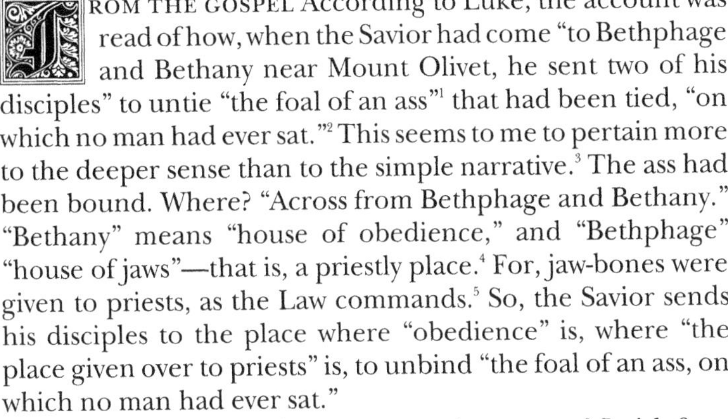

ROM THE GOSPEL According to Luke, the account was read of how, when the Savior had come "to Bethphage and Bethany near Mount Olivet, he sent two of his disciples" to untie "the foal of an ass"[1] that had been tied, "on which no man had ever sat."[2] This seems to me to pertain more to the deeper sense than to the simple narrative.[3] The ass had been bound. Where? "Across from Bethphage and Bethany." "Bethany" means "house of obedience," and "Bethphage" "house of jaws"—that is, a priestly place.[4] For, jaw-bones were given to priests, as the Law commands.[5] So, the Savior sends his disciples to the place where "obedience" is, where "the place given over to priests" is, to unbind "the foal of an ass, on which no man had ever sat."

2. But, who else besides a man can sit on an ass? I wish for a moment to give an example, so that what I am going to say can be understood.[6] It is written in Isaiah, "A vision of four-footed beasts in tribulation and straits," and the rest, up to the point where it says, "The wealth of asps will not profit them."[7] Each one of us should consider what a great wealth of asps he has

1. Cf. *Commentary on John* 10.127. 2. Lk 19.29–30.
3. Cf. *Commentary on Matthew* 16.17.
4. Origen also explains the etymology of "Bethany" in *Commentary on Matthew* 16.17; *Frag.* 406 on Matthew (GCS Origenes 12.171); *Commentary on John* 6.40.206; and *Frag.* 80 on John (GCS Origenes 4.547). He explains the etymology of "Bethphage" also in *Commentary on Matthew* 16.17 and *Commentary on John* 10.190.
5. Dt 18.3.
6. On the meaning of the ass, cf. *Commentary on John* 10.185–196.
7. Is 30.6(LXX).

previously carried, what great riches of beasts,[8] and how a rational man has never sat on our ass[9]—not the word of Moses, nor of Isaiah, nor of Jeremiah, nor of all the rest of the prophets. Then he will see that the Word of God, and Reason, have sat upon us, when the Lord Jesus came and commanded his disciples to go and untie "the colt of an ass," which had previously been bound, so that it could walk free. Thus, the "colt of an ass" is untied and led to Jesus. When he sent his disciples to untie it he said, "If anyone asks you why you are untying the foal, say to him, 'Because the Lord has need of it.'"[10]

3. Many people were lords of this colt before the Savior needed it. But, after he began to be its Lord, the many ceased to be its lords, for "no one can serve God and mammon."[11] When we serve wickedness, we are subjected to many passions and vices. Hence, the colt is untied, "because the Lord has need of it."[12] Even now the Lord "has need of" the colt. You are the colt of the ass. Why does the Son of God "have need of" you? What does he seek from you? He needs your salvation. He wants you to be untied from the bonds of sin.

4. Then the disciples lay "their garments upon the ass"[13] and have the Savior sit down. They take the Word of God and put it on the souls of the hearers. They take off their garments and "spread them out on the road."[14] The garments of the apostles are upon us; their good works are our adornment. The apostles want us to tread upon their garments. And, indeed, when the ass imitates the disciples' teaching and their life, it is untied by the disciples, bears Jesus, and treads on the apostles' garments. Who of us is so blessed that Jesus sits on him? As long as he was on the mountain,[15] he dwelt only with the apostles. But, when he begins to descend, a crowd of people runs to meet him. If he had not come to the descent, the crowd could not have run to meet him. He descended, and sat upon the colt of an ass, and the whole people praised God in a harmonious voice.

8. Cf. *Hom.* 8.3.
9. That is, the body; cf. *Hom.* 34.7.
10. Lk 19.31.
11. Mt 6.24.
12. Lk 19.31.
13. Lk 19.35.
14. Lk 19.36.
15. The Mount of Olives, but also the Mount of the Transfiguration.

5. The Pharisees saw this and said to the Lord, "Reprove them."[16] He said to them, "If they are silent, the stones will cry out."[17] When we speak, the stones are silent. When we are silent, the stones cry out.[18] "For, the Lord can raise up from these stones sons for Abraham."[19] When shall we be silent? When "the charity of many grows cold,"[20] and when the prophecy that the Savior uttered is fulfilled, "Do you think that, when the Son of Man comes, he will find faith upon the earth?"[21] We invoke the Lord's mercy, lest we should be silent and the stones cry out. We should speak out and praise God, in Father, Son, and Holy Spirit, to whom is glory and power for ages of ages. Amen.

16. Lk 19.39.
17. Lk 19.40.
18. That is, the Gentiles; cf. *Hom.* 22.9.
19. Lk 3.8.
20. Mt 24.12.
21. Lk 18.8.

HOMILY 38

Luke 19.41–45

On the passage from, "But when he approached, he saw the city and wept over it," up to the point where it says, "He expelled all who were selling doves."

HEN OUR LORD and Savior approached Jerusalem, he saw the city, wept, and said, "If only you had known on that day what meant peace for you! But now it is hidden from your eyes. The days will come upon you when your enemies will surround you with earthworks."[1] These are mysteries that are spoken. If God reveals their significance, we hope we can open to you what is hidden. We must first contemplate his weeping. By his example, Jesus confirms all the beatitudes that he speaks in the Gospel. By his own witness, he confirms what he teaches. "Blessed are the meek,"[2] he says. He says something similar to this of himself: "Learn from me, for I am meek."[3] "Blessed are the peacemakers."[4] And what other man brought as much peace as my Lord Jesus, who "is our peace," who "dissolves enmity," and "destroys it in his own flesh"?[5] "Blessed are they who suffer persecution on account of justice."[6]

2. No one suffered such persecution on account of justice as the Lord Jesus did, who was crucified for our sins. Thus, the Lord exhibited all the beatitudes in himself. For the sake of this likeness, he himself wept, because of what he had said: "Blessed are those who weep,"[7] to lay the foundations for this beatitude, too. He wept for Jerusalem "and said, 'If only you

1. Lk 19.41–43.
2. Mt 5.5.
3. Mt 11.29.
4. Mt 5.9.
5. Eph 2.14–15.
6. Mt 5.10.
7. Mt 5.4.

had known on that day what meant peace for you! But now it is hidden from your eyes,'" and the rest, up to the point where he says, "Because you did not know the time of your visitation."[8]

3. One of the hearers might say, "What you are saying is obvious, and indeed has been accomplished in Jerusalem. For, the Roman army surrounded it, destroyed it, and exterminated the people.[9] And a time will come when a stone will not be left upon a stone in this city." Now I do not deny that Jerusalem itself was destroyed on account of the crimes of its inhabitants. But I ask whether perhaps that weeping pertains also to this Jerusalem of ours. For, we are the Jerusalem that is wept over,[10] since we ourselves have a deeper insight. If, after the mysteries of the truth, after the preaching of the Gospel, after the teaching of the Church, and after the vision of the mysteries of God, one of us sins, Jesus will bewail him and lament over him. For, he does not lament over a Gentile, but over him who was a citizen of Jerusalem and ceased to be so.

4. But he bewails this Jerusalem of ours, because after her sins "enemies have surrounded" her—namely, contrary powers,[11] evil spirits. And they throw up earthworks around her perimeter, and besiege her, "and do not leave a stone upon a stone." This is particularly true if someone is conquered after years of chastity and, enticed by the pleasures of the flesh, loses the will to persevere in purity. If you have fornicated, "they will not leave a stone upon a stone in you." For, in another place Scripture says, "I shall not remember his earlier acts of justice. I shall judge him in his sin, in which he was apprehended."[12] So this Jerusalem is the city that Jesus wept over.

5. Thereafter, the Scripture says, "He went into the temple," and after he entered it, "he cast out those who were selling doves."[13] He did not cast out the buyers.[14] A buyer owns what

8. Lk 19.44.

9. In A.D. 70, under the Roman general Titus.

10. Origen identifies Jerusalem with the Christian soul. Cf. *Commentary on John* 10.174.

11. Cf. *Hom.* 30.3.

12. Ez 18.24.

13. Lk 19.45.

14. Cf. *Commentary on Matthew* 16.22; *Commentary on John* 10.168.

he has bought. Jesus casts out of his Father's temple those who sell what they had, and thus discard it, like that prodigal son who received his inheritance from his father and lost it all by drinking too much.[15] So, if anyone sells, he is cast out, especially if he sells doves. Why did the Scripture mention no other birds except doves? This animal is simple and comely. I fear that a vice of this sort could also be found in us. For, if I display before the common crowd what the Holy Spirit has revealed and entrusted to me, I sell it for a price and do not teach without payment, what else am I doing except selling doves, that is, the Holy Spirit? When I sell the Spirit, I am cast out of God's temple.

6. Hence, we should ask God that all of us might buy rather than sell. For, if we have not sold, we shall know and understand our salvation. Otherwise, enemies will surround our city. Once a hostile army surrounds us, we shall not merit the Lord's tears. So we should rise at daybreak and pray to God that we might be able to eat at least the crumbs that fall from his table.[16] The Scriptures express astonishment that the Queen of Sheba came "from the end of the earth to hear Solomon's wisdom."[17] When she saw his dinner, his furnishings, and the attendants in his palace, she was astounded, and wholly in a state of wonder. If we do not embrace the great riches of our Lord, the great furnishings of his Word, and the wealth of his teachings; if we do not eat the "bread of life";[18] if we are not fed with the flesh of Jesus, and do not drink his blood; if we disdain the banquet of our Savior, we should realize that God has both "kindness and severity."[19] Of these, we should pray more for his kindness upon us, in Christ Jesus our Lord, to whom is glory and power for ages of ages. Amen.

15. Lk 15.12–13.
16. Cf. Mt 15.27.
17. Lk 11.31. See 1 Kgs 10.4–5.
18. Jn 6.35.
19. Rom 11.22.

HOMILY 39

Luke 20.21–40

Concerning the question of the Sadducees, which they proposed to the Lord, about the woman who had seven husbands; and once again about the denarius *that the Savior ordered shown to him.*

HERE IS A SECT of the Jews called the Sadducees. They deny "the resurrection of the dead"[1] and think that the soul dies with the body, so that after death there is no longer any consciousness. These Sadducees put a question to the Lord. They made up a story of a woman with seven husbands. After the first husband died, she married the second to raise up the seed of the first. When he died she also married the third, and again the fourth, and in this fashion reached the seventh. Hence, they ask which of the seven brothers will claim her as his wife "in the resurrection of the dead." The Sadducees proposed this problem as an attack on the Savior's words, at a time when they saw him teaching the disciples about the resurrection.

2. The Savior answered them and said, "You are wrong. You know neither the Scriptures nor the Power of God. For, in the resurrection of the dead they shall neither marry nor be given in marriage, but will be like angels in heaven."[2] Those who will be like angels will thus be angels. We should also learn that angels do not contract marriage. Here, where there is death, both marriage and children are necessary. But, where there is immortality, there is need neither of wedlock nor of offspring. I shall pose for myself a question that is very troublesome and not easily solved. I shall pose it from the point of view of those

1. Lk 20.27 and 35.
2. Mt 22.29–30.

people who are zealous in studying the Scriptures and "meditate on the Law of the Lord day and night."[3] Where, they say, is it written in Scripture that "they shall neither marry nor be given in marriage"? I have gone over both the Old and the New Testaments in my memory and my mind. I have never recalled the phrase mentioned. If I have perhaps erred, one who knows more should teach me. I shall eagerly learn what I am ignorant of. But, as far as I can see, no such phrase will be found, either in the Old Testament or in the New.

3. The Sadducees' whole error arose from their reading the prophetic books, which they did not understand.[4] Among them is this passage in Isaiah: "My chosen ones will not have children who are cursed."[5] And in Deuteronomy, among the blessings, "Blessed are the sons of your womb."[6] And they think that these prophecies are going to be fulfilled "in the resurrection," since they do not understand that it is spiritual blessings that have been prophesied. For, Paul, "the vessel of election,"[7] interpreted all of these blessings, which have been placed in the Law, spiritually. He knew that they are not carnal, and says to the Ephesians, "Blessed be God, the Father of our Lord Jesus Christ, who blessed us with every spiritual blessing."[8] Therefore, all of these blessings will exist spiritually, when we rise from the dead and gain eternal happiness. They also find something similar in the Psalms, and fall into the same error. The Scripture says, "Your wife is like a fruitful vine on the walls of your house. Your sons are like shoots of olive trees around your table," up to the point where it says, "may the Lord bless you from Zion, and may you see what is good for Jerusalem."[9] So, when Jerusalem has been rebuilt and restored to its ancient state, the holy man is going to see the good things that the Scriptures mention.

4. Those who understand "Jerusalem" spiritually and know that Scripture says of her, "She is heavenly, she is above, she is our mother,"[10] they will see the good things of that city. We

3. Ps 1.2.
4. For a similar argument, cf. *Against Celsus* 1.49.
5. Is 65.23.
6. Dt 7.13.
7. Acts 9.15.
8. Eph 1.3.
9. Ps 128.3–5.
10. Gal 4.26.

have often spoken of them. And they will see what we have just quoted from the psalm: "Your wife is like a fruitful vine on the walls of your house. Your sons are like shoots of olive trees around your table."[11] The Sadducees understand all of this corporeally. They were that party of the Jews to whom the Savior says, "You know neither the Scriptures nor the Power of God."[12] That much, briefly, on the question that the Sadducees put to the Lord. And further, the passage about the image of Caesar has been read. So, we should also touch upon this passage. Some people think that the Savior spoke on a single level when he said, "Give to Caesar what belongs to Caesar"[13]—that is, "pay the tax that you owe." Who among us disagrees about paying taxes to Caesar? So the passage has a mystical and secret meaning.

5. There are two images in man.[14] One he received from God when he was made, in the beginning, as Scripture says in the book of Genesis, "according to the image and likeness of God."[15] The other image is earthly.[16] Man received this second image later. He was expelled from Paradise on account of disobedience and sin, after the "prince of this world"[17] had tempted him with his enticements. For, just as the coin, or *denarius*, has an image of the emperor of this world, so he who does the works of "the ruler of the darkness"[18] bears the image of him whose works he does. Jesus commanded that that image should be handed over and cast away from our face. He wills us to take on that image according to which we were made from the beginning, according to God's likeness. And thus it happens that we give "to Caesar what belongs to Caesar, and to God what is God's."[19] Jesus said, "Show me a coin."[20] For "coin," Matthew wrote "*denarius*."[21] When Jesus had taken it, he said,

11. Ps 128.3–5.
12. Mt 22.29. The "Power of God" is Christ.
13. Lk 20.25.
14. Cf. *Commentary on the Canticle*, Prologue 2.4–5.
15. Gn 1.27.
16. 1 Cor 15.49.
17. Jn 12.31.
18. Eph 6.12.
19. Lk 20.25.
20. Lk 20.24.
21. Mt 22.19. Origen errs. Matthew has, "Show me the coin"; Mark and Luke have, "Show me a *denarius*."

"Whose inscription does it have?" They answered and said, "Caesar's." And he said to them in turn, "Give to Caesar what is Caesar's, and to God what is God's."

6. Paul also uttered this conclusion and said, "As we bear the image of the earthly man, we should also bear the image of the heavenly man."[22] When Christ says, "Give to Caesar what is Caesar's," he means this: "Put off the person of the earthly man, cast off the earthly image, so that you can put on yourselves the person of the heavenly man and give 'to God what is God's.'" God seeks us. What does he seek? Read Moses: "And now what does the Lord your God seek from you?"[23] and the rest that follows. So, God seeks from us and entreats us, not because he needs something that we have to give him, but, after we have given it to him, he will credit that very thing to us, for our salvation. To make it clearer, I shall recall the parable of the *minas*.[24] A man received one *mina*, earned ten, and brought them to the Lord, who had entrusted the one *mina* to him. He received in addition another *mina* that he had not had before.

7. For, the Lord orders the *mina* of the man who had not increased what he had received to be taken away and given to him who has the other *minas*. He says, "Take the *mina* and give it to him who had ten *minas*."[25] And, in this way, God will restore to us the very things we have given to him, along with what we had not had before.[26] God asks and demands from us, both so that he might have an occasion for giving and so that he himself might return what he had demanded. For, by his graciousness the *mina* is doubled, and more than he hoped for is given to anyone who is worthy. Hence, let us rise up[27] and pray to God to be worthy of offering him gifts that he can restore to us, and in place of earthly things bestow heavenly things on us, in Christ Jesus, to whom is glory and power for ages of ages. Amen.[28]

22. 1 Cor 15.49.

23. Dt 10.12.

24. Lk 19.12–27. Cf. *Hom.* 35.11 and the note there, as well as *Frags.* 227, 228, and 231.

25. Lk 19.24.

26. Cf. *Commentary on Matthew, series* 69.

27. Cf. *Homs.* 12.6 and 36.3.

28. The manuscripts end with this note: "End of the thirty-nine homilies of Adamantius Origen on the Gospel of Luke, translated by the blessed presbyter Jerome from Greek into Latin."

FRAGMENTS ON *LUKE*

FRAGMENTS ON LUKE

95. Luke 4.5

This is what we can understand about the Lord's temptation: when he learned the Evil One's intention, he went into the desert and was willingly hungry.[1] The Evil One thought that, if Christ were hungry, he could deceive him with food, as he had deceived Adam. And, again in accord with the Evil One's intention, Christ went up to the pinnacle of the temple. The Evil One said, "If I could also bring him up to the mountain, I would show him 'all the kingdoms of the earth.'"[2] It follows that Christ went up willingly. Thus too, long ago, God beheld the Evil One thinking this: "If it were possible for a snake to speak, I would approach the first couple through a snake to deceive them." God agreed to this, and allowed his own creature to speak. So too, in the case of Job, God agreed to the destruction of a great deal of property, since the Evil One thought this: "If my plan were agreed to, I would prove that Job's virtue is false, for he only appears to be virtuous because of his wealth." For, the dialogue in that passage has great power because of its clarity; Scripture expresses its intent by the way it arranges the discourse.

96. Luke 4.3–4

Mark and Luke say that Jesus "was tempted for forty days."[3] It is clear that during those days the devil first tempted him

1. Origen is concerned with free choice and with exploiting all its possibilities, even to the point of defending the devil's freedom and God's allowing him to use that freedom.

2. Lk 4.5.

3. Mk 1.13 and Lk 4.2.

from a distance[4]—to sleep, acedia,[5] cowardice, and other such sins. Then, since he knew that Christ was hungry, the devil came closer to him and attacked him openly. Notice what he does. He had heard, both from John and from the voice that came from above, that "this man is a son of God."[6] He did not know that "the Son of God" had become man, for the ineffable Incarnation was concealed from him. So, he assumed that Christ was a man who was pleasing to God because of his virtues.[7] He was also jealous of him because of this honor, just as he had been jealous of the old Adam; he was eager to cast this man down, just as he had cast Adam down. So he comes near and introduces the first temptation, that of gluttony, through which he had also captured the first Adam. And, since there was no food anywhere, because the whole region was a desert, he knew that bread would satisfy Christ's hunger. He himself does not produce bread, because Christ was not going to take it from the enemy. But he commands him to make bread from the stones that he points to. And—behold his wiles and his great wickedness—he tried to keep Christ from knowing his plot. He did not simply say, "Turn the stones into loaves of bread," but he prefixed it with, "If you are a son of God."[8] He did this to show that he wanted this act done to prove that Christ is a son of God. For, he was thinking that Christ would be provoked by his words and offended by the suggestion that he was not a "son of God." He thought that Christ would not recognize the deception and, as a man who has power from God, turn the stones into bread. And then, when he saw the bread, he would yield to his stomach, since he was very hungry.

4. Origen wants to distinguish the forty days during which Jesus fasted and was tempted (Lk 4.2) from the three specific temptations that Luke narrates (Lk 4.3–12). So, he first has the devil at a distance, and then nearer to Jesus.

5. "Acedia," which means "discouragement," "restlessness," "ennui," and the like, is often mentioned by monastic authors as a vice, particularly of monks. It figures in the catalogues of the seven deadly sins in antiquity and the Middle Ages.

6. Cf. Jn 1.34, which has "the Son of God," with the definite article. Here Origen quotes the words without the article, but in the phrase that follows includes it, to distinguish "a son of God" from "the Son of God."

7. Origen makes the devil an Adoptionist.

8. Lk 4.3.

But the devil did not escape the notice "of him who lays hold of the wise in their villainy."[9] Christ answered him and said, "It is written, 'Man shall not live by bread alone,'"[10] and the rest, because he knew the devil's villainy. He did not perform the sign that the devil sought, because his signs were worked to help those who beheld them; but the devil would not have profited from the sign. For, even later, when the devil saw everything that Christ did, he was not converted. Christ defends himself against the devil's secret purpose and answers him from Scripture, with the Book of Deuteronomy. He speaks thus: "Why do you bid me to make bread from stones? Only on account of the hunger that oppresses me, so that I might be entrapped by visible things. 'But man shall not live by bread alone.' There will be another sort of food, for 'every word that comes from God's mouth'[11] to the hungry man sustains his life as food does and suffices for him." Thus did he patiently repel the deceit of gluttony.

97. Luke 4.5

(a) The evangelist says that the devil "showed him all the kingdoms of the world in a moment of time";[12] he means that "he described the world in words." In a certain way, he displayed it in Christ's mind, as he thought. He who made all things is ignorant of nothing.

(b) For, if this is not so, how was he able to bring the places at the edges of the world to one place, to be seen corporeally?

98. Luke 4.5–6

Perhaps he mentioned the kingdom of the Persians or the Indians, and in that way showed him the glory of the whole world and all the kingdoms. But "he showed him the kingdoms of the world,"[13] and how he was strong enough to rule

9. 1 Cor 3.19.
10. Lk 4.4.
11. Mt 4.4.
12. Lk 4.5.
13. Lk 4.5.

them. The devil goaded him on, as a mere man,[14] since he wished to prevail over him, just as over the rest of men.

99. Luke 4.10

But I think that the fact that Jesus needs the angels of God to take him up "upon their hands" so that he will not strike "his foot against a stone"[15] concerns the surrender of his glory rather than the affirmation of his divinity.

100. Luke 4.18–19

I. For, he set free those who were captives, and overpowered the rebellious tyrant—that is, Satan. He shined the intelligible, divine, and heavenly light upon those whose hearts had been darkened, as he himself says: "I, the light, have come into the world."[16] He freed from bonds—clearly, from bondage to sin—those whose hearts had been shattered. He manifested the life to come and threatened just judgment. He proclaimed "a year acceptable to the Lord,"[17] in which the announcement of the Savior took place. For, I think that the "acceptable year" means his first coming, and "the day of reward"[18] means the day of judgment. He proclaimed a "year acceptable to the Lord," which the all-wise Paul mentions when he says, "Behold, now is the acceptable time, now is the day of salvation."[19]

II. ". . . and deliverance to captives."[20] What captives does he mean, except those whom the devil had just taken prisoner and put in chains? Christ came and overpowered the impostor and the rebellious tyrant, Satan, and liberated the captives. Luke says that these same people were blind and broken. For, Christ shined the intelligible light upon those whose minds had been darkened. He forgave "the broken ones"[21]—or

14. Origen's term for "mere man," ψιλὸς ἄνθρωπος, was already established in the third century as a designation for a christological heresy, sometimes called "Psilanthropism," that denies Christ's divinity. Again, Origen makes the devil a heretic.

15. Lk 4.11.
16. Jn 12.46.
17. Lk 4.19.
18. Cf. Col 3.24.
19. 2 Cor 6.2.
20. Lk 4.18.
21. Lk 4.18.

rather, he loosed them from the bonds of sin, as he also loosed those broken in heart—that is, crushed by the weight of sin or humbled in spirit. To them he proclaims "a year acceptable to the Lord." What sort of year is it? Either one in which the proclamation of the Savior took place, or one in which the True Lamb was offered for the sins of the world.

101. Luke 4.39

[The Savior stops at the house of Simon and finds his mother-in-law ill with fever.] (a) "And he stood over her and rebuked the fever, and it left her."[22] In Matthew's and Mark's versions, "the fever left her,"[23] and in the whole phrase nothing is ever suggested about a living being that causes the fever.[24]

(b) In the phrase recorded by Luke, "he stood over her and rebuked the fever, and it left her," I wonder whether we are not forced to say that what is rebuked and departs is a living being that yields to the power of him who rebukes it. For, it is not reasonable to say that a lifeless thing, which cannot perceive a rebuke, was rebuked.

(c) It is not surprising that there are some noxious powers in the human body, and we shall not wholly blame the soul of the sufferers as being deluded by them. For, after the devil had had his sport with Job, to his grievous loss, he received the power to test him through his body. Job was free from blame in this matter, for he did battle and nobly endured the suffering. If we are ever tried by corporeal labors, let it only be said, "But do not touch his soul,"[25] as the Lord, too, gives a rebuke and heals those who are ill.

103. Luke 4.40

About sunset, or after the day ended, they brought the sick. Either they were ashamed, or they feared the Pharisees, or they were also engaged in other matters, or perhaps they

22. Lk 4.39.

23. Luke omits "the fever."

24. See the next two paragraphs. Since in Luke Jesus addresses the fever, Origen wonders whether the fever is personal.

25. Jb 1.12.

thought it was impossible to heal on the Sabbath. For, the evangelist indicated that "he was teaching them on the Sabbath."[26] Therefore, their relatives brought the sick at sunset, and "he healed them."[27]

104. Luke 5.1

And he "stood at the Lake of Gennesaret,"[28] or—according to both Matthew and Mark—"he was walking by the Sea of Galilee."[29] The evangelists might seem to make contradictory statements, but the one who works at the Scripture can say what follows about this passage. If God called the bodies of water "seas" at the beginning of creation,[30] and the rivers are also bodies of water,[31] according to this meaning these rivers, too, are "seas." So too, the sweet and drinkable Lake of Gennesaret is now called the Sea of Tiberias in the Gospels,[32] surely because it is itself a body of water. Gennesaret is a place in the middle of Canaan. When the Lord dwelt in the region near the sea, he found the men gathered around Peter and John, and he called them after the catch of fish;[33] previously, they were disciples of John the Baptist.[34]

106. Luke 5.14

Bidding the leper keep his mouth sealed[35] makes it clear that he must condemn himself to silence until he has converted and purified himself. It is not inappropriate to use the passage in regard to those who are guilty, and to teach the elect about divine things.

26. Lk 4.31.
27. Lk 4.40.
28. Lk 5.1.
29. Matthew and Mark both name this body of water the "Sea of Galilee" twice (Mk 1.16 = Mt 4.18 and Mk 7.31 = Mt 15.29). Luke calls it the "Lake of Gennasaret," only here (Lk 5.1). John mentions it once, as the "Sea of Galilee, which is the Sea of Tiberias" (Jn 6.1).
30. Cf. Gn 1.10.
31. Cf. Ez 31.4.
32. Cf. Jn 6.1.
33. Cf. Lk 5.9–10.
34. Cf. Jn 1.35.
35. That is, Jesus tells the leper he has cured not to reveal the cure until he shows himself to the priest.

107. Luke 5.14

If you wish, consider living beings that have reason, at a time when reason is not present to the soul. If this ever happens, the sinner is not blamed, for he is in the condition of someone without reason. But, if reason is present, he is responsible. But, why is his whole body affected? Perhaps it figuratively reveals excitement or melancholy, or the condition of the age of infancy? For, at the time when reason offers no help and consciousness is not present, nothing that is done or said is a sin. Sin is possible only when consciousness is present. The passage should be read in this way. We are pleasing to God in a double fashion. For, if we live for God, let there be nothing dead in us. If we die to sin, let there be none of it living in us.[36] For, since we live in him, let us beg for death to sin; when we die to the world, let us not rush back to the passions. We die to sin when we kill the parts that are earthly. "We have died to sin; how shall we still live to it?"[37] So, defilement exists even if it happens in a small matter and is impure according to the Law, just as wholly dying to sin is clean. Scripture says, "For, a little leaven leavens the whole lump."[38] Some said that the state of death that comes from a disposition to evil, such as from intemperance or injustice, is unclean. But the state of death that sets apart something bodily, which is not brought about by moral evil, is clean—for example, a marriage outside one's tribe, except because of licentiousness; food, except if it is spoiled; work on the Sabbath, except work for profit. According to some again, the Law makes the wholly leprous man clean, showing how God hates what is of a mixed character. The Old Law makes this more manifestly clear in the passage, "You shall not plant a mixed vineyard. Avoid a cloak that is adulterated, made of two sorts of fiber. And you shall not mate your flocks to different sorts of animals."[39] You must always prefer simplicity, which is seen even in the wholly leprous man.

36. Cf. Rom 6.11–12.
37. Rom 6.2.
38. 1 Cor 5.6 and Gal 5.9.
39. Lv 19.19.

108. Luke 5.27

So, the Scripture says, "He went out and saw a tax collector named Levi."[40] This man is Matthew the Evangelist. Mark and Luke conceal his name by using his earlier name,[41] whereas Matthew makes his own name known when he says, "He saw Matthew the tax collector."[42] He says this so that we might wonder at the skill of the God who healed him and might believe in [God] fully.

110. Luke 6.21

Christ announces the laughter that comes from joy and cheerfulness, as Scripture says in the Book of Job: "He will fill the truthful mouth with laughter."[43] Perhaps this is why even one of the patriarchs is called "Laughter"[44]—because the name signifies divine cheerfulness.

111. Luke 6.24

The seed of the rich fell among briars and was choked off.[45] "Those who wish to be rich fall into temptation";[46] they have been told "not to place their hope in uncertain wealth."[47] "Do not be fearful when a man grows rich";[48] "if wealth abounds, do not commit your heart to it";[49] "a good name is preferable to great wealth."[50] The rich man will be punished after his death; and a rich man is told, "You fool, this night will they require your soul of you."[51]

112. Luke 6.43

"The good tree" is the Holy Spirit. The "bad tree" is the devil and his underlings. The man who has the Holy Spirit

40. Lk 5.27.
41. Cf. Mk 2.14.
42. Mt 9.9.
43. Jb 8.21.
44. Isaac; cf. Gn 21.6.
45. Cf. Lk 8.14.
46. 1 Tm 6.9.
47. 1 Tm 6.17.
48. Ps 49.16.
49. Ps 62.10.
50. Prv 22.1.
51. Lk 12.20.

manifests the fruits of the Spirit, which the Apostle enumerates when he says, "The fruit of the Spirit is love, joy, peace, patience, kindness, goodness, faith, gentleness, self-control."[52] The one who has the opposing power[53] brings forth briars and thistles, the passions of dishonor.

113. Luke 7.37

The more perfect soul, which serves the Word of God well, has the freedom[54] to go to the head itself, and "the head of Christ is God."[55] So, the soul pours out its perfume and spreads about a sweet smell to the glory of God; God is glorified by the sweet smell of the life of the just. But the less perfect woman—that is, soul—is at the feet and occupies herself with humbler things. We are near her, for we have not turned from our sins. Where are our tears? Where is our weeping, so that we can approach at least Jesus' feet? We cannot go first to the Head himself. After our sins, it is enough to be able to bring the good odor of repentance, so that we can be the second one, the woman who anoints the feet, but not the head—that is, the woman who touches not what is more perfect and exalted, but the lowest and the least.[56]

114. Luke 8.4

Scripture deliberately says, "When a very large crowd came together. . . ."[57] For, it is not many but few who enter through the narrow path[58] and "who find" the way "that leads to life." Hence, Matthew says that outside the house he taught in parables, but within the house he explained the parables to the disciples.[59]

52. Gal 5.22–23.
53. On the "opposing power," cf. *Hom.* 6.5 and the note there.
54. παρρησία; cf. *Hom.* 27.3.
55. 1 Cor 11.3.
56. Origen often interprets details in the Gospels as indicating stages of progress in the spiritual life. Here, progress is from Jesus' feet to his head; in *Frag.* 124 the demoniac cannot yet sit at Jesus' feet, but can proclaim him to others.
57. Lk 8.4.
58. Cf. Mt 7.13–14.
59. Cf. Mt 13.1 and 36.

120. Luke 8.16

Scripture says this not about a sensible lamp, but about an intelligible one. No one "lights" the lamp and conceals it "with a vessel,"[60] or puts it "under a bed, but upon the lampstand" within himself. The vessels of the house are the powers of the soul. The bed is the body. "Those who go in" are those who hear the teacher. The lampstand is the intellect,[61] since it is the place of reason—or rather, it is the mouth, whenever someone opens it to speak the word of God. For, in both cases those who have approached God will see "the light"—and "light" is knowledge, which illuminates by itself.

121. Luke 8.16

(a) He who wants to apply "the lamp" to the most perfect of Jesus' disciples will put us to shame by the words spoken about John, that "he was the lamp that burns and shines."[62] But, also, "the eye is the lamp of the body";[63] "the eye" refers to each one's mind. The phrase, "let your lamps be burning,"[64] was spoken to all of Jesus' disciples. Accordingly, one should not conceal the burning, intelligible lamp of the soul, but place it on a lampstand. Moses "placed" a type of this lampstand "in the tent of witness."[65]

(b) Let the fellow-slaves be given portions of grain with a bushel by the "faithful and prudent householder."[66] Let "all those in the house"[67]—that is, those in the Church—look upon the brightness of the lamp placed on the lampstand, which draws them into clear knowledge by the Word.

60. Lk 8.16 has "with a vessel or under a bed" (as the RSV translates the passage) and not the more familiar "under a bushel basket," found at Mt 5:15, Mk 4.21, and (in some manuscripts) Lk 11:33. Origen goes on to interpret "vessel" as "spritual capacity."

61. Origen uses τὸ ἡγεμονικόν, which means "the leading part," "the authoritative part of the soul," a term that the Stoic philosophers used for "reason." Cf. *Frag.* 244.

62. Jn 5.35.

63. Cf. Mt 6.22.

64. Lk 12.35.

65. Ex 40.24.

66. Lk 12.42.

67. Mt 5.15.

(c) But they do not place the lamp "under the bed," where someone might lie down to rest, or "beneath" some other "vessel." For, the one who does that has no concern for those who come into the house. The lamp should be put where it benefits them.

(d) Those who attach their minds to the "true light,"[68] and the shining Word, and the rays of wisdom (the mind has the nature that the Creator gave it) need the lamp of wisdom and truth from the Word, the illumination of the true light.

(e) And we should realize that the command, "Let your lamps be burning," is fulfilled by those who, by Providence, have in their souls a clear-sighted mind that participates in him who says, "I have come into the world as a light."[69] For, those who burn the lamp and place it "upon the lampstand," so that it may shine "upon all in the house," will also persuade those in the house who see the lamp's shining to burn brightly in their own lampstands.

122. Luke 8.16

Perhaps the Lord calls himself a "lamp" that gives light to all those in the house—that is, in this world. He was God by nature, and became flesh in the economy,[70] just as in the case of a lamp, light was, in its essence, uncircumscribed in his soul, but, like fire coming through a wick, it was held[71] in by the earthen vessel of his flesh. He names the Holy Church "lampstand." By its proclamation, the Word of God gives light to all who are in this world, and illuminates those in the house with the rays of the truth, filling the minds of all with divine knowledge. He calls the synagogue of the Jews a "bushel" figuratively. He means the somatic worship prescribed by the Law, and the old symbols of the letter of the Law; for the synagogue was wholly unable to discern the light of true knowledge contained in the concepts. [That worship meant that the light of

68. Jn 1.9.
69. Jn 12.46.
70. On "economy," cf. *Hom.* 6.3 and the note there.
71. Reading κρατούμενον.

the true, intelligible knowledge could not be distinguished from the symbols in the letter of the Old Law.] The Word does not will to be held under this bushel, but desires to be placed on the height, and upon the pinnacle of the Church's beauty.

123. Luke 8.16

The devil held all of them[72] captive with the letter of the Law, as under a bushel,[73] and deprived them of the eternal light. Nor did he give spiritual contemplation to those who strove to put aside sense perception as something deceptive. "But places it upon the lampstand." I mean the Church, or rather, rational worship in spirit, so that it may shed light upon all and teach those in the whole world to live and conduct themselves by reason alone. We should not light the divine lamp—that is, the illuminating Word—by contemplation and action, and place it under a bushel, lest we be condemned for circumscribing, by the letter, the uncircumscribable power of wisdom. "But upon the lampstand"—I mean the Holy Church in the height of true contemplation, which casts the light of the divine teachings on everyone. (But something is also said about this in the *Commentary on Matthew,*[74] so it is redundant to speak about it here.)

124. Luke 8.39

Jesus sends the possessed man back "to his house." For, the man did not have enough power to go and sit "clothed at Jesus' feet"[75] and "be with him."[76] Although those from the surrounding region had no place for Jesus' presence, Jesus nonetheless provided for the salvation of those who were able to hear him there. He dismissed the man who voluntarily sat

72. That is, the Jews.
73. See *Frag.* 120 and the note there.
74. This part of the *Commentary on Matthew* is lost.
75. Lk 8.34.
76. Lk 8.38.

at his feet so that the man could teach what "God had done" for him. There might be some hearers and disciples of a man like him. He did not have the capacity for more, but he did preach from the little he was able to receive.

You might also apply the passage to the nature of a man outside Israel, on whose account Jesus sails down to the land of the Gerasenes and for whom he comes upon the earth. Scripture says that the man "did not clothe himself with a cloak."[77] For, he did not put on what would conceal his shame. "And he did not dwell in a house."[78] For he was not, like Jacob, "a simple man, who dwelt in a house."[79] So Jesus "released him, saying, 'Return to your house.'"[80] And "he dwelt in the tombs"[81]—not with the living, but with the dead. Scripture also says, "There was a large herd of swine feeding on the mountainside."[82] Do swine ever feed on a mountainside? So, how was "the herd rushing over the cliff"?[83] Do not the lovers of pleasure, and the friends of the belly and what is under the belly, feed where there are tombs, and near the legion of demons? But Jesus, in his goodness, destroys the life of the swine in water, and keeps the sins of loving pleasure and the body from breathing again with the help of demons. Perhaps such a man becomes temperate; but, if anyone is temperate, he is with Jesus. But the one who just begins to practice temperance is "at his feet."[84]

125. Luke 8.41–44

Such is the narrative[85] of the miracle.[86] Perhaps we should contemplate it more subtly and more closely. Let the simpler and less sophisticated people admire God's great deeds in

77. Lk 8.27.
78. Lk 8.27.
79. Gn 25.27(LXX); the Hebrew has "dwelling in tents."
80. Lk 8.39.
81. Lk 8.27.
82. Lk 8.32.
83. Lk 8.33.
84. Lk 8.35.
85. I.e., *historia,* or the first level of meaning.
86. I.e., the raising of Jairus's daughter and the cure of the woman who had a flow of blood.

themselves. For, those deeds edify, even when they are taken literally. But we are able to pass on to vision, to seeing that "these things happened to them as types, and they were written for our sake."[87] Let us pray to God and ask his Word to come and explain these things: why Jesus went first to the daughter of the synagogue leader and not to the woman with a flow of blood who met him on the road; and why, although he intended to go first to the synagogue leader's daughter, this woman was healed first. For, the Son of God went first to the synagogue leader's daughter—that is, to the synagogue of the Jews—and found her sick and dying, for Israel's transgressions made her die. The woman with the flow of blood, who was along the road, who was filled with uncleanness, whose blood flowed "not in the time of menstruation"[88] but was always flowing, and who was sick with sins of scarlet.[89] She is the Church of the Gentiles. She believes in the Son of God before the other woman. Jesus walks by her, and she follows, wishing to touch even "the hem of his cloak."[90]

Luke added what Matthew did not say: that the synagogue leader's daughter was twelve years old. The woman with the flow of blood had the flow for twelve years.[91] So the woman's flow of blood began when the girl was born. As long as the synagogue lives, the woman is in a state of disobedience. And the time for the death of the girl and for the beginning of the woman's salvation is the same. For, the girl dies when she is twelve, and the woman believes and is healed after twelve years of suffering. "She could not be healed by any"[92] of the physicians. For, many physicians promise to heal the Gentiles. If you see the philosophers proclaiming truth, they are physicians trying to heal. But the woman spent all she had and "could not be healed by any" of the physicians. But, when she touched the hem of Jesus,[93] the only physician of souls and bodies, she was healed immediately through her fiery-hot faith. If we see our faith in Christ Jesus and know how great the Son of God

87. 1 Cor 10.11.
88. Lv 15.25.
89. Cf. Is 1.18.
90. Lk 8.44.
91. Lk 8.43; cf. Mt 9.20.
92. Lk 8.43.
93. Origen omits "cloak" here.

is, and who it is we touch, we shall realize that we have touched only a bit of the hem of his garment. But at the same time the hem heals us and lets us hear from Jesus, "Daughter, your faith has saved you."[94] And, if we have been healed, then the daughter of the synagogue leader will rise up also; for Scripture says, "When the full number of the Gentiles has entered, then will all of Israel be saved."[95]

126. Luke 8.44–45

His disciples touched and grasped him, but the woman with the flow of blood did not touch him, for she did not dare to. Rather, out of reverence, she touched only the hem of his cloak.

127. Luke 8.47

(a) The flow of blood was an affliction. Thus, you will say that other somatic sufferings are also afflictions of God, who afflicts those who are worthy of his training through such sufferings. "He afflicts every son whom he accepts."[96] So he said to the paralytic, when he freed him from the affliction, "See, you have become healthy; sin no longer, lest something worse should happen to you."[97]

(b) Previously, out of reverence, she did not dare to encounter him directly and expect a cure. But, after he had sought her out, she encountered him in a suitable way—reverently, respectfully, and showing the appropriate awe. And she makes the confession of cure openly to all—not to him who knows all things, but to those who do not know—and acknowledges the cure openly. For, Mark says this, too: "She knew by her body that she was healed of the affliction."[98]

(c) And here the Savior also confirmed by his word the cure that the woman had received by touch: "Go in peace, and

94. Lk 8.48.
95. Rom 11.25–26.
96. Prv 3.12.
97. Jn 5.14.
98. Mk 5.29.

know that you are cured of your affliction."[99] And he first cured the soul by faith, and then the body as well.

129. Luke 9.25

There is a sin that is the death of the soul; John calls it "sin unto death."[100] There is also a sin that is a weakness of the soul, and a sin that is a loss of the soul, since the word "to forfeit"[101] is used here. The Apostle also says, "If anyone's work is burned, he will suffer loss."[102]

138. Luke 9.28

"About eight days passed after these words." Matthew says "six,"[103] since he counts neither the day on which the words were spoken nor the day on which Jesus was transfigured, but only the six in between. But Luke includes all the days.

139. Luke 9.28

(a) Let us find out how Luke can say, "After these words there passed about eight days," whereas Mark says "after about six days."[104] As far as the saying, "there passed about eight days," Luke counts the day itself on which the event took place, whereas Mark counts only the days in between. There is no disagreement in what they say.

(b) But I would say, summarizing the argument, that what the Savior proclaimed was not without a plan; he did it not immediately, but after six days.

(c) The six days are a symbol of creation[105]—that is, the Transfiguration comes after this world. For, then Jesus has anyone who is Peter or James or John go up "the high mountain."[106] No one else besides the three goes up to see Jesus,

99. Mk 5.34.
100. 1 Jn 5.16.
101. Or "lose"; Lk 9.25.
102. 1 Cor 3.15.
103. Cf. Mt 17.1.
104. Mk 9.2.
105. Cf. *Homilies on Leviticus* 13.5.
106. Mk 9.2.

who was transfigured, and Moses and Elijah, who were seen in glory.

140. Luke 9.28

The Transfiguration on the mountain manifested to the disciples a token of the Savior's future glory. And he was manifested corporeally, to give their mortal eyes a vision, even if they could not bear the exceeding greatness of his splendor, which was untempered and could not be borne by our eyes. The disciples showed that the glory that befits the divine essence is invisible to, and unapproachable by, any created nature; they were unable to bear even this corporeal vision manifested to them upon the mountain, but fell to the earth. But, when someone goes up with him, and is exalted with him, he sees the Word gloriously transfigured, and sees him as the Word Itself and as the High Priest who both takes counsel with the Father and prays to him.[107] But, since he was not yet bringing his body into unchangeable incorruptibility, he was seen shining with perishable clothing, along with Moses and Elijah. For, when the just arise in glory at Christ's second coming, they will not have garments that the senses perceive,[108] but some gleaming coverings will be put around them. Just as the bodies of these men did not become other at the Transfiguration, so at the resurrection the bodies of the saints will be far more glorious than the ones they had in this life, but will not be different from them.[109] Those with Jesus appeared in glory to the disciples. Moses showed the face of the Law, Elijah the face of the prophets. Jesus himself was Lord of the Law and the prophets. So, whoever understands the spiritual law and

107. Origen succinctly describes Christ's two natures. As the Father's Word, he and the Father are of one mind; the Greek term translated "take counsel" is, literally, "to have word in common." As High Priest, he offers worship to the Father in the name of all creation.

108. Origen might mean clothing, but more probably, "spiritual bodies," as Paul writes in 1 Cor 15.44.

109. Origen affirms the continuity of the resurrection body with the earthly body.

"the wisdom hidden in mystery"[110] in the prophets sees Moses and Elijah in glory.

141. Luke 9.30

And they conversed with each other—that is, they say things that are in mutual agreement. He clearly joins the men of the Old Covenant to the apostles, because at the second coming of Christ all the just will be joined together.

146. Luke 9.31

When Peter heard that Christ was going to suffer and thought he had found the right time to say that he did not want it to happen, he asked the Lord to remain always above, on the mountain, lest the Jews find him when he came down and kill him. He does not know the good things that will come from the Passion and the Resurrection for all men. "As he said this, a cloud overshadowed them."[111] The cloud put an end to their eagerness to seek something beyond their power. Through this event he prefigures the truth that all the saints—both those before the Lord's coming and those after the coming—will be together. The Law and the prophets and the Gospel will set up the same tents—three in number, but looking toward one goal. At the resurrection the saints will be "taken upon the clouds to meet the Lord and to be with him"[112] forever.

148. Luke 9.36

Jesus does not want the evidence of his glory to be spoken of before his glorification, which followed his Passion. Otherwise, his hearers, and especially the crowds who would see the one who had been so glorious crucified, would be injured. The evidence was not concealed grudgingly, but out of con-

110. 1 Cor 2.7.
111. Lk 9.34.
112. 1 Thes 4.17.

cern that it would not be believed. For, Luke says, "And they kept silent and proclaimed to no one in those days anything of what they had seen."[113] When did they "proclaim"? After the Ascension, and after the coming of the Spirit. For, then they were filled with the freedom to speak, and were deemed worthy of the Spirit. They had the voice of the Spirit manifested in signs, and the Spirit served as their advocate. And everything that they said was well received.

151. Luke 9.45

This is what he says: "Even if you do not understand these words in the present time, at the time of salvation, when you are perfectly converted to me and are stripped of the veil that I strip from you in the Passion itself, you will put your ignorance aside and understand them. You will see the symbol of it: the veil of the temple torn asunder."[114] But perhaps, among disciples in general, teachers' words must at first not be understood, and their speech veiled, so that later, after the hearers have applied the words to their ears, the clarity of the words, transported from the ears to the heart, can be manifested. But see how Jesus first spoke in parables, even to the disciples themselves, who listened along with the outsiders. Then, after that, "he explained everything privately"[115] to them. We, too, often, when we carefully study the Scriptures and do not understand them, look up, as it were, with fixed attention as, for a moment, the Word shines "in our hearts to illuminate the knowledge of his glory";[116] and "he" is Christ. The phrase "he will be handed over,"[117] recorded by Matthew and Luke, gives no clear answer to the question, "by whom?" So, as we said, one will say, "by Judas"; another, "by the people." But, since Judas and the people were human beings, let us realize that it is perhaps better for us to follow Paul, who says of the Father that he "did not spare his own Son, but handed him over on

113. Lk 9.36.
114. Cf. Lk 23.45.
115. Mk 4.34.
116. 2 Cor 4.6; cf. 2 Cor 4.4.
117. Mt 17.22 and Lk 9.44.

account of us all,"[118] and thus to say that the words, "to be handed over," need "by God." Proceeding from that point, you will inquire whether the meaning of "to be handed over" is the same when the words are applied to Judas and to God. Anyone who says that they are the same as regards their end will grant this difference: Judas betrayed him for the sake of money and handed him over as an act of treachery, whereas the Father did it out of beneficence. Still, consider how it is said so that they do not understand it. In the case of sense perception, not being perceived often occurs because of a defect on the part of those who perceive. So it is also possible either not to perceive words and speech reasonably or to perceive them wrongly. Since "fear of the Lord is the beginning of perception,"[119] it is not the fear that frightened the disciples, like the trivial fear that came upon them from their ignorance of the word and of the veil that prevents them from learning by asking questions. For, the master guides their lack of understanding and conceals the word from them; the Savior saw from their asking questions that, if he answered when he was questioned, they would be stripped of their ignorance and the veil. At the same time, compare these points: first, that "the disciples asked him privately"[120] about the parables, and did not "fear to ask";[121] but now, "they were afraid to ask him about this saying."[122] Like a householder, he was bringing about both ignorance and revelation in them. He was managing, at the suitable time, the removal of ignorance and of the veil, since he was going "to be given over into the hands of men."[123]

154. Luke 9.58

"But, if you are ready, o man, to be like me, who have nowhere 'to lay [my] head,'[124] you will accept what is uncertain

118. Rom 8.32.

119. Cf. Prv 1.7(LXX). Origen may have rearranged the verse to suit his purpose. The usual form is, "Fear of the Lord is the beginning of wisdom," as in Ps 111.10, Prv 9.10, and Sir 1.14.

120. Mk 9.28.

121. Lk 9.45.

122. Lk 9.45.

123. Lk 9.44.

124. Lk 9.58.

here below in hope of the Kingdom of Heaven, because of my teaching. You will not expect rest here, but rather in the age to come. For, my disciples, who practice justice, 'will suffer tribulation in this world.'"[125] "Evil men and impostors,"[126] who are compared to foxes and birds of the sky in this life, "will go from bad to worse, deceiving and being deceived."[127] The words, "the Son of Man has nowhere to lay his head," correspond particularly well to Paul's expression, "we are homeless";[128] Christ was speaking in him.[129]

155. Luke 9.58.

What he says is this: "If you will not set yourself free from the birds and the beasts—really, from the demons—I cannot dwell in you. And you, if you are that sort of man, cannot take on the apostolic office."

156. Luke 9.59–60.

The passage has a more profound interpretation: when the father had died to the young man, and was dead,[130] then the young man was called by the Savior. I think that, just as the world was crucified to Paul, and he was dead, since the concerns of the world were dead to him[131] (for, he was no longer aiming at them as "things that are seen and are passing"[132]), so the devil has died to every just man, who lived for him when he was a sinner. For, everyone "who commits sin is born of the devil,"[133] and the evil father lives for every sinner who lives for the things of this world. But, to every one to whom the evil one has died, may the Savior say this: "Follow me."[134] And perhaps the need for us to hate our father[135] should be understood

125. Jn 16.33.
126. 2 Tm 3.13.
127. 2 Tm 3.13.
128. 1 Cor 4.11.
129. Cf. 2 Cor 13.3.
130. The next sentences explain this odd usage. Origen is imitating Paul's idiom in Gal 6.14: "But far be it from me to glory except in the cross of our Lord Jesus Christ, by which the world has been crucified to me, and I to the world."
131. Cf. Gal 6.14.
132. 2 Cor 4.18.
133. 1 Jn 3.8.
134. Lk 9.59.
135. Cf. Lk 14.26: "If someone comes to me and does not hate his father. . . ."

mystically in this way, if we are going to become worthy of Jesus. The words, "to bury the dead,"[136] mean, allegorically, only our own dead. For, somehow the dead bury "their own dead" in themselves and become their own graves and monuments. Finally, the one who obeys Jesus leaves the dead man behind and no longer touches him. For, he knows that the one who touches a corpse is defiled.[137]

157. Luke 9.62[138]

Each of us is the plowman of himself. As land, he has his own soul, which he must renew with an intellectual plow. He gathers the hard-working oxen from the pure Scriptures. Then he will renew his soul, which grew old through long idleness during the passing of time and brought forth much evil and fruitless deeds. He cuts them down with the plow of the Word, makes the ground fallow, and from the divine teaching sows the seeds of the Law, the prophets, and the Gospels, and remembers and attends to them. So, the God of the universe says through the prophet Jeremiah, "Plow for yourselves fallow ground, and do not sow among briars."[139] For, it is not enough simply to receive divine seed and to bear fruit without first purifying your souls and casting out every passion, and the cares about life[140] and its pleasures, which are the briars. For, Scripture says, "Turn away from evil and do good."[141]

158. Luke 10.1

But Luke says this about the seventy disciples, whereas Mark says, "He called the Twelve and sent them out two by two, and gave them power over unclean spirits."[142] Serving the Word "two by two" by God's will seems to be an ancient practice,

136. Lk 9.60.
137. Nm 19.16.
138. In this fragment, Origen reproduces part of his own *Homilies on Jeremiah* 5.13.
139. Jer 4.3.
140. Cf. Lk 8.14.
141. Ps 37.27.
142. Mk 6.7.

beginning from Moses and Aaron, when the people "went out of the land of Egypt,"[143] for God led Israel out "in the hand of Moses and Aaron."[144] And "Joshua son of Nun and Caleb son of Jephunneh,"[145] both of them of the same mind, restrained the people when they were provoked by the ten.[146] And Eldad and Medad, being of the same mind, both prophesied in the tent.[147] And later, God sent Paul and Barnabas out to the Gentiles, and such men were a model of those who agree, "two upon the earth."[148] You can add to these examples the verse, "Brother helped by brother is like a fortified city,"[149] and, "Two are good, better than one."[150] Matthew also shows that the apostles were ordered two by two, in his list of them, for he arranges them in pairs.[151]

159. Luke 10.8–9

Just as you heal bodies, so also save souls by teaching. He now calls himself the Kingdom of God, as if he were saying, "King and God." "'It has come near,'"[152] he says, "and will now dwell within you. Make yourselves worthy and be prepared to receive him." I think that the difference between a house and a city[153] has been expressed in the Psalms, where we read, "Unless the Lord builds a house, and unless the Lord guards the city, the guard has kept vigil in vain."[154] He watches over the Gentiles, because what has already been built is called a "house," and what is already worthy of defense and a garrison is called a "city." Thus, he intended the phrase, "they receive you,"[155] to apply to to the better house, which is a city.

143. Nm 33.1.

144. Nm 33.1.

145. Nm 14.6.

146. According to Nm 13, Moses sent twelve men to reconnoiter the land of Canaan. When they returned, ten of the spies discouraged the people, but Caleb "quieted" them (Nm 13.30).

147. Cf. Nm 11.26. Origen errs. Eldad and Medad prophesied in the camp, and not at the tent.

148. Mt 18.19.

149. Pv 18.19.

150. Eccl 4.9.

151. Cf. Mt 10.2–4.

152. Lk 10.9.

153. Lk 10.5–12 speaks first of a household receiving Jesus' disciples, and then of a city that receives them. Origen seeks the meaning of the distinction.

154. Ps 127.1.

155. Lk 10.8.

160. Luke 10.11

He says this, "Say, 'May the dust of your sins justly return to you.'" But the dust had to be taken up by those who could wash it away, so that the hearers would neither have it nor themselves be injured by it.

161. Luke 10.11

(a) Observe that the cities that do not receive the apostles and their sound teaching[156] have broad streets, analogous to the passage, "Wide is the gate and broad the way that leads to destruction, and many are those who pass through it."[157]

(b) One should know that the city that does not receive the apostles is filled with earth that is stirred up and makes the air dusty and stifling. The city that receives them does not have dust as its foundation or, if it has the dust of some sins, it puts off the dust and is cleansed of its sins.

162. Luke 10.21–22

As Word, he wills to reveal rationally, and as Wisdom wisely, and as Justice justly.[158] According to his rank, he knew the proper times for revealing and the bounds of revelation. He reveals when he strips off the veil that lay upon the heart[159] and the "darkness" that was put "to conceal him."[160] For, thus, someone—like Moses—will be able "to enter into the darkness where God was."[161] The heterodox[162] think that they can construct their impious dogma from this starting-point: that the Father of Jesus Christ was unknown to the saints of the Old Covenant. We say to them that the words "to whom the Son wishes to reveal"[163] apply not only to future time, about which the Savior spoke these words to us, but also to past time.

156. Cf. 1 Tm 1.10.

157. Mt 7.13.

158. Titles of the Second Person. For "Word," cf. Jn 1.1; "Wisdom," 1 Cor 1.24; and "Justice," 1 Cor 1.30.

159. Cf. 2 Cor 3.15.

160. 2 Sm 22.12.

161. Ex 20.21.

162. In this case, Marcionites.

163. Lk 10.22.

For, the words, "to reveal," in the aorist tense,[164] apply to anyone in the past. To refute them, we should use the Scripture passage that reads, "Your father Abraham rejoiced to see my day; he saw it and was glad."[165] When they heard these words they said, "You are not yet fifty years old and you have seen Abraham?" The Savior says, "Amen, I say to you, before Abraham was, I am."[166] Therefore, he who spoke these words put himself into Abraham's power, so that Abraham would see his day. But, if they do not wish to accept the assertion that the word, "to reveal," applies to the past, we should say this to them, that knowing is not the same thing as believing. "For, to one is given the word of knowledge through the Spirit, to another faith, in the same Spirit."[167] So, some would be among the believers but not among the knowers. Let it be granted to them that Abraham did not know the Father, but only believed in him; for, the one who does not know him does not know both how he is God and how he is Father. And the many, indeed, have knowledge of God as Creator, but do not confess him as the Father of the Son.

163. Luke 10.21

The perception of the present need is a preparation for the foulness to come. He who does not perceive that he needs real beauty, because he has apparent beauty, is obviously left in need of true beauty. So too, Christ shows forth the Father's good will, of which God also said in the past through the prophet, "Upon whom shall I look, except upon the meek and quiet man, who always trembles at my words?"[168] And so, God did not respect folly over wisdom. He preferred humility to arrogance, and naturally deserted the man who obstructs kindness to himself through his insensibility. But the humble and childlike man says, "Teach me the truth according to yourself, for I am unable to learn from man if I do not learn

164. "Aorist" means "without boundaries," a verb tense in Greek that simply indicates past action without specifying it further.

165. Jn 8.56.

166. Jn 8.57–58.

167. 1 Cor 12.8–9.

168. Is 66.2.

from you." For, who should teach about God if not God himself? So the revelation was from above, after the determination according to merit.

164. Luke 10.22

There is no great difference between, "All things have been given to me by my Father,"[169] and, "All power in heaven and on earth has been given to me."[170] "All power" is given to him so that "through his cross he might reconcile both what is upon the earth and what is in heaven."[171] He has not yet reconciled everything, as is clear from the fact that war is still being waged from the side of evil. But perfect peace will exist perfectly. The Father handed over to him all that is wholly just, since the Son himself was handed over "for the sake of all men."[172] "He is the Savior of all men, most of all of believers,"[173] and, "He is the expiation for all our sins, not only for ours, but also for the sins of the whole world."[174] He was handed over in that he became man,[175] "so that at the name of Jesus every knee should bend—of those in heaven, on the earth, and under the earth, and every tongue confess that Jesus Christ is Lord to the glory of God the Father. Amen."[176]

165. Luke 10.23–24

Why are "the eyes" of Jesus' disciples "blessed," since "many prophets wished to see" what these men saw, but "did not see, and wished to hear" what they heard, "and did not hear"?[177] Let us look at the mind of these men. The simpler believers think the words mean "many prophets who prophesied about me wished to live during my times, in order 'to see what you see and hear what you hear.'" But they did not succeed in reaching these times, which you have been found worthy of.

169. Lk 10.22.
170. Mt 28.18.
171. Col 1.20.
172. Rom 8.32.
173. 1 Tm 4.10.
174. 1 Jn 2.2.
175. Origen here takes the phrase, "handed over," not of Jesus' death sentence, but of the Incarnation.
176. Phil 2.10.
177. Lk 10.23–24.

But, what is the reason why "many" prophets desired these things, but not all? We have already said of Abraham, that "he saw the day of Christ and rejoiced."[178] It is possible that a similar thing took place in the case of other prophets and just men also—not many, but a few. They anticipated the vision and the understanding that Jesus' disciples had. Inasmuch as these men saw what the apostles saw, and heard what Jesus' disciples heard, they did not desire, because they had vision and understanding "as those who have not."[179] But there were other prophets and just men who had less vision and understanding than the apostles, and they did not obtain what they desired. But now eyes are "blessed"—and I think it follows reasonably that other bodily members of the saints are blessed, too, as the phrase, "blessed is the womb that bore you, and the breasts that nursed you,"[180] shows. And how are "the feet" not blessed that neither stumble nor totter but are "welcome—the feet of those who proclaim the Good News."[181] And blessed are the hands whose "raising up is an evening sacrifice,"[182] and whose raising up means Israel's victory but Amalek's defeat.[183] And blessed is the heart from which "there flow rivers of water springing up for eternal life."[184] And blessed are the knees that "bend at Jesus' name";[185] blessed too the tongue that "confesses that Jesus Christ is Lord, to the glory of God the Father."[186] And blessed is the mouth that serves the Word of God,[187] and the nose on account of which it is said, "We shall run behind you for the smell of your perfumes."[188]

166. Luke 10.27–28

These words are spoken against the disciples of Valentinus and Basilides, and those of Marcion, for they too have these words in their "Gospel." We shall say to them, "When Jesus agreed with the young man who quoted, 'You shall love the

178. Jn 8.56.
179. 1 Cor 7.29.
180. Lk 11.27.
181. Is 52.7 and Rom 10.15.
182. Ps 141.2.
183. Cf. Ex 17.11.
184. Jn 7.38.
185. Phil 2.10.
186. Phil 2.11.
187. Cf. Acts 6.4.
188. Song 1.4.

Lord your God,'[189] as a commandment of the Law, he took it as applying to none other than the Creator. And in response the Savior said to him, 'You have answered rightly.'"[190] What else does he want each of us to do so that we might have eternal life except to love the God of the Law and the prophets "with our whole heart and our whole soul and our whole strength and our whole mind"?[191]

170. Luke 10.38

The Savior lodged with holy women in a certain village. Luke is silent about its name, but John specifies it and says it was "Bethany."[192]

171. Luke 10.38

You might reasonably take Martha to stand for action and Mary for contemplation. For, the mystery of love is lost to the active life unless one directs his teaching, and his exhortation to action, toward contemplation. For, there is no action without contemplation, or contemplation without action. But we should rather say that Martha received the word more somatically, in her house—that is, in her soul—whereas Mary heard it spiritually, even if she sat "at his feet." This means that she had already passed beyond what was handed down by way of introduction according to the plan of salvation, since she "had put aside the things of a child"[193] but had not yet received what is perfect. Martha can also be the synagogue of circumcision, which received Jesus in his own territory, because it was engaged in worship according to the letter of the Law. But Mary is the Church of the Gentiles, which has chosen the good part, the "spiritual law,"[194] which is not to be taken from her and cannot be destroyed, like the glory upon the face of Moses.[195] From the Law she takes the few beneficial things—or rather,

189. Dt 6.5 and Lk 10.27.
190. Lk 10.28.
191. Lk 10.27.
192. Jn 11.1.
193. 1 Cor 13.11.
194. Rom 7.14.
195. Cf. 2 Cor 3.7.

she sums all of them up in one commandment: "You shall love."[196] And, corresponding to the expression "one thing is necessary,"[197] you will understand, "you shall love your neighbor as yourself."[198] And, to the expression, "there is need of few things,"[199] "you understand the commandments: You shall not commit adultery. You shall not murder,"[200] and what follows. Still another interpretation: Martha can be the believers from among the circumcised, and the Judaizers, who keep the precepts of the Law in Jewish fashion, while Mary can be those among them who have been evangelized, and are "Jews in secret."[201] They sit only at Jesus' feet, and "seek the things that are above, not the things upon the earth."[202] For, interpreting the passage in another way, you will find that Martha is more somatic and busy "with many things,"[203] while Mary is concerned only with contemplation and spiritual things.

172. Luke 11.1

Then, to show that he was urging his disciples to follow his teaching about prayer, he adds the comment that even John (of whom you taught us that "no man born of woman is greater than he"[204]) was not unconcerned with teaching about prayer. Also consider the phrases, "we do not know how to pray as we ought,"[205] and, "You have commanded us to ask for great and eternal things. How is it possible for us to know them, except from you, our God and Savior?"[206]

173. Luke 11.1.

This is the same prayer as in Matthew,[207] but it is said here in an abridged form, unless one prefers to think that the

196. Lk 10.27.
197. Lk 10.42.
198. Lk 10.27.
199. Cf. Lk 10.42, the critical apparatus.
200. Lk 18.20.
201. Rom 2.29.
202. Col 3.1–2.
203. Lk 10.41.
204. Lk 7.28.
205. Rom 8.26.
206. A non-canonical saying attributed to Jesus. Cf. *On Prayer* 27.1, where Origen also quotes this saying.
207. Cf. Mt 6.9–13.

prayers are different but have some common phrases. As "the will" of God "is done in heaven, so also upon the earth"[208] whenever we do nothing against his will. How can the one who says we should ask for heavenly and great things bid us to ask for bread? He means the bread that is true, intelligible, and spiritual.

174. Luke 11.2

I think that no one can call God "Father" unless he is filled with the "spirit of sonship."[209] And a son who glorifies his Father calls him "Father," and keeps the commandment that says, "Love your enemies, pray for those who persecute you, so that you may be sons of your Father in heaven, because he makes his sun rise upon the wicked and the good, and sends rain upon the just and the unjust."[210] Again, someone who "does justice"[211] is begotten of God. And one who is begotten of God calls him "Father"; he has received "the seed" of God "in himself,"[212] so "he is no longer able to sin."[213] Again, someone is begotten of God, "not from perishable seed but through the living and abiding word of God,"[214] according to what is written. For, John says, "as many as received him, to them he gave the power to become children of God, to those who believe in his name. They were begotten, not from blood, nor from the will of flesh, nor from the will of man, but from God."[215] This means, not that he takes us up into God's nature, but that he gives us a share in grace and bestows his own dignity upon us. For, he tells us to call God "Father." Then to the words, "Our Father," Matthew adds, "in heaven."[216] He is discoursing about the Kingdom of Heaven[217] and recounts that, after the Beatitudes, the Savior also teaches his word

208. Mt 6.10.
209. Rom 8.15.
210. Mt 5.44–45.
211. 1 Jn 2.29.
212. 1 Jn 3.9.
213. 1 Jn 3.9.
214. 1 Pt 1.23.
215. Jn 1.12–13.
216. Mt 6.9.
217. Matthew's Gospel often has "Kingdom of Heaven" where Mark and Luke have "Kingdom of God." "Heaven" is a common Jewish circumlocution for "God."

about prayer to all those present. But Luke, who teaches about the Kingdom of God in his whole Gospel, omitted the words, "in heaven," thus teaching that the divine is more exalted and better than any place. According to Luke, Christ taught the disciples personally about prayer, since they were more exalted than the rest of the people. Nor does Luke add, "deliver us from the evil one,"[218] as Matthew says.

175. Luke 11.2

Or perhaps the phrase means this: if the name "god" is given to carved objects and demons by those who fall from the truth and rank "the creature above the Creator,"[219] then the name of God is no longer hallowed, and God has not been distinguished from things he is distinct from. He teaches us to pray that the good end might come more quickly, so that the name of "God" might be applied to the Lord as the "only true God."[220] Clearly we can also harmonize the following phrase with this interpretation. What is it? "May your kingdom come."[221]

176. Luke 11.2

"Let death reign"[222] over me no longer. May it not hold me prisoner through sin, but "may your kingdom come"[223] upon me, so that the passions, which now hold sway and reign over men, may cease to exist. Someone might also ask these things about the kingdom that exists in each individual.

177. Luke 11.2

"May your kingdom come,"[224] so that "every rule and authority and power,"[225] and even every kingdom of the world,[226] and

218. Mt 6.13.
219. Rom 1.25.
220. Jn 17.3.
221. Lk 11.2.
222. Cf. Rom 4.14 and 17.
223. Lk 11.2.
224. Lk 11.2.
225. 1 Cor 15.24.
226. Cf. Mt 4.8.

the sin that reigns in our mortal bodies, might be abolished, and God might reign over all of them.

180. Luke 11.3

Since Marcion's disciples have this reading, "Give us your substantial bread each day,"[227] we shall raise an objection to them, for they avoid allegories and anagogical senses. What is God's bread? For, if they explain it as we have proposed, then they are clearly allegorizing. But, if they suppose it means material bread, how, according to them, can this the bread come from the good God? The words, "each day," must apply to "bread." For, thus our true life is restored, so that "the inner man"[228] might live for God.

181. Luke 11.3

Luke's phrase, "each day," is more emphatic than Matthew's "this day."[229] The outer man,[230] who is properly substance, does not obtain living bread and exists for the enemy of life, namely, death, since the body is not nourished. Lowly people think of corporeal bread when the Teacher is says that we should not "care about tomorrow,"[231] especially if they read "the substantial bread" instead of "the bread that 'will come' or 'is coming.'"[232] This is clear from the saying, "For, you do not know what the next day will bring,"[233] that is, the one coming tomorrow. The followers of Mani will either allegorize it, which is not proper, or they will ask for the bread of the Demiurge.

227. Marcionites read "your bread" instead of "our bread," which is the standard reading in Lk 11.3.

228. Cf. Rom 7.22 and 2 Cor 4.16.

229. Lk 11.3 and Mt 6.11.

230. Cf. Rom 7.22 and 2 Cor 4.16.

231. Cf. Mt 6.34.

232. Both Matthew's and Luke's versions of the Lord's Prayer contain the word ἐπιούσιον, the meaning of which is obscure. Origen interprets it in *On Prayer* 27.7–9, and takes it to mean "substantial," in the sense of "adapted to one's substance or nature." He also reports two variant readings here.

233. Prv 3.28(LXX), with ἐπιοῦσα for "next."

182. Luke 11.5

The phrase, "who of you," is addressed to the disciples, but the words, "has a friend," imply that God is a friend to the saints, as he was to Moses and to Abraham.[234] And "midnight" is this "time" of life "that has grown short,"[235] when the destroyer comes to every house of Egypt—that is, this world—where the doorposts were not anointed with Christ's blood.[236] The disciple asks his friend for "three loaves."[237] He wishes to nourish his visitor "from the way" with divine knowledge about the Trinity, as Scripture says: "Apart from me you can do nothing."[238] But, why does the friend answer from within, "Do not make trouble for me"?[239] You will inquire whether we, "who labor and are heavily burdened,"[240] should not present our burdens to the Savior, because "he bears our weaknesses and suffers on our account."[241] Or, does it mean that, just as God is said to sleep for one man and for another, a sinner, to grow angry, he is also said to bear the burden of one who approaches him?

183. Luke 11.9

The Savior's statement, which says, "Ask and it will be given to you,"[242] is true. It is confirmed by his words, "Every one who asks receives."[243] Someone might ask why some people pray and are not heard. To this one should answer that the one who comes to ask in a suitable way and neglects none of the things that contribute to obtaining what he is concerned about, he will surely receive what he asked to be given to him. But, if one who moves outside the aim of the prayer that has been handed down to us appears to ask, but does not ask as he should, he does not ask perfectly. If he does not receive, the words, "everyone who asks receives," are not wrong. For,

234. See Jas 2.23 and Ex 33.11.
235. 1 Cor 7.29.
236. Cf. Ex 12.22–23.
237. Lk 11.5.
238. Jn 15.5.
239. Lk 11.7.
240. Mt 11.28.
241. Is 53.4 and Mt 8.17.
242. Lk 11.9.
243. Lk 11.10.

as the Teacher also said, "everyone who comes to me on account of my teachings will receive" knowledge "of them."[244] We take the words, "to approach the teacher," pragmatically—that is, it means giving earnest attention to the teacher's words, putting them into practice, and studying them. To the one who does not approach him in this way, we should say, "You have not approached him as you were urged to." James makes this point more clearly when he writes his letter that, "Some seem to ask but do not receive, for they ask wrongly, for the sake of wicked pleasures."[245] But someone will say, "Some even ask for divine knowledge and the reception of virtues and do not receive." To him we should say that they did not want to receive the good things themselves, but to be flattered on account of them. Lovers of pleasure exult in praise. So God does not give to them, since they want to squander the things they desire on pleasures.

185. Luke 11.24

What does it mean that the evil "spirit wanders through waterless places, seeking rest and not finding it"?[246] The waterless places were formerly the Gentiles. But now they have been filled with divine water and no longer offer rest to the evil spirit. So, Satan turns his attention to his former home, the people of Israel. When they were in Egypt, the evil spirit dwelt among them, because they lived by the customs and laws of the Egyptians. But, after they were redeemed by God's mercy through Moses, he left them. But now, since they have not believed in Christ but have rejected the Redeemer, "the unclean spirit"[247] has assaulted them again. He found that they no longer had anything divine in them; they were deserted, and ready for him to dwell in them. Clearly he dwelt in them with all his power. The passage seems to make this clear when it says that "seven other spirits"[248] were with him. The divine

244. Source unknown.
245. Jas 4.3.
246. Lk 11.24.
247. Lk 11.24.
248. Lk 11.26.

Scripture usually applies this number to a multitude, as when it says that "the sterile woman bore seven children, and the woman with many children has grown weak."[249] For, those "who have not believed in my son"[250] have not only the kind of "unclean spirit" that the Jews had in Egypt, but are filled with other evil spirits too; and, for them, "the last" became "worse than the first."[251] For, they now suffer worse things than they did in Egypt, since they have not believed in Jesus Christ, but "have killed the pioneer of our life,"[252] and hence have been deprived of life. A prophet no longer says among them, "Thus says the Lord." There is no longer a sign among them, no longer a wonder, no longer a sign of God's manifestation and presence. For, the good things have passed over to us, the Gentiles, according to the word of Jesus, who said, "The kingdom of God will be taken from them and given to a people that bears its fruits."[253] We are that people to whom "the kingdom of God," the commonwealth of the Gospel, has been given.

186. Luke 11.33–34

It seems to me that in the phrase, "the lamp of the body is the eye,"[254] something like the following is revealed. The mind is the organ of sight for the whole soul and the whole man. In order to draw our attention to this point, Scripture has said, "Let your lamps be burning."[255] As if we were lighting the lamp within us, we are made aware of our intellectual power. The verse, "No one lights a lamp and puts it in a hiding place, but upon the lampstand,"[256] is similar. Those who care about wisdom and reason and the practice of divine things light a lamp to become perfect. Perfection comes to be in a man in no other way than by his exercising his faculties on divine and intelligible things. Paul made this clear when he said, "Solid food is for the perfect, who have trained their faculties by

249. 1 Sm 2.5.
250. Source unknown.
251. Lk 11.26.
252. Acts 3.15.
253. Mt 21.43.
254. Lk 11.34.
255. Lk 12.35.
256. Lk 11.33.

practice to distinguish good and evil."[257] These are they to whom one can speak of wisdom, which is spoken of to the perfect; of wisdom Scripture says, "we speak wisdom among the perfect."[258] In the strict sense, Scripture calls our mind an "eye." The beginning of wisdom is in the mind, in the man concerned solely for simplicity, who has no duplicity, guile, division, separation, or divergence in him. But in the evil man the mind is the principle of vice and every sort of sin. Consider whether you can also interpret the word "body" figuratively, corresponding to "eye." In that case, either "the body" is taken to mean the whole soul, even though it is not somatic—for God put the mind into man's soul—or "the body" means whatever exists in man apart from the mind—that is, the combination of the rest of the soul and the body. For, in the proper sense the whole soul is illuminated by the mind; but one might say that either the simplicity of the mind affects the body, for the body is led by the mind, or sin affects it, for the mind uses the body as an instrument for sin. You should not be surprised if in the verse, "the lamp of the body is the eye,"[259] we take the body as a figure of the soul, even though, in the proper sense of the word, the soul is invisible and incorporeal, for it is made in the image of the invisible God. We find that even the powers of the soul, which are not "bodies" but named that, are named figuratively, using parts of the body. For, in the phrase, "enlighten my eyes,"[260] the eyes are clearly not corporeal; and in the verse, "he gave me an ear,"[261] the discourse is not about bodies; nor is it whenever Scripture says, "Let him who has ears to hear hear."[262] And, in the Song of the Bride,[263] hair, teeth, lips, cheeks, the neck, and breasts[264] are praised by the bridegroom. The bride is either the soul of man, which enters into marriage with Christ, or the Church. The parts of the body are interpreted figuratively: if they are said of the soul, then they apply to its powers. You can also find the verse, "Let

257. Heb 5.14.
258. 1 Cor 2.6.
259. Lk 11.34.
260. Ps 13.3.
261. Is 50.4(LXX).
262. Mt 11.15, 13.9, 13.43; Mk 4.9, 4.23, 7.16; and Lk 8.8, 14.35.
263. That is, in the Song of Songs.
264. Song 4.1–5.

my foot not stumble,"[265] applied to the soul's power to progress. If you attend to the Scriptures, you yourself will find many such examples there. From them you will be able to avoid stumbling over the explanation of what the "body" means in the verse, "the lamp of the body is the eye,"[266] and in other passages like this one. In the Book of Proverbs, you will find the phrase, "divine sense-perception,"[267] recorded in a promise, as distinct from perception that is not divine. For, "sense perception" itself is not divine. Even irrational beasts share in it; they see, hear, taste, smell, and touch. Not all men participate in the divine perception, but those who so act that the words, "you will find divine perception,"[268] are applicable to them. So, do not wonder if the noun, "body," like the names of parts of the body that are applied to the powers of the soul, is applied to the whole soul in the verse, "the lamp of the body is the eye."[269] We do not mean to say that the word "body" in the Scriptures is always to be interpreted allegorically. We know that the word "body" is also applied to other things, as in the verse, "Do not fear those who kill the body,"[270] and, "You are the body of Christ."[271]

187. Luke 11.34

I think that the meaning of the next expression is this: "your body" has become "light" once you are illuminated by the lamp of the body. There is no longer any dark part in you, for you no longer sin at all. Thus the whole body will be light. Its rays can be compared to a lamp with a gleaming flash; the lamp illumines, but it does not dispell the darkness. For, illumination from the mind is like a gleaming flash, and the light in the body is like a lamp with gleaming rays. The body is by nature darkness, a thing to be led where the mind wills. So, if the minds of those who are unlearned and ignorant, which

265. Ps 91.12.
266. Lk 11.34.
267. Prv 2.5. The same reading is found in *Against Celsus* 1.48, 7.34; *Commentary on John* 20.33; and Clement of Alexandria, *Stromateis* 1.27.2.
268. Prv 2.5.
269. Lk 11.34.
270. Lk 12.4.
271. 1 Cor 12.27.

are by nature light, are in fact darkness, then the whole body is too—that is, the passionate part of the soul, which is the spirited and appetitive part; and the darkness is much worse.

188. Luke 11.35

"See to it that the light in you is not darkness."[272] So it is necessary for you, he says, to render your mind pure and thus to make both your words and your deeds gleam. But you do the opposite. Where you should bring forth light, you produce darkness, and bring forth envy from wicked thoughts.

191. Luke 12.2

So, Scripture says of this time, "God judges the hidden things of men,"[273] and, "He will illumine what is hidden in darkness and make clear the plans of hearts."[274] I mean that, however much one may try to hide the good by making an accusation, the good is by nature revealed.

192. Luke 12.6

Notice that Luke does not mention the fall of a sparrow upon the earth, as Matthew does.[275] Now, "five sparrows" suggests the senses of a just man, which perceive even the things exalted above a man. These senses see divine things, hear the voice of God, taste "living bread,"[276] smell the good odor of Christ's perfume,[277] the "oil of gladness,"[278] and touch a living word. Although they are greatly disparaged by those who judge that the "things of the spirit"[279] are foolish and cheap, "they are not forgotten in the eyes of God."[280] If the Word was sold for thirty pieces of silver,[281] it is no wonder if the divine senses are sold for two pennies. The obvious meaning is that

272. Lk 11.35.
273. Rom 2.16.
274. 1 Cor 4.5.
275. Cf. Mt 10.29.
276. Jn 6.51.
277. Cf. Eph 5.2.
278. Ps 45.7.
279. 1 Cor 2.14.
280. Lk 12.6.
281. Mt 26.15.

the smallest sparrow is not "forgotten in God's eyes." Search beyond the obvious meanings: God forgets some of them on account of sin. In the literal sense, the detailed treatment of Providence, and knowledge of even small details, is manifest in these words, while in the spiritual sense the mind falls to the earth like sparrows when it ought to be borne upward; it seeks what is below because it is caught in the evils of the flesh, was handed over "to the passions of dishonor,"[282] and has destroyed its freedom along with its honor. Such is the one who was lifted up by the Word but thinks of earthly things.[283] According to the literal sense, again, the words, "it will not fall to the earth without your Father,"[284] do not show his will, but his foreknowledge. For, of those events that happen, some happen according to his will, other according to his good pleasure, and still others according to his consent.[285]

193. Luke 12.19

"You have many goods laid up." As he lay down he said, "You have goods laid up for many years."[286] But he erred in his judgment about the goods, for he did not know that the real goods are not on the earth, which was cursed,[287] but in heaven. There the rest of the blessed and the joy in Christ Jesus do not last "for many years" but for endless ages.

195. Luke 12.35–37

"The loins" of those who live in chastity "are girded."[288] And, since our life is night, we need a lamp. The lamp is the mind, which is the eye of the soul. And, if watchfulness belongs to the "inner man,"[289] with good reason do we need watchfulness in this life—on account of the "principalities and powers,"[290]

282. Rom 1.26.
283. Cf. Phil 3.19.
284. Mt 10.29, which reads, "without your Father's will."
285. Origen distingushes among God's efficacious will (βούλησις), his positive will for good (εὐδοκία), and his permissive will for evil (συγχώρησις).
286. Lk 12.19.
287. Cf. Gn 3.17.
288. Lk 12.35.
289. Rom 7.22 and Eph 3.16.
290. Eph 6.12.

I mean, that lie in wait. We struggle against them,[291] "so that we might find a place for the Lord, a dwelling place for the God of Jacob,"[292] so that we might open to the Lord when he knocks. But consider that a reward is also given for watchfulness. For, Scripture says, "he will gird himself"[293]—that is, "he has girded his loins," following the saying, "The Lord has put on power and girded himself."[294] He will make each one recline according to his worthiness, and according to his worthiness[295] he will serve each one, rewarding "each one according to his works."[296]

196. Luke 12.36

There are, of course, sleep and watchfulness for the "outer man" as well as for the "inner man."[297] And we ask to be watchful, as the Savior says: "Be watchful and pray, lest you enter into temptation."[298] And in Proverbs, Scripture says, "Do not give sleep to your eyes or slumber to your eyelids."[299] But we ask to sleep when the Savior says, "Sleep now and take your rest."[300] And Solomon says, "For, if you are seated, you will be without fear; but, if you lie down to sleep, you will fall asleep sweetly, and you will not fear any terror coming upon you."[301]

197. Luke 12.36

But in this life we must be very watchful indeed, because the enemies are lying in wait, and they are not "flesh and blood, but principalities and rulers of this world and spirits of evil."[302] By our watchfulness, "we must be saved, like deer from snares and like a bird from a trap";[303] and, once we have girded our loins and have had our lamps lighted, we may be "like

291. Cf. Eph 6.12.
292. Ps 132.5.
293. Lk 12.37.
294. Ps 93.1.
295. Cf. Mt 16.27.
296. Rom 2.6.
297. Cf. 2 Cor 4.16, Rom 7.22, and Eph 3.16.
298. Mk 14.38.
299. Prv 6.4.
300. Mk 14.41.
301. Prv 3.24–25.
302. Eph 6.12.
303. Prv 6.5.

men awaiting their lord, so that when he comes and knocks we may open for him immediately."[304] And take care, lest he require an account during the first, second, and third watch of the night, and the fourth as well. We must be watchful at every hour, as Solomon said: "Consider your heart at every watch."[305]

198. Luke 12.37–38

So I think that Christ "will gird himself"[306] and will make those recline whom he finds watching, since, according to Isaiah, "he will gird his loins with justice."[307] What of the words, "He will come and serve them"?[308] See whether you can speak of two kinds of service. One is in this life, according to these words of Christ: "I am in your midst, not as the one who reclines to eat, but as the one who serves."[309] The other is the service of which he says here, "If he comes in the second watch, and if he comes in the third watch, and finds them thus, blessed are those servants."[310]

199. Luke 12.39

The scheming thief still comes to the soul of each man; and the Word of God appears, to guard his own. So be watchful. If the thief comes and finds the master of the house watching, he will not dig through the master's house. But, if the Son of Man comes, the master should watch, so that he can open for him immediately when he knocks. For, if the Son of Man finds him sleeping, and he does not open to the knock, he leaves him behind and departs. After this life, the one who has been watchful in it "will sleep sweetly and will not be terrified by any terror that comes to him."[311] Thus "David slept with his fathers,"[312] as did the others who followed. We find this

304. Lk 12.36.
305. Prv 4.23.
306. Lk 12.37.
307. Is 11.5.
308. Lk 12.37.
309. Lk 22.27.
310. Lk 12.38.
311. Prv 3.24–25.
312. 1 Kgs 2.10.

expression applied to none of the holy men born from foreign seed, but only to the present instance. This is perhaps why the Apostle says, "Not all of us shall fall asleep."[313] If all of us shall fall asleep, "then blessed are the servants whom the Lord will find watching when he comes."[314] He gives them their wages, even to excess; "he will gird his loins with justice."[315] He holds authority over the time when each one is asked for his soul, no matter what sort he is. And, if he rules over him who says, "I shall tear down my barns and build bigger ones," and, "He said to him, 'You fool, this very night do they demand your soul of you,'"[316] how much more will he rule over the blessed and holy ones who will be with the Lord after "the departure."[317]

200. Luke 12.42

Now, it seems to me that I hear the words "faithful" and "wise," but the Savior does not apply the word "faithful" to one of the virtues, "faith" in its proper sense according to the Scriptures; nor does he apply "wise" to another virtue, since the faithful man is wholly wise and, conversely, the wise man is faithful, by the reciprocal implication of the virtues.[318] But the word "wise" is sometimes applied not to one who has acquired the virtue of wisdom, but as in the dismissal of the wily steward.[319] The word can sometimes even mean "crafty," as in, "The serpent was the craftiest of all the beasts upon the earth."[320] Thus too in this case, the faithful man is not perfect in giving his assent to his faith in God. In this regard, the faithful man may not be wise in all things, and the wise man may not be faithful in all things. Even according to the divine Scriptures themselves, the steward is wise, but not faithful.

313. 1 Cor 15.51.
314. Lk 12.37.
315. Is 11.5.
316. Lk 12.18 and 20.
317. Phil 1.23.
318. Origen uses a Stoic term for reciprocity among virtues.
319. Cf. Lk 16.8. In the parable of the unjust steward, the master tells the steward that he has acted "wisely."
320. Gn 3.1. The LXX uses the word that Origen is concerned with here, φρόνιμος.

This is clear from what follows. It was not proper to a wise man to waste the rich man's goods, and to call in each of his master's debtors and reduce their debt.[321] And that he was not faithful is also clear, since according to one sense of the word he was "wise"—that is, crafty. For, the master praises his craftiness but censures his unfaithfulness, and for this reason says to him, "You shall no longer be able to be my steward."[322] And perhaps faith, as we have already said, suffices for salvation for the many, but in the stewards there is a need for both—for faithfulness and for wisdom. And, since he is not such a man, he will not be able to contemplate both the time for giving the measure of grain to the servants, and what is fitting for each. But, since many stewards of the churches are faithful, but not wise too, or the opposite,[323] therefore the Lord asked a rhetorical question, to show as clearly as possible the scarcity and rareness of stewards who are both faithful and wise at the same time. When he found one, the master placed him over his servants. In the same way the Savior chose Judas. He was not unaware that Judas would later oppose him, but he made use of him in the time before his fall and in his providential plan that led to virtue for the work of apostolic service. The hidden good is greater for a faithful and wise man than what was promised to the man who increased his *minas* tenfold or fivefold.[324] And it is no surprise why the reward of those who differ from them is greater. For, cities are to be given to those who increased the amount of their *minas*, and abundance to those who double the *talents*. For, much more belongs to these—not only to be set over an abundance, but "over all the master's substance,"[325] which is laid up by the faithful and wise steward. He himself is worthy of the whole substance by persevering in his faith. You will seek to learn whether, if many faithful and wise persons are found, each of them can be set

321. Lk 16.1–7.

322. Lk 16.3. Luke has the present, Origen the future, "shall be able."

323. Origen is again critical of bishops.

324. Origen will contrast the parables in Lk 19.11–27 and Mt 25.14–30. See *Hom.* 35, note 37.

325. Lk 12.44.

"over all the substance" of the master. For, if he is set "over all," how can another be placed over ten cities? And, even more so if there are many? Let this be said as an exhortation.

201. Luke 12.46

What Daniel said to the second of the two elders who accused the holy Susanna, "For, God's angel is already taking you," and, "By God he will divide you in half,"[326] as interpreted by Origen, means that this will happen to him fully in the judgment, according to the word spoken by the Lord: "And he will cut him in pieces."[327]

202. Luke 12.51–53

The persons named in the Gospel are six in number.[328] But one person, the daughter-in-law, counts for two. The daughter-in-law and the daughter, who oppose the mother and the mother-in-law, are the same person. And thus he opposes three to contend against two, and two to contend against three. By way of comparison, in a house (that is, a man), the five senses are unanimous in their pleasures before the Word comes to them, but divided when the Word dwells there. Two are the more philosophical senses: sight, by which we see the world and its order and wonder at the Creator; and hearing, through which the Word of God makes us disciples. Then there are the other three senses: taste, smell, and touch, which are servile and not by nature suited for philosophy. The three usually oppose the two.

But the phrase, "father will be divided against son,"[329] should be read from another principle, not from the one just explained. Literally, the phrase makes clear the division of be-

326. Dn 13.55. 327. Lk 12.46.

328. In Lk 12.52, Jesus says that five in one household will be divided, three against two and two against three. Then, in verse 53, he names six persons: father, son, mother, daughter, mother-in-law, and daughter-in-law. In this *tour de force,* Origen tallies the account.

329. Lk 12.53.

lievers from unbelievers. Symbolically, however, "father," the mind, is divided against "son," worthless passion, and does not give assent to it. "And son against father": the son does not bury his dead father.[330] "Mother against daughter": the soul does not receive the daughter's worthless fruit. "Daughter against mother": the soul has not yet united matter with itself. "Mother-in-law against daughter-in-law": the mother of the soul, who lived under the Law as her husband[331] (by "the mother of the soul" I mean the Holy Spirit), deserts the people of the circumcision. "Daughter-in-law against mother-in-law": the people separated from the Spirit through sin.

203. Luke 13.6

He appears to compare them to a fig tree (Titus of Bostra).[332] —[The fig tree stands for] all the nations; or, in another interpretation, humanity was the fig tree (Isidore of Pelusium).—"Cutting them down." This, then, is the first rejection[333] (Isidore of Pelusium). A prayer for grace. But others consider it the three-fold prayer[334] (Cyril of Alexandria).—And the tree was rejected.[335] I think this other, fourth rejection[336] is the time of the Incarnation, toward which he spurs Israel on, and digs around it, and warms it,[337] to perfect those who are warmed by the Spirit. But, since they remained fruitless after such threats, the fig tree was cut down and the Gentiles were grafted on to the root of those people;[338] for, the root remained. Or, one can take the farmer to be an angel commanded by God to preside over Jerusalem, which is also compared to an unfruitful fig tree.

330. Cf. Lk 9.59.
331. Cf. Rom 7.1–3.
332. The fragment collects opinions on the meaning of the fig tree. The editor judges that most of it is Origen's work.
333. Of the Jews.
334. That is, the *Trisagion* of the Greek liturgy.
335. Here Origen's comments begin.
336. The man in the parable had sought fruit from the tree three times in three years, and allows it one more year to bear.
337. Manure warms, as Origen suggests.
338. Cf. Rom 11.17–24.

204. Luke 13.6

So, we can delineate the saying concisely: the fig tree is either the city of Jerusalem, or the synagogue of the Jews, or the whole of humanity.

The master of the household, to whom the fig tree belonged, was God the Father, or the Savior himself.

The worker in the vineyard was the Son of God.

He says he has come a third time: that is, through Moses, through the prophets, through himself. Or, the first year was the one in which the command was given to Adam, "From every tree in the garden shall you eat food," and the rest.[339] The second year was the one in which God gave the commandments to Israel in the Law that came through Moses. The third year was the one in which he himself gave the perfect law in the Gospel. Or, the first year was the time when Moses and Aaron lived; the second was the time when Joshua son of Nun and the judges lived; the third was the time when "the prophets, up to John"[340] the Baptist lived; the fourth year was the time of the Incarnation, in which he himself proclaimed to all the kingdom of heaven through the Gospel.

205. Luke 13.21

In another way, it is possible to take the woman for the Church, the leaven for the Holy Spirit, and the three measures for body, spirit, and soul.[341] These three are sanctified by the leaven of the Holy Spirit, so that by the Holy Spirit they become one lump, in order that "our whole body and spirit and soul may be kept blameless in the day of our Lord Jesus Christ,"[342] as Paul the divine says.

209. Luke 14.12–14

So, taken literally, we are bidden not to invite friends and neighbors, but "the poor and the crippled, the lame and the

339. Gn 2.16.
340. Lk 16.16.
341. Cf. *Hom.* 4.5.
342. 1 Thes 5.23.

blind."[343] If these words are understood not by way of accommodation and as parables, so that even the simpler people can profit by his words as far as possible, then he is rejecting the prevailing customs. For, a wise man docs not invite poor people who are not believers, nor does he refuse to invite friends who are believers, even if they are poor. So, perhaps "friends" is meant figuratively, as those who, by their reason, rejoice in the doctrines of the truth.[344] "Brethren" are those who hold fraternal doctrines. "Relatives" are those who are further away but wish to come closer to us in doctrine. "Neighbors" are those who have, not in a very different way, the structures of our doctrines. We should understand "rich people" as applying to all of them.[345] The man who is wealthy in the doctrines he believes are true but, when he is called to the really true Word, contradicts the truth, is like one who invites the teacher. But, since there are "not many wise men"[346] among us, but there are some, we have to find out whether they are to be invited also. For, those who proclaim what they have heard invite "the rich," and not the poor, but he who serves the Word for true glory has been set free from idle opinion.

"Invite the poor,"[347] he says, those who are poor in words, so that you can make them rich. Invite "the crippled," those whose minds are injured, so that you can heal them. Invite "the lame," those who limp in their reason, so that they can make "straight paths."[348] Invite the blind, who do not have the faculty of contemplation, so that they can see the true light.[349] But the words, "they do not have the means to repay you,"[350] are equal to, "they do not know how to arrange an argument dialectically, by question and answer."

"Luncheon" means the introductory words, or the moral

343. Lk 14.13.

344. Origen begins to apply the four words in Lk 14.12 to Christian groups that are closer to, or further from, the Great Church in their beliefs.

345. Cf. *Hom.* 32.5 and the note there on the figure ἀπὸ κοινοῦ.

346. 1 Cor 1.26.

347. Lk 14.13.

348. Prv 4.26 and Heb 12.13.

349. Jn 1.9.

350. Lk 14.14.

ones,[351] or the words of the Old Covenant. "Dinner" means the mystical words, made in progress, or those of the New Covenant. He says "resurrection of the just" here, which John first mentions in the Apocalypse.[352]

210. Luke 14.16

And "a man," acclaimed for his generosity, is God the Father; as "a man" he makes "a dinner" in the kingdom of God for those not yet able to eat even a luncheon. And the dinner was "great," for it surpassed the "luncheon."[353] For, "luncheon" means the introductory or moral arguments,[354] or the Old Testament. "Dinner" means the mystical words spoken by those who advance, or the words of the New Testament. But, behold the advent of his "dinner." Christ is sent as a servant to serve the Father, and summons everyone. "For, he did not come to be served, but to serve,"[355] and, "I am in your midst as one who serves,"[356] "taking the form of a servant."[357]

211. Luke 14.18

The guests were invited because they were prepared by nature, but in three ways they fall away from their call: by imagining that opinions are more persuasive than intelligible things; by pursuing sensible, and not intelligible, things; and by love of pleasure. For, some have bought a field and ask to be excused from the dinner. They receive other opinions about divinity, which have great persuasive power and elaborate expression, and they despise the field, which has in it "treasure"[358]

351. A lower sort of discourse. Aristotle, in the *Nicomachean Ethics* 1.103a5 and elsewhere, distinguishes ἠθικός, "ethical," from διανοητικός, "intellectual," as lower from higher. Elsewhere, Origen writes of the book of Ecclesiastes as physical, Proverbs as moral, and the Song of Songs as theological. Cf. *Frags.* 210 and 218.

352. Rv 20.5–6.

353. Cf. Lk 14.12, where Jesus says to his host, "When you make a luncheon or a dinner. . . ."

354. Cf. *Frag.* 209 and the note there.

355. Mt 20.28.

356. Lk 22.27.

357. Phil 2.7.

358. Cf. Mt 13.44.

and powers. The one who neither sees nor tests the word he acquired, on account of being preoccupied out of necessity and not voluntarily, goes out from the dinner and from him who invited him—and perhaps even from himself. The words, "I ask you," mean that they respect the man who invited them only in words.

212. *Luke 14.18–20*

The man who bought five yoke of oxen did not first try out what he bought. He disdains intellectual nature and philosophizes about sensible things, as the Ebionite Jews do.[359] He does not take the oxen seven by seven, as clean animals, but two by two, like the unclean animals that came to the ark.[360] For, the Savior makes "the two into one new man,"[361] and says, "I and the Father are one."[362] But, if two is the number of matter, this man reveres sensible and material things. Hence, he too excuses himself from the intelligible banquet. So, in some copies, instead of "I ask you," the words, "and for this reason I am unable to come," are found.[363] For, those who chose sensible things say that they cannot grasp the incorporeal. The other man is he who says, "I have married a wife." He appears to have found wisdom and lives with her. But he excuses himself from true wisdom; or, he is united with flesh, a lover of pleasure rather than a lover of God.[364] "Those who are in the flesh cannot please God."[365]

214. *Luke 14.21–22*

The people in the streets[366] are those who proceed along the broad way. They live without teaching and doctrines. The ones

359. Cf. *Hom.* 17.4.
360. Cf. Gn 7.2.
361. Eph 2.15.
362. Jn 10.30.
363. Lk 14.19. Modern critical editions also note this variant.
364. Cf. 2 Tm 3.4.
365. Rom 8.8.
366. In this passage, Origen tries to account for the differences among the four words for "street" that Luke uses in this parable, here translated "streets," "lanes," "roads," and "paths."

in the lanes are those who restrain evil for such-and-such a reason. The city is the earthly world. The poor and the lame and the blind are "the foolish and ignoble and weak things of the world."[367] The rest are those invited last from the roads and the paths. This third group is the souls in Hades, for many are the roads of those who depart this life. To these souls, the Savior proclaimed the Gospel after he put off the body.[368] He is a lover of men and by necessity approaches those who are not yet free.

215. Luke 14.28

The tower, which has majesty and nobility and grandeur, would be discourse about God. Through the parable, the Savior intimates that, if you are going to speak of God, you must consider whether you can begin. The Word seeks to perfect everything for discourse about God, lest you begin with the doctrines of piety and leave the discourse about God unfinished and do not build a parapet at the top. For, if he did not build a parapet, someone will fall from the tower and die.

216. Luke 15.16

You can understand the desire of the prodigal son to be sated with pods in this way. When rational nature exists in irrationality, it desires; and, if it does not get more convincing reasons, then it accepts any at all. Since the pods taste sweet and make the body fat, they do not bind the bowels. They are the specious words of lovers of matter and the body, who say that pleasure is a good, "itching at their ears and running after myths."[369] ". . . and no one gave him any."[370] For, lowly people do not present their unsound teachings to the clever, lest they be refuted. Or, the words of outsiders are not nourishing, and cannot satisfy the need for rational food.

367. 1 Cor 1.27–28.
368. Cf. 1 Pt 3.19.
369. 2 Tm 4.3–4.
370. Lk 15.16.

217. Luke 15.20–21

"I have left heavenly things behind, and have also been irreverent towards you."[371] In the literal sense, the account shows the human suffering and describes the son's desertion and estrangement. His father does not bring him back to his original good fortune until he perceives the misfortune he is in, comes to himself, and attends to the words of repentance. For, he says, "I have sinned,"[372] and the rest. He would not add the sin "against heaven" to his confession if he did not believe that heaven is his fatherland, and that he did wrong when he left it. So, such a confession makes his father well disposed to him, so that he runs to him and welcomes him with a kiss on the neck.

218. Luke 15.23

If we can understand the deeper meaning of the passage, it begins with ethical arguments[373] like food, in the word, "eating," and then with the higher mysteries like wine, in the words, "let us be glad." For, "wine is the beginning of gladness,"[374] as Scripture says.

219. Luke 15.25, 27

In the literal sense, the word "music"[375] applies to the musical harmonies of voices. There are also sounds that are harmonious with musical sounds and discordant with other sounds. And the evangelical Scripture knew the name for the musical harmonies, as shown here. But, in the Book of Daniel, too, Nebuchadnezzar is portrayed as commanding that, whenever those who were gathered heard "the sound of the trumpet, pipe, lyre, sambuca, and psaltery, and of every sort of musical instrument, they should fall down and worship the

371. Lk 15.21. 372. Lk 15.21.
373. Cf. *Frag.* 209 and the note there.
374. Ps 104.15.
375. Greek συμφωνία, "concord of sound."

golden image."[376] "Because I have received him back in good health. . . ." "In good health"[377] means he had cast off his sickness by repentance.

221. Luke 16.17

"One dot"[378] is not only the letter *iota* among the Greeks, but also, among the Hebrews, the letter they call *iodh.*[379] It is possible that Jesus said, "one *iota* or one tittle,"[380] symbolically, since the beginning of his name, not only among the Greeks but also among the Hebrews, begins with the letter *iodh.* And "one *iota* or one tittle" is Jesus, the Word of God in the Law. He does not abolish the Law "until all things come to pass,"[381] and he does not fall.[382] For, he falls for the sake of salvation, to bear "much fruit."[383] But, when he falls, it is an easier thing "for heaven and earth to pass away"[384] than for "one tittle to fall" of what concerns him in the Law. But, "he fell into the earth"[385] and died, to bear more fruit. He was not conquered; he "humbled himself and became obedient unto death, death on a cross."[386]

222. Luke 16.19

"There was a certain rich man."[387] What seemed better to him was not really better. According to Solomon's words, "a good name is better than much wealth."[388] The opposite seemed better to him: great wealth rather than a good name. So, he is named by what he loved; he is called "rich," not "holy" or "just." But the poor man, who had nothing in this world, is called by the simple name of "Lazarus." But, see how the Savior of all describes the characteristic qualities of the rich man. He

376. Dn 3.5.
377. Lk 15.27.
378. Mt 5.18 has "one *iota* or one tittle"; Luke has only "one tittle."
379. Origen has *ioth.*
380. Mt 5.18.
381. Lk 21.32.
382. Luke has literally "one tittle will not fall" from the law. Origen associates this "fall" with the seed falling into the ground and dying in Jn 12.24.
383. Jn 12.24.
384. Lk 16.17.
385. Jn 12.24.
386. Phil 2.8.
387. Lk 16.19.
388. Prv 22.1.

says, "And he was clothed in purple and linen, and he feasted splendidly each day."[389] He did not give the man's proper name, but said, "There was a certain man," to bring out the element of uncertainty by this common designation, and to stress the common, insulting element by the unclarity. But it is not so with the just. How is it? Scripture says, "There was a certain man in the land of Uz named Job."[390] And, "There was a man in Jerusalem whose name was Simeon."[391] Why? Because Scripture adds about Job, "And that man was blameless, without evil, just, truthful, and God-fearing; and he refrained from every evil deed."[392] And about Simeon, "This man was just and reverent, and awaited the deliverance of Israel, and the Holy Spirit of God was with him."[393] Job was also rich, but he did not pass his life in luxury and lack of compassion. His house stood open to every needy person by his loving will. He treated no one unjustly, but helped those who suffered unjustly; he furnished the things needed for life to widows and orphans. For, these are the just deeds of just rich men.

223. *Luke 16.23.*

Someone wished to reject the narrative about the rich man and the poor man and, in ignorance of the Gospel, posed this difficulty: if Lazarus was placed in Abraham's bosom, someone else was lying in Abraham's bosom before Lazarus departed this life; and before that one, someone else. And, when another just man dies, Lazarus, the poor man, will be displaced. The one who poses this difficulty has not seen Abraham's bosom, and does not realize that tens of thousands can rest in Abraham's bosom at the same time, since they partake in what was revealed to him. Even John, the beloved disciple, according to the narrative, rested "on Jesus' bosom"[394] during the Supper; he was deemed worthy of this gift because the Master judged him worthy of exceptional love. But, taken figuratively, the phrase means that John rested upon the Word, and reposed upon more mystical things. He lay back on the

389. Lk 16.19.
390. Jb 1.1.
391. Lk 2.25.
392. Jb 1.1.
393. Lk 2.25.
394. Jn 13.23.

bosom of the Word, just as the Lord himself is called the "Only-Begotten" Word "in the bosom of the Father."[395]

226. Luke 18.21

Madness is evident in the thought of Marcionites and Manichees, who say that the Law is alien to Christ. For, Mark says that "Jesus looked upon him and loved him."[396] He would not have loved one who spoke of observing the Law of an alien god. But, we should ask why he loved the man who would not follow him to life. It is possible that he who observed the Law—and that from his youth—was worthy of love under the Old Covenant. But, by his contempt for perfection, he did not allow his love for the Old Law to become perfect. Hence, having grasped all that was incomplete in the Law, Paul hastened on to perfection.

227. Luke 19.12

"The man who set out for a great place to receive a kingdom for himself"[397] is Christ after the Ascension. He returns in the Second Coming. Consider whether the ten servants can be the ten apostles; for we exclude Judas the traitor, and "James the brother of John," who did not work for very long because he was soon killed by Herod's sword.[398]

228. Luke 19.22

All of us will be judged on our whole lives, when an account is demanded and "every idle word that men have spoken"[399] shall be revealed openly. But, if anyone ever "gave a cup of cold water in the name of discipleship,"[400] this will also be revealed, when the Scripture written by Daniel comes to pass,

395. Jn 1.18.

396. Mk 10.21.

397. Lk 19.12. On Lk 19.11–27, cf. *Hom.* 35.11 and the note there; *Hom.* 39.6–7; and *Frags.* 228 and 231.

398. Cf. Acts 12.2. Origen gives an unusual interpretation of the number ten, applying it to the apostles.

399. Mt 12.36.

400. Mt 10.42.

which says, "Books were opened and he sat down to judgment."[401] For, it is as if a copy of all we have said and done and thought existed, and by divine power every one of our secrets shall be exposed, and everything we have hidden shall be revealed.[402] "For, all us must stand before the judgment seat of Christ, so that each one may receive either good or evil, according to what he did in the body."[403] No one should think that long ages are needed for such an examination of the accounts of all men and their whole lives here on earth. For, God wills in one moment to recall to the memories of all men those things, good or evil, done during their whole lives. He will do this by ineffable power, and will remind each one of what he did, so that we shall perceive what we have done and comprehend why we are punished or rewarded. For, we should take courage, and say that the hour of the expected judgment has no need of time. Just as the resurrection is said to happen "in a moment, in the twinkling of an eye,"[404] so will the judgment, I think. So, in this parable, ten servants are found receiving ten *minas*; each one receives one. In the other parable, one servant receives five *talents*, another two, another one.[405] In another place, one servant owes five hundred *denarii*, the other fifty.[406] If anyone considers the complexity of the human soul and its differing disposition or indisposition for more or fewer of the virtues, and for some virtues rather than others, perhaps he will understand how each soul has come to what it deserved, and with what coins of the Master, which appeared with the fulfillment of the Word, and the care and training that lead to the fullness of the Word.

230. Luke 20.25

(a) It is necessary to give those things back to Caesar that do not injure piety. For, if this were not so, we should not

401. Dn 7.10.
402. Cf. Mt 10.26, Lk 8.17, and 1 Cor 14.25.
403. 2 Cor 5.10.
404. 1 Cor 15.52.
405. Cf. Mt 25.15; *Hom.* 35.11 and the note there; *Hom.* 39.7; and *Frags.* 227 and 231.
406. Cf. Lk 7.41.

have been commanded to be obedient to kings and to every superior power.[407]

(b) And, simply, if there is an image of deceit, it is to be attributed to the craftsman of evil. But, if there is a symbol of virtue, this is to be attributed to God. What is perfect has been stated in Matthew.[408]

231. Luke 19.24

He says to those standing there, "Take the *mina* from him."[409] The *mina* is the grace of the Holy Spirit, and the one who has this grace cannot be punished unless he is first stripped of it. "And give it to the one who has ten *minas*."[410] For, God bestows good things on us with interest. The one who made ten *minas* from one is given the ten *minas* in return, and God adds another *mina*, too, the one that belonged to him who did not work.

232. Luke 19.26

The Savior says, "He who has"[411] a virtue as the fruit of his labors and sweat also receives something more from God, just as to the one who has the faith that we can muster will be given the gift of faith. And simply, if someone has one of those things that come to be by effort, and that are bettered by attention and care, God will give what is lacking. But, the one who is useless and does not pass the Word on to many will be deprived of what he had, and punished.

234. Luke 19.30

This place is a village, where an ass stood tied, and a colt; this fact, I think, is not without meaning. For, in comparison with the whole heavenly world, a village is despised upon the

407. 1 Pt 2.13.
408. Cf. Mt 5.48.
409. Lk 19.24. Cf. *Hom.* 35.11 and the note there; *Hom.* 39.7; and *Frags.* 227 and 228.
410. Lk 19.24.
411. Lk 19.26.

whole earth, and is mentioned without the addition of proper name.

235. *Luke 19.30*

For, the work of the disciples who loose the bound colt is to lead the beast they loosed to Jesus, and to throw their cloaks (that is, their deeds and words) with which they were clothed onto the colt, and then to put Jesus upon the colt and seat him there, and again to spread their cloaks in the road, so that the colt they loosed, upon which Jesus was riding, might walk upon the disciples' cloaks.

236. *Luke 19. 37, 40*

When "the crowd of disciples" praises "God in a loud voice,"[412] the stones are silent. But, when the disciples of the crowd are silent, which happens "when the apostasy comes,"[413] the stones shall cry out.

237. *Luke 19.40*

(a) What sort of stones are those that do not become children for Abraham?

(b) Which are the stones of which it is said, "Is it not possible for God 'to raise up children for Abraham from the stones'"?[414]

238. *Luke 19.41–43*

(a) In the hardening that has happened to a part of Israel "until the full number of Gentiles comes in,"[415] there is hidden from the eyes of Jerusalem "the things that belong to [her] peace."[416] She did not know them, and this in the day of Jesus' visitation. But days are coming upon her when her "enemies will cast up a wall"[417] around her, and what follows.

412. Lk 19.37.
413. 2 Thes 2.3.
414. Lk 3.8.
415. Rom 11.25.
416. Lk 19.42.
417. Lk 19.43.

(b) This is the sense of the words: since you did not recognize your peace, namely myself, you were handed over to your enemies. Now, since peace "has been hidden from your eyes,"[418] you have no peaceful thoughts, nor do you love what has happened, but you look to contradiction. "Days will come upon you" in which "your enemies"[419] will lord it over you—and intelligible enemies instead of sensible ones. For, externally, the Jews were conquered by Romans, but internally by unclean demons. Thirty-five years after Christ's Ascension the city was conquered by Romans.[420]

239. Luke 19.45

It is characteristic of sellers to give the things that are useful for life, which they made by their God-given skill, and to take human things that, in themselves, are useful for nothing.[421]

240. Luke 20.29–30

For, they say that seven brothers were joined to one woman by the law of marriage. Clearly she was lawfully married to each of them, once the other had died. But they say that, last of all, the woman died.

241. Luke 20.36

Jesus says, "like angels of God in heaven."[422] He does not say that they will be men in heaven, but that they will be like the angels in heaven, just as Mark, too, had spoken and said, "But they are like angels in heaven."[423] For, just as the angelic host is many, but is not increased by generation but exists by an act of creation, so too is the host of those who are raised.

418. Lk 19.42.

419. Lk 19.43.

420. In A.D. 66 the Jews in Jerusalem rebelled against the Romans; in 70, the city fell to a Roman army under Titus and Vespasian.

421. That is, money.

422. Mt 22.30.

423. Mk 12.25.

242. *Luke* 20.38

But we know that the followers of Marcion and Valentinus still struggle against this passage and apply the saying to souls. For, they say that these souls live, and that the Lord said of them that God was the God of these souls. But the point of controversy for the Sadducees was never about souls but about bodies, so that the answer applied to bodies. For, the dead man is said to rise when the soul joins the body and not during the period in between, when the soul is separated from the body and does not have the properties of life that accompany the body. Both of them, a man and ordinary life,[424] form a unity, and each of them is needed to restore life again after death.

244. *Luke* 22.10

But we ought to know that those who live in feasting and worldly cares do not ascend into that upper room, and hence do not celebrate the Pasch with Jesus. For, after the discourses of the disciples, with which they catechized the head of the household (that is, the mind), divinity, as already mentioned, comes into the house and feeds the disciples.

245. *Luke* 23.17

Why did they have to release one criminal at the feast? It was probably because the Jews were then bound to the Romans by a treaty that the favor was granted to them at the feast. Saul, too, granted Jonathan to the people and shows them this sort of ancestral custom.

246. *Luke* 23.18, 21

The Jews think and do the things of robbers, and they made the house of God "a den of thieves."[425] So, Jesus expelled them

424. Origen means biological or corporeal life.
425. Lk 19.46.

from God's house, and they shouted about the thief Barabbas: "Release Barabbas to us."[426] But, about the Savior of the world they said, "Crucify, crucify him."[427] So, up to this day the Jews do not have Jesus, for they have not believed in the Son of God. Instead, they have among themselves Barabbas, the thief, who comes from "the spirits of evil."[428] They deemed him, who had been captured and thrown into prison among them, worthy of release. So, Barabbas the thief rules the unbelieving Jews.

248. Luke 23.43

The expression so troubled some people as discordant that they dared to suspect that the phrase, "Today you shall be with me in paradise,"[429] was inserted into the Gospel by some people who lived an easy life. But we say, more simply, that perhaps, before he departed for the so-called heart of the earth,[430] he established the believing thief in the paradise of God.

250. Luke 23.45

John did not mention this event. Matthew and Mark specify neither the sun nor the eclipse. But Luke says, "The sun was eclipsed."[431] Perhaps the event shows us either that there was a dark cloud, or clouds passed under the sun's rays that shone upon the land of Judea, or the air there grew thick and joined in grieving for what had happened, just as the land around Judea, and the rocks and the tombs, did. For, the Scripture mentions the whole land of Judea in many places.[432] [This happened so that they might know that the man who was hanging on the cross is he who took on himself the world when God "fought against the Egyptians on their account,"[433] and eclipsed the light of the sun, when darkness spread over their whole land.][434]

426. Lk 23.18.
427. Lk 23.21.
428. Eph 6.12.
429. Lk 23.43.
430. Cf. Mt 12.40.
431. Lk 23.45.
432. Cf. Gn 13.9, Jer 1.14, and Jl 1.2.
433. Ex 14.25.
434. Cf. Ex 10.22. The passage in brackets may be by Cyril of Alexandria.

251. Luke 23.45

It is likely that the event also suggests something else to us: that the hidden things of the Law were revealed in Christ through his Passion. For, the concealing veil hung within the Holy of Holies of this age. The shadow of the Law had to be lifted. It was torn off and shows that the Holy of Holies was opened to those justified by faith in Christ. He shows the things of God to the saints, so that in the future we may approach the interior tent, with nothing barring the way. You will seek out which of the two veils, the one within and the one without, "was divided."[435]

252. Luke 23.46

"And crying out with a loud voice Jesus said, 'Father, into your hands I commend my spirit.' And after he said this, he expired."[436] He said this because he wished to sanctify our own deaths by these words, so that we, too, as we depart the present life, may commend our spirits "into the hands" of the heavenly Father.

253. Luke 23.46

This word, which he spoke on the cross, "Into your hands I commend my spirit,"[437] teaches that the souls of the saints are no longer shut up in the underworld, as they were previously, but are with God, once this event has happened, as in the firstfruits in Christ. For, they departed and were detained below, but the Lord in his own person changed their journey to an upward one. [For, when human nature was found in him to be rich in sinlessness, he brought it about as something new for us that souls were released "into the hands of the living God."[438] And St. Stephen knew this when he said, "Lord Jesus, receive my spirit."[439]][440] The word "I commend" teaches us that

435. Lk 23.45.
436. Lk 23.46.
437. Lk 23.46.
438. Cf. Heb 10.31.
439. Acts 7.59.
440. The passage in brackets may be by Cyril of Alexandria.

his Passion was voluntary and shows that the soul does not perish. [The words, "I shall lay down (my life),"[441] make it clear that he will take it up again.][442]

254. *Luke 24.2*

After the Resurrection the stone was removed on account of the women, so that they would believe that the Lord had risen. They saw the tomb—empty and devoid of the body. Then there follows, "And they entered and did not find the body of the Lord"[443] Jesus.

255. *Luke 24.15*

What is the glory of the Lord's body, which Paul mentioned,[444] that was revealed to the disciples in the Transfiguration on the mountain?[445] Since, after the Resurrection, he had to appear to the apostles and the five hundred disciples[446] to confirm their faith in the resurrection, they saw him as they were able to. Just as they had known him before his Passion, he showed them the scars of his wounds.[447] Notice that, since he was leaving, he left peace with them, as John wrote; when he came to them again, he gives peace, something sweet in deed and in name.[448]

256. *Luke 24.32.*

After the Savior had spoken, Simon and Cleopas[449] confess

441. Jn 10.18.
442. The passage in brackets may be by Theodore of Mopseustia.
443. Lk 24.2.
444. Cf. Phil 3.21.
445. Cf. Mk 9.2.
446. Cf. 1 Cor 15.6.
447. Cf. Jn 20.27.
448. Origen tries to discover the difference between two verbs used in Jn 14.27, in which Jesus both "leaves" (more literally, "sends") peace and "gives" it.
449. Origen regularly identifies the disciple on the road to Emmaus with Cleopas as Simon. Cf. *Commentary on John* 1.5.30 and 1.8.50; *Against Celsus* 2.62 and 68; *Homilies on Jeremiah* 20; Joseph H. Crehan, "St. Peter's Journey to Emmaus," *Catholic Biblical Quarterly* 15(1953) 418–426; Rupert Annand, "He Was Seen of Cephas: A Suggestion about the First Resurrection Appearance to Peter [Mk 16:2;

that "our hearts were burning,"[450] and so on. They show that the words were spoken by the Savior out of the love that held a flame of fire to those who heard him. They set them afire, kindling the hearts of the hearers for love of God.

257. *Luke 24.50*

Something of this sort has also been written about Aaron in the book of Leviticus, namely that "He raised up his hands over the people and blessed them."[451] I gather from this that the saying expresses a mystery, namely, that the one who blesses someone must be adorned with works that distinguish him from the many and raise him above them. For, when he is going to bless the people, the hands of Aaron are raised on high. So, if someone has his hands down toward earthly things, he does not intend to bless anyone. So, too, the hands of Moses did not help the people when they were down, but when they were raised up.[452] The raising up of the Savior's hands was a symbol of this. By his actions on behalf of men, he raised his hands for the sake of man, and saved the believers. Perhaps, therefore, everyone who is raised up by his deeds has been crucified, as Paul wrote: "I am crucified to the world and the world to me."[453] That is to say, the word about the world has been conceived, thought, and raised on high, and no longer lies below. For, to the one who does not understand the account of creation, the word has not been crucified. For, I consider that mystical crucifixion beautiful which Paul, too, suffered—to be crucified together with Christ. And the world was, in Paul's mind, exalted and thought by him. But, the Lord also lifts up his hands in another way, and bestows power on the disciples through his blessing.

Lk 24:33–34; 1 Cor 15:5; John 21:1ff]," *Scottish Journal of Theology* 11 (1958) 180–187.

450. Lk 24.32.
451. Lv 9.22.
452. Cf. Ex 17.11.
453. Gal 6.14.

INDICES

GENERAL INDEX

f refers to Fragments, h to Homilies (for which <Homily#>.<Section#> are indicated), pr to the Preface (Jerome's Letter), and n to notes.

INDEX OF HOLY SCRIPTURE

f refers to Fragments, h to Homilies (for which <Homily#>.<Section#> are indicated), pr to the Preface (Jerome's Letter), and n to notes.

Books of the Old Testament

Books of the New Testament

CPSIA information can be obtained
at www.ICGtesting.com
Printed in the USA
BVHW03s1103140818
524469BV00001B/105/P